THE TIMELINE OF MEDIEVAL WARFARE

THE TIMELINE OF MEDIEVAL WARFARE

THE ULTIMATE GUIDE TO BATTLE IN THE MIDDLE AGES

Phyllis G. Jestice

THUNDER BAY
P·R·E·S·S

San Diego, California

Thunder Bay Press
An imprint of the Advantage Publishers Group
10350 Barnes Canyon Road, San Diego, CA 92121
www.thunderbaybooks.com

ISBN-13: 978-1-59223-859-0
ISBN-10: 1-59223-859-9

Project Editor: Sarah Uttridge
Picture Research: Natascha Spargo
Design: Andrew Easton at Ummagumma Design

Printed in China

1 2 3 4 5 12 11 10 09 08

Contents

Early Medieval Warfare

When Germanic invaders seized control of the western Roman Empire in the fifth century AD, they brought an attitude toward warfare that the Roman-ruled populace had not seen for centuries. Much of Germanic culture revolved around free men's abilities as warriors. A king who could not command troops in battle was despised and unlikely to live long; the follower of a king who proved cowardly in battle was disgraced for life.

Small Germanic Successor states replaced the unified Roman Empire, and neighbour fought against neighbour in a struggle for prestige, advantage and loot, which would provide the means to repay loyalty. Unfortunately, it is impossible to uncover most specifics of early medieval warfare in Europe. Our written sources are few and far between. What makes it even harder to understand warfare in the period following the Germanic

Left: The Battle of Lechfeld, 955, giving a romanticized view of Otto I's victory over the Magyars.
Right: A typical medieval school scene. The teacher, a member of the clergy, teaches by reading to the boys.

invasions is that, even when a source exists, it is usually frustratingly vague – for example, saying that one army defeated another, but without details. Alternatively, an early medieval tale may have such strong legendary elements that we cannot reconstruct the historical reality. Nobody, for example, would argue that an early medieval warrior had the abilities of a Beowulf, although the poem does give some important clues about arms and armour. In part, such vagueness can be attributed to the fact that most accounts were written by monks who were usually isolated from the fighting of secular society. To a great extent, though, the authors probably assumed that everyone *knew* how a battle would have played out, what fighting techniques were used and what tactical

possibilities were available to the opponents.

Nonetheless, a few basic points can be made about early medieval war, which hold true, to a great extent, for the military history of the Middle Ages more generally.

Tactics and Strategy

A first important point to make, especially since Hollywood so often caricatures medieval military engagements, is that medieval commanders often displayed

an excellent grasp of both strategy and tactics. The Middle Ages had no words equivalent to either term, yet there are many examples throughout the medieval centuries of clever commanders who repeatedly won impressive victories that can be attributed only to a good sense of what to do with troops on the battlefield and how to bring a war to a successful close.

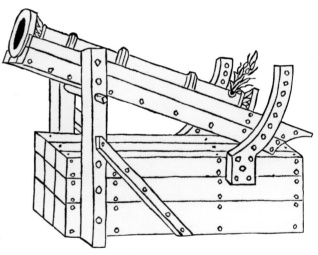

A medieval monk hand-copying a text; production costs were high in the Middle Ages.

A fourteenth-century illustration of a cannon, from a copy of Vegetius' treatise De re militari *(a Roman handbook on war).*

774

Charlemagne defeats the Lombard king, Desiderius, and becomes king of the Lombards.

772–785, 792–793, 798–803

Charlemagne conquers the Saxons.

778

15 August Battle of Roncesvalles. As Charlemagne's army withdraws from Spain, Basques ambush and destroy the rearguard, led by Count Roland.

Right: This romantic painting of Vikings landing on the English coast suggests some of the horror that the northern raiders invoked.

Bottom: Count Geoffrey V of Anjou (1113–1115), the only commander known to have read the treatise De re militari *in a military context during the Middle Ages.*

What the Middle Ages *didn't* have was any sort of system for training generals in the art of command. There was a single Roman handbook on war, *De re militari* (On military matters), written by Vegetius in the late fourth century AD. It was copied frequently throughout the Middle Ages, and was eventually translated into French, English, Italian, German, Spanish, Portuguese and even Hebrew. The last language listed suggests that perhaps Vegetius' readers were not, in fact, using his treatise to help plan campaigns, but rather had an

788

Frankish annexation of Bavaria.

782

Massacre of Verden. The Franks under Charlemagne slaughter thousands of Saxon prisoners.

789

First known Viking raid, against the southeast coast of England.

antiquarian interest in Roman matters. There is only one mention of a commander in the field actually making use of Vegetius: Count Geoffrey V of Anjou in the early twelfth century is reported to have been reading the treatise while besieging a fortress.

The Size of Armies

A second basic problem when studying war in the Middle Ages is the size of the armies involved. Until the thirteenth and fourteenth centuries, when royal account books report specific payments to troops, estimating how many men fought in a given encounter is a matter for guesswork, and historians' estimates vary considerably. Medieval narrative sources are of little help in reckoning armed forces, because their authors were fond of very large round numbers, which are clearly impossible given the resources of the time. At the other extreme, we find definitions such as that included in the laws of the West Saxon king Ine (c. 700), saying that up to seven men should be regarded as thieves; 7–35 as a 'band'; and any more, an army. Indeed, a force of 36 well armed men could have raided most early medieval

An idealized fifteenth-century drawing of a military camp. Only knights and nobles would have enjoyed the luxury of tents.

villages successfully, and many early medieval 'battles' appear to have started as raids that encountered resistance.

In general, historians of war argue that armies before the eleventh century must have been small – not because kings could not raise more men, but rather because of logistical considerations. Even an army of 2000–3000 would have encountered major supply difficulties. Early medieval fighters were expected to provide their own weapons and food. But how could large quantities of food and animal fodder be transported long distances? Much of Western Europe still had an infrastructure of Roman roads, and there is evidence that they were mended and maintained in some regions. Much fighting, however, took place on frontiers where the Romans had rarely penetrated. Transport issues were so intractable that kings usually travelled with their retinues from place to place even in peacetime, to eat resources where they were produced, rather than having provisions brought

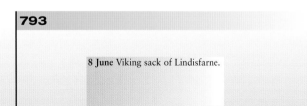

789–795

Charlemagne defeats the Avars in the Balkans.

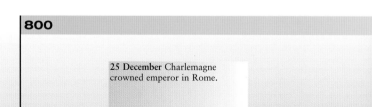

793

8 June Viking sack of Lindisfarne.

800

25 December Charlemagne crowned emperor in Rome.

to their courts. The longer the campaign – and the larger the number of troops engaged – the more cumbersome such supply problems would have been. The problem was aggravated even more by the fact that most early medieval campaigns took place in the spring, when the fighters could not have hoped to live from the bounty of the country. Admittedly, the Carolingians in the late eighth century moved the annual gathering of the war host from March to May, apparently to make it more likely to find grazing for their increasing number of cavalry horses. But it was still necessary to carry food for the men and grain for the animals.

Who Fought?

It is also questionable that the largest army was the most efficient and effective army, at least in the early Middle Ages. Early Germanic society, as described by the Roman historian Tacitus in the early second century AD, was a society dominated by war, in which all free men bore arms and took their place in the battle line. All men were not, however, equally useful in battle. The average freeman fighter was a relatively poor man, as measured by his military

For much of the Middle Ages, the best roads were the surviving Roman Roads that crisscrossed Europe.

equipment. This was a metal-poor society, and his body armour, if he had any at all, would have been made of leather, as was his helmet. His shield would have been made of wood, and he would have fought for the most part with a spear – the spearhead often constituting the most metal he carried on his person. His secondary weapons would have been a dagger, or perhaps an axe.

Compare the effectiveness of such a man to the retainers of an important lord, many of whom would have been clad in chain mail hauberks, with metal helmets, and stronger shields reinforced with a metal boss and rim. Such a man would probably have

Beginning in the twelfth century, knights adopted personalized coats of arms, as in the earl of Oxford, right.

805–807

Danish construction of the Danevirke, a rampart and ditch 19km (12 miles) long, built across the base of the Jutland Peninsula.

Muslim conquest of Cyprus.

initiated a military engagement using his spear, but he was also likely to have a sword – an expensive investment, which, according to one early Germanic law code, was worth three oxen. These 'professional' military retainers were also likely to have horses, so at the least they had greater speed and mobility in getting to a battle, and in some early medieval cultures served in the battle as cavalry. And, of course, these men had no profession but

....

Charlemagne (768–814), who restored the western Roman Empire, was crowned emperor on Christmas Day, 800.

Secular and sacred scenes were often mixed together, as in this tenth-century manuscript illustration from St Bertin, showing a boar hunt in the bottom panel.

....

fighting, so were likely to have been trained better and more able to fight as a unit.

By the time extant sources allow us to see who participated in battles, rulers clearly preferred a smaller army of better-armed, better-trained fighters to peasant levies. The reign of the great Frankish emperor Charlemagne (768–814) is often taken as a turning point in this regard. In the year 807, Charlemagne legislated that every three (later four) *mansi* of cultivated land had to provide a well-equipped fighting man. A *mansus* was roughly the amount of land necessary to feed a family, and the owner of such a large estate was expected to come and fight himself, while poorer freemen banded together to equip and send one of their number. But was this an innovation, or a codification of existing practice, as was the case with so much Carolingian legislation? We simply do not know the answer. We do, however, know that

808

Charlemagne introduces a system for poorer freemen to pool their resources to equip representatives for military service.

814–817

Bulgar siege of Constantinople.

Godfrey de Bouillon (1058–1100) and his knights departing for the First Crusade. Godfrey became the first ruler of the Christian kingdom of Jerusalem.

Charlemagne did not call troops from all over his large empire for every campaign. Sometimes only the fighting men of the nearest region would be summoned for military service. At other times there would be a proportional levy. For example, the Saxons were expected to send only one in every six fighters to campaign in Spain, and one in three against the Bohemians, while the whole force was required to take to the field against the neighbouring Elbe Slavs.

By the 830s, the Frankish *Annals of St Bertin* make it clear that peasants were not expected to fight. The monastic chronicler reports that commoners of his region made a pact to defend themselves against Viking raiders. The local aristocrats, however, attacked and slaughtered the peasants for their presumption. It was the duty and right of the aristocrats and their bands of followers to do the fighting – not uppity peasants who, if given the chance, might also take up arms against their lawful lords.

827–902

Muslim conquest of Sicily from the Byzantine Empire.

829–843

Frankish civil war.

834

Viking sack of Dorstadt and Utrecht.

By the tenth century in France, kings and great lords could probably each raise about 200 heavy cavalry and 1000 foot soldiers.

A fanciful illustration of the Viking assault on Paris in 845. Like all galleys, Viking longships would not have employed oars and sail simultaneously.

King Louis IX of France (1226–1270). Although an unsuccessful commander, Louis' two crusades helped unify France for the first time in centuries.

Lesser aristocrats would at least have had enough men to enforce their will on their own estates. Such bands of retainers would have been a motley assortment of muscular peasants plucked from the fields and younger sons of privileged fighters who had their own way to make. It was only gradually, as it became the custom to give these retainers lands (*fiefs*) from which they could equip themselves, that such men became privileged minor nobility, the 'knights' that emerged in the tenth and eleventh centuries.

Why Fight?

Why did people wage war in the early Middle Ages? To some extent, the reasons were the same as they have always been in the history of warfare: men fought to defend what was dear to them, to prove their loyalty and honour, and for gain. In

843

August The Treaty of Verdun partitions the Kingdom of the Franks between Lothar, Louis and Charles, sons of Louis the Pious.

845

28 March Viking sack of Paris.

847

Muslim raiders attack Rome, looting St Peter's Basilica. Pope Leo IV (847–55) responds to the threat by constructing a wall around the Vatican.

the ninth and tenth centuries, the dominant concern of the elite classes was warfare. Kings were expected to command their armies in person; if that was impossible, the commander was usually a close relative, preferably a son. Early medieval kings who could no longer successfully command their armies rarely lasted long, though.

Much of warfare was clearly private war, in the form of vendettas between rival clans or simple attacks attempting to seize land from a neighbour. Private war was only gradually outlawed: in France, for example, it was outlawed in the thirteenth century by Louis IX (1226–1270); in Germany, it remained acceptable throughout the Middle Ages.

Rulers waged war to gain or protect territory; their followers fought to hold onto their privileged positions, for the chance of

....

Left: Troubadour Bertran de Born (1140s–c. 1215) provides some of our best evidence about the chivalric world of the twelfth and thirteenth centuries.

Right: St. Augustine of Hippo (354–430) was a father of the Church.

850

Viking conquest of Utrecht.

851

Battle of Sandwich. The king of Kent defeats a large Viking force.

852

Battle of Givald's Foss. Vikings defeat West Frankish king, Charles the Bald.

booty (or a share of the lord's generosity after the fight), and for the fun of it. Many fighting men must have found winters boring, looking forward to the opening of the campaigning season to relieve the tedium. They would have agreed with the twelfth-century troubadour Bertrand de Born, who said he loved to see the fresh flowers and grass of spring because war could begin again and encourage the generosity of lords. An annual campaign was normal in the early Middle Ages, only gradually dying out in the later Middle Ages, except on frontiers or in disputed regions.

Regulating War

Early medieval warriors were most different from their Germanic forebears in one respect: they were Christian, and Christian ethics had an odd way of insinuating themselves into societal affairs, even on the battlefield. Not that early medieval churchmen convinced warriors to turn

Sixteenth-century German nationalists looked to figures like Louis the German (c. 806–876) as the founders of the German state, as in this illustration.

858

Louis the German invades Aquitaine, but is repelled by his brother Charles the Bald, of France.

860

Russian attack on Constantinople driven off by the Byzantine fleet.

865–878

Viking 'Great Army' conquers most of England.

the other cheek – or even attempted to do so. After all, the clerics were born and bred in this warrior society, and for the most part accepted its values as their own. Nonetheless, there was a gradual trickle-down effect of notions about 'proper' warfare from the theologians to the warriors. Thus in ninth-century Francia the practice of enslaving defeated enemies died out (except when the losers were pagans). Similarly, killing captured enemies after victory died out (except when the losers were pagans; in a notorious case, Charlemagne massacred 4500 defeated Saxon warriors at Verden in 782).

The blessing of banners marked the departure of a king and his army, while elaborate Christian liturgies encouraged the fighters, who by the ninth century probably confessed their sins and took communion before any important engagement. By the second half of the tenth century, rituals had even evolved to bless the sword of a new knight, as part of a 'consecration' with strong religious overtones. Churchmen had also elaborated a theory of 'just war', explaining that warfare was praiseworthy when defending one's homeland against barbarians and society in general against

outlaws. Church fathers, most notably St Augustine of Hippo, established rules for when to fight, emphasizing the need for a war

The Saxon duke Widukind's submission to Charlemagne in 785, from Versailles, France.

870

Battle of Hoxne. The Viking Great Army defeats and kills King Edmund of East Anglia.

Charles the Bald and Louis the German divide Lotharingia in the Treaty of Mersen.

871

The West Saxons fight nine battles with the Vikings.

875–885

Byzantine reconquest of southern Italy.

King Offa of Mercia holding a model of the monastery of St. Albans. The twelfth-century illustration catches well the king's combination of armed force and piety.

to be formally declared and waged on the authority of a prince, in defence of religion and justice. Nonetheless, the Church's position on war was ambivalent at best. Church councils repeatedly ordered clerics not to bear arms themselves (the repetition suggesting that many churchmen were indeed out on the battlefields of Europe with their kinsmen). And soldiers who killed in war were expected to perform penance, although this demand seems to have been enforced rarely, and the penance was light anyway (a mere forty days).

The 'Core Land' Advantage

By about the year 800, our evidence for early medieval warfare begins to improve, and one point becomes particularly clear: the settled Germano-Christian successor states of western Europe, the 'core lands' of the medieval West, had a clear military advantage over the 'barbarians' of the frontiers. This core land/periphery distinction remained in general true throughout the Middle Ages. The Germanic successor states, impoverished though they were by comparison to the Roman Empire, nonetheless provided enough stability to create an impressive military establishment. By c. 750, towns were on the rise again in much of the formerly Roman territory. Iron implements, though expensive, were readily available. Kings and great lords could equip their retinues with helmets and with hauberks of iron chain that provided good defence, at least against glancing blows on the battlefield.

Horses were also becoming more readily available in the core lands, and a significant part of the successor states' armies at least rode to the battlefield, even if they may have dismounted to fight. By the eighth century, the traditional Frankish military muster date of 1 March had been moved to 1 May, apparently so that the larger numbers of horses used on campaign could find sufficient fodder. Evidence suggests that by the late eighth century the Franks also fought on horseback, employing striking and throwing weapons, rather than the couched lance that became the hallmark of the 'knight' by the twelfth century.

876

8 October Battle of Andernach. Louis the Younger of East Francia defeats the invasion of Charles the Bald of West Francia.

878

6 January Battle of Chippenham. The Viking king, Guthrum, defeats the West Saxons in a surprise attack. King Alfred flees, leaving most of Wessex in Viking hands.

Treaty of Wedmore. In a treaty with Alfred the Great of Wessex, the Viking king, Guthrum, agrees to make peace and convert to Christianity.

May Battle of Edington, England. The army of Wessex, led by Alfred the Great, defeats the Viking Great Army under Guthrum, opening the door to negotiation.

A great deal of ink has been spilled arguing about the date of the introduction of the stirrup to western Europe, the premise being that only this technological innovation made effective cavalry possible. Currently, though, most military historians regard the debate as misguided. Stirrups were apparently introduced into Europe in the late sixth century, but took centuries to become popular among horsemen everywhere.

A new generation of war historians has actually *tried* ancient and medieval cavalry practices, instead of just theorizing from behind a desk. It has established that stirrups do not, in fact, make for better cavalry, nor are they necessary for a knight to charge with a couched lance. The key element in giving cavalrymen a more secure seat is a supportive saddle, raised at front and back – an invention that had already developed by the later Roman Empire.

By the second half of the eighth century, as the military became more efficient, ambitious rulers of the core lands began to create impressive states at the expense of the 'savages' who dwelt along their frontiers. The military careers of the Frankish king Charlemagne (768–814) and the Anglo-Saxon Offa of Mercia (757–796) illustrate the state of affairs well.

Of the two, sources are much better for Charlemagne. Building on the successes of his father and grandfather, Charles the Great spent most of his long reign fighting the neighbours in all directions in 53 major campaigns, of which he personally led just under 30. He defeated the Lombards (probably equal in military equipment, but inferior in organization), the Bavarians, the Saxons and, finally, the Avars, doubling the size of the Kingdom of the Franks and garnering enough loot to initiate major cultural and governmental reforms.

Charlemagne had such great advantages in equipment, mobility and sheer numbers that most enemies could not hope to meet his army in open battle, so he had to make do with raids and sieges. In fact, Charlemagne fought only three major pitched battles, one of which – the Battle of Roncesvalles, in 778 – ended in the destruction of his entire rearguard in a Basque

880s

Construction of burhs, fortified points of refuge from Viking raids, throughout Wessex.

881

3 August Louis III of West Frankia defeats the Vikings in a pitched battle at Saucourt.

ambush (better equipment did not count for everything). Charlemagne could bring together impressive military resources. At the sieges of Pavia (773) and Barcelona (802), he is reported to have had heavy siege equipment and massive supply trains. In general, though, the ability of the ruler to provide logistical support for the army was strictly limited. Charlemagne normally demanded that his troops supply themselves, bringing carts with three months' provisions when he called them to campaign. And the Franks' willingness to fight depended in large part on the rich rewards of successful campaigning. Eventually, Charlemagne was the victim of his own success, running out of profitable enemies and leaving his heirs to cope with the repercussions of a state that had been built on a foundation of war with very little of the mortar of bureaucracy and institutions.

Similarly, in England, King Offa of Mercia was able to parlay good military equipment and a powerful personality into a major state. Indeed, if as many written sources existed for Offa as for Charlemagne, the former might also have gone down in history as 'the great'. Mercia had always been one of the strongest kingdoms of Anglo-Saxon England, and Offa was able to build on his father Aethelbald's creation of a strong military force, taking advantage of a long

Left: Part of Offa's Dyke, a massive earthwork built between England and Wales in the late eighth century by King Offa of Mercia.

Emperor Louis I the Pious (814–840), whose reign was plagued by civil war and Viking invasions.

882

Battle of Ashloh. Vikings defeat an East Frankish army commanded by King Charles the Fat.

885–886

Viking siege of Paris. The Vikings are eventually bribed to depart after an 11-month siege.

Prince Arpád (c. 845–c. 907), second leader of the Magyar confederation that troubled central Europe in the ninth and tenth centuries.

Mercian/Welsh border. This high earthwork and ditch structure was nearly 240km (150 miles) long, and required at least 5000 workers to erect. But, as in the case of Charlemagne, the Mercian state was built on a foundation of individual charisma and success, and fragmented rapidly after Offa's death.

The Last Wave of Invasions

Charlemagne's great Frankish state did not need any outside help to cause it to collapse; by 829, civil war had broken out as his grandsons, the children of Louis the Pious, squabbled for their shares of the Carolingian Empire. Ultimately, they partitioned Charlemagne's state into three parts: what became the separate kingdoms of France and Germany, and an amorphous strip of territory between the two (Lotharingia, Provence and northern Italy), which remained a bone of contention between the two stronger states for centuries. The chaos of this ninth- and

civil war in the kingdom of Wessex to the south. Offa defeated several of the small kingdoms around Mercia – as in the case of Charlemagne and the Lombards, defeating equally equipped forces that were less organized and worse-led than his own. He also launched at least three major raids into Wales, taking advantage of his own superior equipment over a people of the frontier. He showed his ability to command the services of his people and also his ambitions in the great wall, Offa's Dike, which he had constructed along the entire length of the

---

886

The army of Wessex captures London from the Vikings, the first sign that the reconquest of England is possible.

---

c. 890

Battle of Hafrsfjord. King Harold Finehair defeats a coalition of nobles, uniting Norway for the first time.

Invention of nailed horseshoes.

891

1 September Battle of the Dyle (modern Belgium). An East Frankish army under King Arnulf defeats the Danes in a surprise attack on their fortified camp.

The Magyars were a serious threat to Germany, especially because of their horse-borne mobility and use of compound bows.

Right: The German king Henry I (919–936) began the military reorganization that finally ended the Magyar threat in the reign of his son Otto the Great.

....

tenth-century period of internal strife for pre-eminence was greatly complicated, though, by the last waves of 'barbarian' invasion into Western Europe.

The threat was threefold. Sailing from northern Africa, Muslim pirates, as well as state-controlled forces, conquered Sicily, attempted to establish control of southern Italy, and launched devastating raids against the west coast of Italy and south coast of France. From the north, Scandinavians – both pirates and, later, state-sponsored armies – raided, especially in France and the British Isles, seizing and settling parts of France, England, Scotland and Ireland. Perhaps the least threatening challenge was that of the Magyars (Hungarians), mounted nomadic raiders who laid large swathes of Germany, northern Italy and modern Switzerland waste, but at least did not try to settle in Western European territory. In all cases, the invaders tended not to be as well armed as

896

Battle of Bulgarophygon. Tsar Simeon I of Bulgaria defeats a Byzantine army.

897

Alfred the Great of Wessex designs and builds warships to fight the Danes at sea.

HEINRICH I.

GIOVANNI DECIMO: 126

IOANNES · PP · X · ROMANVS
126

Pope John X (914–928) personally led an Italian army to a major victory against the Saracens at Garigliano.

the people of the lands they were invading. With the exception of the conquest of Sicily, all preferred to operate by means of sudden raids, avoiding pitched battles whenever possible. The new threat put a premium on two elements already developing in western warfare: mobility and the construction of fortifications, both of which would dominate military life until the end of the Middle Ages and beyond.

Germany and the Magyars

The case of Germany and the Magyars illustrates the situation well. The nomadic Magyars moved into the Carpathian basin in the 890s and proceeded to launch at least 32 major raids into Western Europe between 899 and 955, often operating in

conjunction with Slavic allies. The Magyars were light horse archers who fought in the traditional fashion of the steppe, skilfully employing sudden attacks and simulated flights to break their enemies' cohesion. Because they had no siege equipment, they rarely took fortified places, although they sometimes attempted a blockade.

The Magyars came in large enough numbers that the army of a single German duchy was rarely effective against them, even if they were able to muster in time. Thus in 907 the Magyars defeated the Bavarians, going on to destroy a force of Franks and Thuringians the next year and to subdue a combined German army in 910. The 910 victory at Augsburg was particularly impressive, as the Magyars first came to grips with two supporting German divisions, then drew out the German centre with a feigned flight, only to turn and strike the disorganized troops in the flanks and rear. Some victories against the invaders were possible, as in 913, when an allied force of Swabians and Bavarians managed a convincing victory. But in general, the advantage lay with the Magyars in the early years of the tenth century.

898–955

At least 32 major Magyar raids into Germany and northern Italy.

899

26 October Death of Alfred the Great of Wessex.

903

Muslim conquest of the Balearic Islands.

In 924, however, King Henry I of Germany was fortunate enough to capture a Magyar prince, providing him with the opportunity to arrange a nine-year truce in return for the prince's return and regular tribute payments. During the truce, Henry set to work on a plan to foil future raids. He built fortified places of refuge (*burgs*) on the Elbe frontier, and also dedicated most of his resources to building up a heavy cavalry force. Nobles and their retainers were probably already horsemen, but it is likely that before this time German horsemen mixed in with their infantry while fighting, rather than forming a separate wing mobile enough to take on the mounted Magyars before and during battle. Thus what Henry accomplished was probably much more consolidation than innovation, but the result was still impressive. When the force was ready, Henry broke the truce by refusing to send more tribute. When a large Magyar force invaded, he defeated them handily at Riade in March 933. According to

This nineteenth-century depiction of the Battle of Lechfeld (955) gives equal credit to the Church (Bishop Ulrich, bearing his cross) and state (King Otto I).

907

Magyar raiders defeat the Bavarians in the Battle of Pressburg.

908

Magyar raiders defeat the Franks and the Thuringians.

910

Battle of Augsburg. Magyar raiders defeat an East Frankish army led by King Louis III.

Battle of Tetlenhall. King Edward of Wessex defeats an army of the Danelaw (Danish-held England).

This more secular early-twentieth century painting of the Battle of Lechfeld puts King Otto I at center stage.

defeat of a Slavic coalition at Lenzen in 929 and of rebellious Saxons and Lotharingians in 939.

At first, the contingents of heavy cavalry in Germany must have been small; an encounter as late as 955, in which Slavs killed a troop of 50 of these new cavalrymen, was regarded as a horrible setback. After all, the new fighting style was expensive: horses had traditionally been the transport of rich men, and had to be bred in larger numbers. Mail hauberks, helmets and swords were also an enormous expense – as were the horseshoes needed to protect warhorses' hooves in Northern Europe. By 955, though, Henry's son Otto I 'the Great' was able to muster heavy cavalry by the thousand.

The year 955 might well be regarded as the year when the army of the Ottonian state (which took its name from Otto I) came of age. Otto had already defeated rebels and gained the submission of northern Italy. But in 955 he had to face a major twofold threat from the east, in the form of Magyar and Slavic armies. In July

one chronicle, the Magyars fled instead of engaging the heavily armoured cavalry with which they were confronted. Another tells that Henry masked his new heavy cavalry with more lightly armed horsemen, and then overset the enemy with a sudden charge. The effectiveness of his new army can be seen not just in this victory against the Magyars, but also in his

911

Autumn Treaty of St-Clair-sur-Epte. King Charles the Simple of France accepts Viking settlement in what will become Normandy, with the Viking leader Rollo as first count.

913

A Swabian and Bavarian army defeat Magyar raiders.

915

An Italian Christian League led by Pope John X drives Muslims from their stronghold at Garigliano.

A sinister illustration of Viking longships approaching the English shore.

955, the Magyars invaded Bavaria and began a siege of the city of Augsburg. Otto marched rapidly to the Danube with his Saxon household troops (he was duke of Saxony as well as king), but had to leave most of the Saxon force he had raised behind to deal with an attacking Slavic coalition. Joining him in Bavaria, though, were forces from the other German duchies as well as a contingent of Bohemians under their duke. The total size of his army is estimated as anywhere from 3000 to 10,000; extant sources simply do not allow us to be more specific. Two points seem certain, though: the Magyars outnumbered Otto's force, but the majority of Otto's force was heavy cavalry.

The two forces met beside the River Lech near Augsburg on 10 August 955, in one of the most decisive battles of European history. And German mobility and armour, combined with good leadership, won the day. The Germans approached the Magyar force in column, and the Magyars attempted their usual tactic of encircling the enemy and attacking the rear. But

The Oseberg Viking ship, about 22m (72ft) long and 5m (16ft) broad, built in AD 820 and used for a woman's burial in 834.

918

King Edward of Wessex defeats and kills the Danish king Guthrum II of East Anglia at the Battle of Tempsford.

923

15 June Battle of Soissons. King Charles the Simple of France defeats his rival Count Robert of Paris.

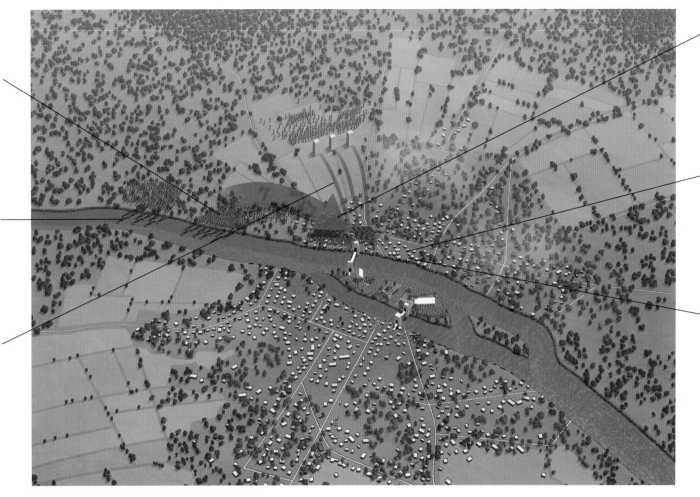

2. After landing, the Vikings prepare three siege towers for an assault on the fortified northern bridge.

1. The Viking force approaches, sailing up the Seine toward Paris in about 700 ships.

3. The Vikings roll their siege towers forward and attack the northern tower of the fortified bridge for three days, but fail to take it.

5. In a second major offensive, the Vikings land on the north bank and attempt to take the fortified bridge in a surprise assault, but fail once again.

4. The Vikings establish camps, but do not try to seal off the city completely.

6. King Charles the Fat sends a Frankish relieving force, but the Vikings defeat it and kill its leader.

Siege of Paris, 885

924

Battle of Lemnos, Greece. The Byzantine navy destroy the fleet of the Muslim pirate chief, Leo.

929

Battle of Lenzen. A Germany army led by Henry I defeats the Slavs.

Alfred the Great overseeing the reconstruction of London's walls after he took the city from the Danes in 886.

showing the ability of the new cavalry to manoeuvre quickly, enough German troops repositioned that they held the Magyars off. When the invaders started to plunder the German baggage, they were driven off in confusion; after all, most of the Magyars had no defensive armour. What made the battle decisive was the long pursuit that ensued. Much of the Magyar army was killed. The Magyar princes were captured, too – and hanged, instead of being held for ransom, as was customary. The Magyar threat to Europe was ended, and Otto I emerged from the Battle of Lechfeld with enhanced prestige, which rose even higher when he defeated the Slavs at Recknitz a few weeks

A later depiction of King Alfred the Great of Wessex (871–899), who saved his land from Danish conquest and began the unification of England.

later. Within a few years, Otto was crowned in Rome as emperor of a newly revived western empire (on 2 February 962) – a title held by most all German kings from then until 1806.

The Vikings

The Northmen, who burst onto the consciousness of Europe's core lands with the Viking sack of Lindisfarne in Northumbria in 793, posed rather different problems that varied from region to region. Speakers of Germanic languages, they were not perceived to be as 'alien' as the Magyars were (Magyars were accused of cannibalism and other atrocities; Vikings were simply feared for their cruelty). Thus, rulers were sometimes ready to make

929

16 January. Establishment of the independent Umayyad caliphate of Spain by Caliph Abd er-Rahman III.

933

15 March Battle of Riade (Allstedt), near Erfurt. King Henry I of Germany defeats a large Magyar army, using his newly developed heavy cavalry force.

934

King Aethelstan of England invades Scotland by both land and sea.

Sack of Genoa, Italy, by a Fatimid fleet.

alliances with Scandinavian raiders against their 'civilized' neighbours, most notably in non-Germanic Ireland, where the large number of independent kingdoms put a premium on fighting men. And Vikings were excellent fighting men. Helmets and armour were rare among them, because of the cost and rarity of iron, and swords were the domain of the rich. But the average Viking marauder seems to have gotten a great deal of practice in warfare, even though the Norse raiders avoided pitched battles when possible. It

···

Above: Otto I of Germany (936–973), crowned on 2 February 962 as emperor of a revived European imperial state, later known as the 'Holy Roman Empire'.

Left: King Hugh Capet of France (987–996), whose initially weak dynasty took centuries to create a unified French state.

was far preferable to strike suddenly against undefended monasteries or villages, gathering up loot (including slaves) and then departing before a force could be organized against them. Because they came by sea in ships that could reach speeds above ten knots, and often rowed up rivers with their flexible, shallow-draught ships, there was usually little advance warning of their coming.

The suddenness of Viking onslaughts meant that mobility could only go so far to help the Christian western Europeans who suffered them, although the French at least appear to have been more advanced in the development of cavalry than the Germans. Most historians now agree that the lords and their retainers in Anglo-Saxon England were also mounted, citing evidence such as the Battle of Maldon in 991, when the Northumbrian commander Byrhtnoth

937

In a major battle of Brunanburgh (Northern England or Southern Scotland), King Aethelstan of England defeats a Scot, Welsh and Viking coalition, uniting England.

939

Battle of Birten. King Otto I of Germany defeats rebel Saxons and Lotharingians, securing his claim to the throne.

dismounted and sent away his horses before the fight began, to prevent flight. With the exception of the Great Army that operated in England from 865 until the late 870s, Viking bands would also have numbered in scores or low hundreds, rather than in the thousands of a Magyar raid. These circumstances made fortified structures rather than cavalry units the essential element against the Vikings.

Western Europe was, for the most part, unfortified when the Vikings began their raids. Town walls left by the Romans had been allowed to crumble, the stones used for other building projects. Most monasteries had only spiritual defences, in the form of a simple hedge or boundary stones that marked the beginning of sacred space. Even the manor houses of nobles were not usually defensible, much less the villages where most of the population lived. People soon started to create impressive fortifications, however. Town walls were built or rebuilt throughout the area of Viking

An eighteenth-century 'portrait' of German emperor Otto II (973–982), who suffered a major defeat at the hands of the Saracens and a major Slavic revolt.

When the Byzantine emperor Basil II Bulgarochthonus won a major victory over the Bulgarians, he is said to have blinded his 10,000 prisoners, leaving every hundredth man with one eye to lead the others home.

penetration. Fortified bridges were constructed to deny the raiders access to major rivers, and were in some cases successful. One can see the difference that fortifications made in the defence of Paris in 845 and in 885. In 845, a Viking fleet numbering at least 120 vessels sacked the city; in 885–886, by contrast, a large Scandinavian force besieged the town for 11 months. A contemporary account tells how the attackers tried to build siege equipment, including a large siege tower, but did the job so badly that the tower collapsed, killing many of them. Finally the force was bought off, because the king of France could not gather a sufficient army to raise the siege. The next year, the same Viking army besieged Sens for six months, but eventually had to depart, leaving the city untaken.

The most impressive series of fortifications erected against the Vikings was the *burhs* of

941

Battle of Andernach. Otto I of Germany defeats a rebellion led by Duke Giselbert of Lotharingia, Duke Eberhard of Franconia and his own brother Henry.

Russian attack on Constantinople, stopped by the Byzantine fleet.

946

German invasion of France.

947

Siege of Senlis. First written mention of crossbows in the medieval West.

c. 950

Construction of Doué-la-Fontaine, the first known stone castle in Europe, in the Loire valley southeast of Angers.

950–952

First Italian expedition of King Otto I of Germany.

Wessex, constructed by order of King Alfred the Great in the 880s and 890s. A *burh* was a place of refuge, apparently a simple wooden palisade in most cases, with enough room inside for a thousand or more people and their animals. They were sited throughout Alfred's territory so that most of his subjects were within one day's journey of a place of safety. A document of the early tenth century, *The Burghal Hideage*, reveals the extent of the king's plans. He was able to rally his subjects to build and man the *burhs*, which were instrumental in stopping the Vikings when they attacked Wessex again in the 890s. The Vikings did not have the siege technology necessary to take the *burhs*, at least quickly, and the West Saxons used them as bases from which to wage guerrilla war against the invaders. As in the case of

....

Left: Otto I's victory at Lechfeld led to his coronation as emperor in 962.

Right: A Byzantine dromon, the standard warship of the Mediterranean for centuries.

Otto I and the Magyars, Alfred the Great and his dynasty came through the Viking invasion with enhanced prestige and authority, beginning the path whereby the kings of Wessex became kings of all England.

Reaping the Invasion Advantage

The greatest importance of the ninth- and tenth-century invasions lies in the way they

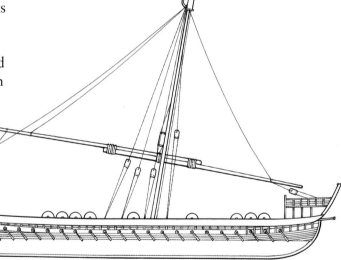

954

Battle of Stainmore. An English force ambushes and killes Erik Bloodaxe, Viking king of York. The kingdom of York is integrated into England.

955

10 August Battle of Lechfeld, Germany. A German army of 8000–10,000 men under King Otto I 'the Great' decisively defeat invading Magyars near Augsburg, marking the end of Magyar incursions into Germany.

16 October Battle of Recknitz. King Otto I of Germany decisively defeats the Slavic Wends.

960–961

Byzantine reconquest of Crete.

encouraged the development of European states, as rulers created (or failed to create) systems of defence. France came out of the invasion period the most seriously weakened of the European states, although we must remember that this region had to deal with repeated civil war as well as Vikings. The raids encouraged governmental fragmentation, especially as more than one king was deposed for failing to stop a Viking attack. Sometimes nobles, rather than the king, came out of an attack with enhanced prestige, as in 886, when the Capetian Odo successfully held Paris against the Vikings – while the king showed his spinelessness by bribing them to depart. Odo, in fact, was elected king a few years after his defence, and his prestige helped his dynasty in its eventual rise to the throne in 987.

Both the Ottonians of Germany and the house of Cerdic, the ruling dynasty of Wessex, came through the invasion period with new military resources and prestige. By the mid-tenth century, Alfred the Great's successors had united England, about the same time that Otto the Great made new and impressive claims for his dynasty in Germany. Both states were based on military resistance and the need for a single hand at the helm against a major external threat.

Yet both Germany and England depended enormously on the personality and ability of the king/war leader who occupied the throne. Wessex's rise to absorb all the other kingdoms of England was punctuated by setbacks when weaker kings failed to rally support to their cause. This was disastrously true in the case of King Aethelred II 'the Unready' (978–1016), whose unfortunate nickname *Unraed* is better translated as 'lacking in counsel' – itself a blasting indictment of an early medieval king. Indeed, Aethelred's reign witnessed the conquest

Medieval illustrations of majestically enthroned kings, such as this illustration, disguise the reality of weak central authority throughout the Middle Ages.

962

2 February Imperial coronation of Otto I of Germany in Rome.

964

A Byzantine fleet attempting to reconquer Sicily is disastrously defeated by Muslims.

965

Byzantine reconquest of Cyprus.

of England by the Danish king Sweyn and his son Cnut. While it is true that the Scandinavian states were coalescing at this time and thus presented a more serious threat than freelance Viking raiders, Aethelred's troubles were caused mainly by a weak personality and inability to keep the loyalty of his own nobles.

Similarly, Germany's army in the later tenth century was impressive, but could not hold out against feckless leadership. Otto I's son, Otto II, was not of his father's calibre. He became involved in a disastrous war with the Muslim invaders of southern Italy, losing almost his entire army and opening the door to a major Slavic rebellion in the process. It hardly mattered that the retainers of bishops, royal monasteries and secular nobles meant that he was able to field at least 8000 heavy cavalry as well as larger numbers of infantry (the numbers are based on the *Indiculus loricatorum* of 981, a military call-up for reinforcements for Otto's campaign in Italy). He was simply out-generaled at the Battle of Cotrone in 982, when the Germans broke the centre of the more lightly armed Muslim army and killed their commander, but were then thrown into confusion when the Muslim reserve hit them in the flank.

The Byzantine Military Establishment

At the end of the tenth century, despite considerable progress, the armed forces of the western European core lands still lagged well behind the military capability of the Byzantine Empire to the east. After a rocky ninth century, the eastern emperors of the tenth century had made extraordinary military gains, ruling nearly as much territory by the end of the tenth century as they had before the Muslim invasions of the seventh century. Especially noteworthy by land was the conquest of the Bulgars by Emperor Basil II 'the Bulgar-Slayer', in a series of campaigns noted for their brutality. Unlike Western European states, the Byzantine rulers employed large numbers of mercenaries,

....

Right: King Aethelred II of England (978–1016), nicknamed Unraed (ill-advised).

Far right: A rare tenth-century illustration of soldiers on horseback, from a copy of Beatus of Liebana's Commentary on the Apocalypse.

966

Conversion of Duke Mieszko I of Poland to Christianity.

969

Fatimid conquest of Egypt.

973

Muslims are driven from their outpost at La Garde-Freinet in Provence.

c. 974

Battle of Hals (Limfjord), northeast Jutland. A coalition of nobles defeat and kill King Harold Greycloak of Norway.

978

A German invasion of France reaches the outskirts of Paris.

982

Battle of Cotrone (Cap Colonna). Muslims attempting to conquer southern Italy disastrously defeat a German-Italian army led by Emperor Otto II.

including after 986 the famed Varangian Guard, composed of northern and western 'barbarians' who fought loyally for their employers.

The Byzantine Empire also maintained a large and effective fleet, numbering nearly 200 ships in the tenth century, and employing an impressive total of about 40,000 oarsmen and marines. Western Europe had nothing comparable. From Scandinavia, we have brief mentions of sea battles, usually between the many claimants to the Scandinavian thrones. From the time of Alfred the Great, the English also had access to at least some fighting ships, although they proved ineffective in halting Viking raids. And in the western Mediterranean, Muslim ships dominated. The Byzantine fleet, by contrast, destroyed a Muslim pirate fleet at sea in 924, one of what were probably numerous encounters as Byzantine *dromons* patrolled the eastern Mediterranean. This Byzantine fleet retook Crete from its Muslim rulers in 960–961, and went on to seize Cyprus in 965. The Byzantines even still had hopes of

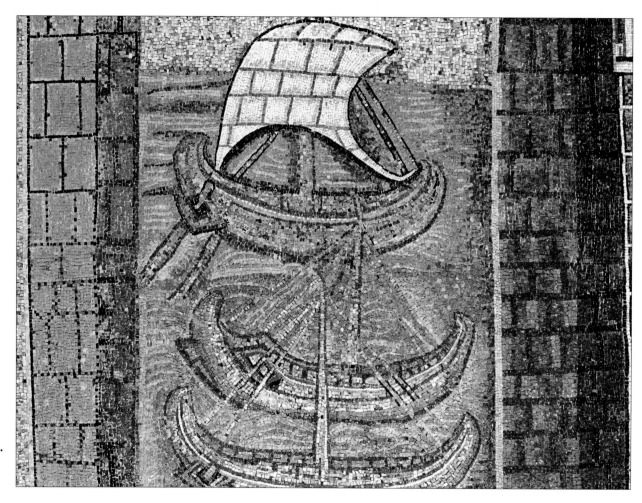

Ships from the Byzantine fleet, which maintained its military importance until the twelfth century.

983

Great Slavic revolt against German overlordship.

986

Creation of the Varangian Guard in Constantinople, an elite imperial guard composed of northern mercenaries.

987

Coronation of Hugh Capet, first French king of the Capetian dynasty.

988

Conversion of Vladimir of Kiev to Orthodox Christianity.

reinforcing their last holdings in southern Italy, but the Muslim forces in Sicily proved to be too strongly entrenched – and Byzantine politics removed the one eastern commander who was proving successful in regaining the island. Nonetheless, the Byzantine fleet proved strong enough to beat off Russian attacks on Constantinople in 860, 907, 941 and 1043.

In the Year 1000

By the end of the tenth century, most of the features that dominated European war for the following centuries were already in place. This can be seen especially in the firmly established contrast between core land and periphery, the pattern of recruitment for military service and the rise to dominance of the heavy cavalryman, the 'knight'.

The ninth and tenth centuries drove home the lesson that the core lands of Europe – France in particular, but also including Germany, northern Italy and England – simply had a material advantage over outlying lands in terms of military equipment. As the last wave of invasions came to an end, warfare became increasingly polarized between two types.

On the one hand was 'civilized' war against Christian neighbours, usually fought with rather low casualties, at least among members of the well-armoured upper class. This was regarded as true and proper warfare. On the other hand was warfare on the periphery, often against non-Christians and certainly against people without the same advantages of equipment enjoyed by the core lands. Such war formed a strong contrast to civilized war. Unable to meet their invaders in pitched battle, the Slavs, the Irish and, to some extent, the Scots, as well as other frontier enemies, fought campaigns of raid and ambush, for which the knights of the core lands found themselves ill prepared.

The pattern of who normally fought was also well established by about the year 1000. Although Western rulers had always employed mercenaries, and the number of mercenaries increased the wealthier a ruler was, the majority of armies consisted of a semi-professional force of nobles and their picked bands of retainers. The military service demanded of each lord was increasingly fixed. For example, the German rulers claimed their customary right to a larger contingent for service in Germany

than when they set out on one of their numerous expeditions in Italy. In France, it is estimated that tenth-century kings and great lords could probably raise a force of about 200 knights and 1000 foot soldiers each. Peasants did not normally engage in battle by the end of the tenth century anywhere within the core lands.

Most significantly for the future, by the year 1000 we have entered the age of heavy cavalry, which would continue to dominate European battlefields for the next half millennium. A majority of any army remained infantry – not only were foot soldiers much cheaper to equip, but an army that consisted solely of cavalry without infantry support would not have lasted long. But the most effective striking force of European armies had become the mounted soldier, who wore a metal hauberk, helmet and, increasingly, a kite-shaped shield, which was easier to manage on horseback than the round shields of the earlier Middle Ages. Thus, by the end of the tenth century, when a contemporary author uses the term *miles*, we can be sure that this is a reference to a mounted soldier, the elite fighting man of later medieval armies.

989	**991**	**992**	**999**
Council of Charroux, France. Beginning of the Peace of God movement, an effort to protect churchmen, women and the poor from endemic warfare.	**10 or 11 August** Battle of Maldon. Danish raiders defeat an Essex force under Ealdorman Byrhtnoth.	**27 June** Battle of Conquereuil. Count Fulk Nerra of Anjou defeats Count Conan I of Brittany, when Conan tries to raise Fulk's siege of Nantes.	Sack of Santiago, Spain, by Umayyad caliph Muhammad al-Mansur.
		King Aethelred II 'the Unready' of England assembles ships to intercept a Danish invasion, but the English fleet is defeated.	

The Eleventh Century: An Expanding Europe

This was a revolutionary age in European history: pope and emperor settled down to a long and destructive fight over governance of the Church; an educational explosion ultimately created a new bureaucratic age; and the core lands of Europe began a process of expansion that shaped the rest of the Middle Ages.

The century was dominated by the beginning of significant population growth and economic revival. In military terms, the eleventh century was a time of war on a larger scale than had been seen since ancient Rome, as a number of rulers turned from a mode of warfare dominated by raiding to a new goal of territorial expansion. Such warfare was often not as profitable as raiding, or only profitable

Left: William the Conqueror leads the Norman charge at the Battle of Hastings, 14 October 1066.
Right: An eighteenth-century impression of the appearance of a Norman footsoldier.

in the long run, so complex state organizations developed to deal with the increasingly expensive pursuit of military glory and gain. Above all, it is a century dominated by the Normans, the descendants of Vikings who settled in northwest France and won an enviable reputation as the greatest warriors of the age.

By about the year 1000, the last invasion period of European history was drawing to a close. The Magyars formed a state (modern Hungary), and integrated with mainstream European society by accepting Christianity. The Slavic states of Poland, Bohemia and Kiev had also taken shape and Christianized in the latter part of the tenth century. This did not

Left: Emperor Henry II of Germany (1002–1024), later canonized as a saint, provoked strong criticism in his lifetime for allying with pagans against Christian Poland.

mean that the neighbouring core lands stopped fighting against Magyars, Poles and so on, but it changed the nature of the campaigns. Defence against raiders gave way to efforts to seize control of blocks of territory, and the rules of acceptable war changed against now-Christian enemies. Thus, Duke Mieszko I of Poland in the late tenth century converted to Christianity, and almost immediately claimed papal protection against German aggression. This did not prevent Henry II of Germany from waging a long war against Mieszko's successor Boleslav Chrobry ('the Brave') of Poland in the first two decades of the eleventh century – but contemporaries were shocked that Henry allied with a non-Christian Slavic coalition against fellow Christians. Similarly, Germany was embroiled in a number of wars with the Magyars, but their purpose was to assert overlordship over the Hungarian state, rather than defence. Indeed,

the German emperor Henry III succeeded in reducing both Bohemia and Hungary to vassalage in the 1040s, although they soon regained their independence.

Highly Organized Invaders

In northern Europe, Viking raids were also transformed into wars of state aggression as the Scandinavian rulers subdued their rivals and converted to Christianity. The transition to a new level of military organization can be seen in the Danish conquest of England in the early decades of the eleventh century. When the English king Aethelred II 'the Unready' (978–1016) proved to be a weak ruler, Viking raids started again, beginning with the great raid of 991, which culminated in a Viking victory at Maldon. But already a difference was visible: the invaders were more highly organized, better armed and some were Christian. Aethelred bought off the raiders several times, which simply encouraged the Danish king Sweyn to look carefully at England's wealth. To compound the problem, Aethelred ordered the killing of all the Danes in England on St Brice's Day 1002. It was a massacre that, according to

1000

Earliest references to *ministeriales*, the 'unfree' knights of Germanic lands.

Conversion of King Stephen of Hungary to Catholic Christianity.

Battle of Svoldr. A Swedish-Danish fleet defeats and kills Olaf Tryggvasson of Norway. Danish overlordship of Norway is restored.

1002

Brian Boru defeats Mael Sechnaill II to become high king of Ireland.

13 November St Brice's Day Massacre. Aethelred II the Unready orders the killing of all Danes in England.

tradition, included among its victims a sister of King Sweyn. In 1003, Sweyn, who had already added Norway and part of Sweden to his empire, attacked in a war that rapidly escalated from retaliatory raid to effort at conquest. It took two major invasions – in 1009 and 1013 – but Sweyn succeeded in driving Aethelred into exile and seizing the throne of England for himself. Sweyn died after only six weeks of rule, but his son Cnut succeeded in becoming king of England (1016–1035) after a further invasion.

Strong Leadership

Cnut won the decisive Battle of Ashingdon against Aethelred's son Edmund II Ironside in 1016, not because the Scandinavians had made up the technological gap between themselves and the core lands (although the gap was rapidly narrowing), nor because of superior generalship – Edmund was a much stronger leader than his father had been. Rather, historians credit Cnut's victory to treachery in the Anglo-Saxon ranks. A key noble, Eadric of Mercia, deserted Edmund at a key point in the battle. The circumstance provides a valuable reminder that the building of stronger, more

A nineteenth-century painting of the depredations of Cnut's army, brings the Middle Ages to life for romantic audiences.

centralized states in the tenth century did not take place without resentment. As late as 1016, many Mercians would have preferred to be ruled by a distant Scandinavian king instead of a scion of the royal house of Wessex. Such disloyalty was the easier to contemplate because Cnut was a Christian.

In Ireland there was a similar hazy transition between repelling raiders and fighting against settled Norsemen who had adopted many of the practices of the lands they had taken. Thus the Battle of Clontarf in 1014, at which the Irish high king Brian Boru won a great victory (although he himself was killed), has been glorified in Irish tradition as a great victory over the evil and ungodly Vikings. In reality, Brian's main opponent was the

1003

King Swein 'Forkbeard' of Denmark raids England.

1003–1017

War between Emperor Henry II of Germany and Duke Boleslav Chrobry of Poland.

1008

English king Aethelred the Unready levies the sea fyrd – every 300 households (*shipsoke*) must provide a ship and crew for service against the Danes. The fleet proves ineffective.

Irish Christian king Maél Schnaill of Leinster. While most of the Norse settlers of the east coast of Ireland sided with Leinster, some fought at Brian's side.

The settled Norsemen of northwest France, the Normans, proved to be the greatest proponents of the fighting style of Europe's core lands in the eleventh and early twelfth century. Thus the Norman conquests of southern Italy and Sicily, and of England, provide excellent case studies for the military trends of the age.

An Age of Conquests

The main rule of war in the eleventh century appears to have been 'take what you can get' – the main players being ambitious and ruthless lords who could mobilize the resources for territorial expansion, rather than the raids that had predominated in earlier centuries. Nowhere is this attitude clearer than in the Norman conquest of southern Italy and Sicily.

In 1016, a group of Norman pilgrims reached Salerno, Italy, only to find the town under siege by Muslims. The Normans took over the defence and defeated the attackers. Their fighting ability so impressed the local

The Battle of Clontarf (1014), one of many battles as minor kings tried to claim the high kingship of Ireland.

Lombard ruler that he invited the Normans to enter his service as mercenaries, as well as any friends and kinsmen they could recruit. By 1018, some Normans had also entered the service of the Byzantine official who governed part of southern Italy. But the Normans soon realized that the patchwork of small states in the region, whether Lombard or Byzantine, were badly governed and ineffectively defended. This was a land of opportunity, and an ambitious family of mercenaries, the Hautevilles (a minor but prolific knightly family of Normandy), decided to take advantage of the situation. Initially working as mercenaries and then striking out on their own, the Normans began to seize the land, winning their first major victories over the local rulers in the 1040s. Their success so worried Pope Leo IX that in 1053 he assembled an army, and at Civitate he personally took the field against the Norman leader Robert Guiscard ('the Wily'), only to be captured and forced to make major concessions.

1009

Major invasion of England by King Swein of Denmark.

Battle of Nairn, Scotland. Danes led by Swein Forkbeard defeat Malcolm II of Scotland.

1010

Battle of Mortlack. Malcolm II of Scotland repels a second Danish invasion.

1011

Muslim sack of Pisa.

By 1071, the Normans of southern Italy had taken Bari, the last Byzantine fortress left on the peninsula, and had begun the conquest of Sicily.

The more famous Norman conquest, Duke William of Normandy's invasion of England in 1066, was a similar bold venture that paid off with a crown. William had apparently won designation as heir to England from his cousin King Edward the Confessor – although their relationship was through Edward's mother, and William did not have a drop of Anglo-Saxon blood. Nonetheless, William had to fight for his promised inheritance after Edward's death in 1066, as Earl Harold Godwinsson claimed that Edward had named *him* heir on his deathbed, and had this selection immediately confirmed by the English nobles present at the time. William staked everything – his prestige, his strong control of Normandy and his life – in the great gamble to gain England. He drew together an impressive army of about 7000 men and ferried them across the English Channel. And luck did indeed favour him. Weather delayed William's departure, so that King Harold's fleet had disbanded by the time they sailed instead of contesting the landing. Best of all, a month

The mausoleum of the crusader prince Bohemund I (c. 1058–1111), at Canosa di Puglia.

earlier, the Norwegian king, Harald Hardrada, invaded northern England. The English Harold had to race northward to fight and defeat Hardrada at the Battle of Stamford Bridge; meanwhile, William landed in the south without resistance. Harold then had to hurry southward again, leaving most of his infantry by the wayside and being trapped into battle before he had assembled a local infantry force. Duke William's gamble paid off. The Normans defeated Harold's force on 14 October 1066, and William was crowned king of England by Christmas.

This degree of territorial grabbing was unheard of before the eleventh century, but was repeated in many regions. It should probably be taken as an outward manifestation of new military confidence from rulers with greater resources than ever before. For the most part, it was a case of trying to seize territory from a clearly defined political entity. The only important exception was the numerous succession and conquest struggles of Scandinavia in the first half of the century, the last stages in the creation of viable states. Scandinavia saw several spirited attempts to

1013–1016

Kings Swein and Cnut of Denmark conquer England.

1014

23 April High King Brian Boru defeats King Maél Sechnaill of Leinster and his Norse allies at the Battle of Clontarf, but is killed during the battle.

29 July Battle of Belathista (Belashita). Byzantine emperor Basil II, 'the Bulgar-Slayer', decisively defeats the Bulgars and blinds his reported 15,000 prisoners. Bulgar czar Samuel dies of shock, opening the way for the final Byzantine conquest of Bulgaria.

1015 (or 1016)

Olaf Haraldsson defeats Swein of Denmark in the sea battle of Nesjar, off the coast of Norway.

A combined Genoese-Pisan fleet drives Muslim pirates from Sardinia.

create a single greater Scandinavian state, most notably under Sweyn of Denmark, who defeated and killed Olaf Tryggvasson of Norway in the sea battle of Svoldr, annexing Norway in the wake of the battle. Sweyn's son Cnut the Great similarly defeated St Olaf of Norway and his ally Onund of Sweden in a sea battle off Helgaá c. 1026. Within a few years, though, Norway was free, and Harald Hardrada of Norway fought 17 years in an ultimately failed attempt to bring Denmark under Norwegian control. But it was just as common in Scandinavia for a king to be defeated and killed by his own people, as when St Olaf was killed in the Battle of Stiklestad in 1030, or when two claimants to the Danish throne fought it out at Aarhus in 1044. (In 1044 the king, Magnus, won over his rival.)

One might expect unsettled conditions and wars of territorial aggression in Scandinavia in the eleventh century. In the core lands of Western Europe, however, the struggle for territorial gain rose to a new pitch. The best example of the phenomenon is the aggressive policy of Fulk Nerra, count of Anjou (987–1040). This was a strong man who seized what he wanted – when on pilgrimage to the Holy Land, he is even reported to have *bitten* off a piece of the sepulchre of Christ to take home as a relic. Fulk waged a series of wars with his neighbour Count Odo II of Blois, including the Battle of Pontlevoy in 1016 with its reported death toll of 3000 to 6000.

....

Left: The most important of a medieval king's duties was protection of the Church, which kings swore to perform when they were crowned.

Below: A scene from the Bayeux Tapestry, the great eleventh-century embroidered narrative of the Norman Conquest of England.

1016

A group of Norman pilgrims reach Salerno, Italy, during a Muslim siege of the city. The Normans defeat the Muslims.

Danish siege of London.

6 July Battle of Pontlevoy. Fulk Nerra of Anjou and his ally Count Herbert of Maine decisively defeat Count Odo II of Blois in one of the bloodiest battles of the century.

18 October Battle of Ashingdon. Cnut of Denmark decisively defeats English king Edmund II Ironside. In the treaty after the battle, England is divided: Edmund keeps Wessex, while Cnut receives the rest of the kingdom.

Left: This illustration of the sea battle at Svold (9 September 1000) vividly depicts the dangers of fighting at sea.

Below right: A nineteenth-century engraving of Counts Fulk III Nerra and Geoffrey II Martel of Anjou.

....

sworn vassals. Thus it was that Henry I of France invaded Normandy in 1053–4 and again in 1057, trying to take advantage of internal Norman problems (although Duke William drove off both invasions).

In 1057, William demonstrated his military skill particularly well. The Norman army shadowed the invading army, led by Henry I and Count Geoffrey of Anjou, until the enemy force was trying to cross the River Dives near Varaville, a process that threw their army into disarray thanks to the tide that was coming in at the time. William then

One reason for Fulk's aggression is that the kings of France of the eleventh century were not strong enough to force their nobles to keep the peace between themselves. The early Capetians were also willing to take advantage of any opportunity that presented itself for territorial expansion, though, even at the expense of their

attacked, inflicting such heavy casualties on the invaders that they had to withdraw. Similarly, William also took advantage of political disarray among his neighbours to conquer the county of Maine in 1063.

The Knights

Duke William of Normandy's main striking force at Varaville and in the invasion of Maine, as in all his battles, was heavy cavalry. In October 1053, he had ended Henry I's first invasion of Normandy at St Aubin-sur-Scie with a ploy that soon became classic: William's cavalry pretended to flee, only to turn and rend

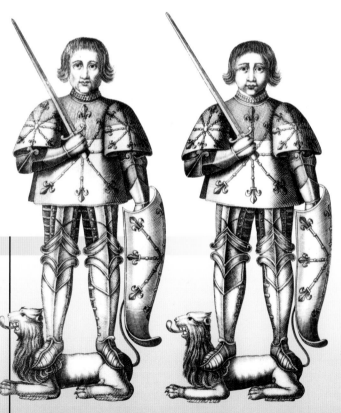

1017

Edmund Ironside dies and Cnut becomes king of all England.

1018

30 January The Peace of Bautzen ends war between Germany and Poland, acknowledging Polish control of Lusatia and Silesia.

Battle of Cannae. A Byzantine army defeats the Lombard count Melus of Bari and his Norman mercenaries on the site of the ancient Roman defeat.

Malcolm II of Scotland invades Northumbria, defeating the English at Carham and establishing the Scottish border at the Tweed.

Norman cavalrymen in the eleventh century normally wore knee-length mail hauberks (slit to allow riding) and conical helmets with a nasal guard.

What, though, was a knight? The term evokes images of courtly society, with young aristocrats jousting to win the hand of fair ladies. The early knight, however, was far from that romantic image. He was a heavy cavalryman, and usually a dependent heavy cavalryman at that. His equipment was prohibitively expensive – a chain-mail hauberk, helmet, shield, lance, sword and, of course, several horses bred for strength and endurance. Using all that equipment was a man with years of training and discipline, a man who could afford to make fighting his main occupation. These conditions meant that early knights could be obtained in only two ways: either a wealthy landowner had to equip himself as a heavy cavalryman (which, to a great extent, he had always been), or he had to equip his military followers. Such followers could be landless younger sons of a significant landowner, perhaps receiving equipment and nothing else

the French force that had lost all cohesion while pursuing their supposedly defeated foes. Similarly, Robert Guiscard's victory at Civitate in the same year was due above all to his knights, which became the striking force of European armies for centuries.

1020

Saxon rebellion against Emperor Henry II of Germany.

1025

18 April Coronation of Boleslav I Chrobry as first king of Poland.

Byzantine emperor Basil II dies while preparing for a Byzantine invasion of Sicily.

1026

A Danish navy defeats the Swedes in the Battle of Stangebjerg.

King Cnut the Great of Denmark, Sweden and England, who finished his father's conquest of England and held a large northern empire together until his death in 1035.

before his parents waved him farewell. More often, though, a lord chose promising peasants with good muscles and took them into service, creating a class of serf-soldiers that are not dissimilar from the slave-soldiers of contemporary Muslim societies. The very name 'knight' is based on an Anglo-Saxon word (*cniht*) that means 'servant'. The more dignified French *chevalier* means 'horseman', with no social connotations originally. Authors of the tenth and eleventh century just called such men *milites* – soldiers.

Such men lived a precarious enough existence, eating at their lord's table, sleeping in his hall and relying on occasional gifts or war loot to get ahead. The luckiest received a *fief* from their lord, a land grant sufficient for the knight to equip himself for war, which was often the simplest thing to do in subsistence-economy Europe. After all, it has been estimated that an eleventh-century knight needed the income from twelve peasant farms to pay for his horses and weapons, and the price rose as armour became more elaborate in following centuries. Probably too much has been made of the idea of medieval knightly armies underpinned by the system of 'feudalism' – the grant of fiefs in return for carefully defined military service. Those who received such fiefs were the success stories of the age; many others received only a money fief, in effect becoming salaried employees of their lords. Knights performing their feudal service apparently did not constitute the majority of any army even in the eleventh century. The traditional 40-day limit to service in most areas, and the quality of fighters provided by a feudal summons, led rulers to seek ways to pay troops of their choice, in the numbers they wanted, and in the proportion of military horsemen and footmen that they regarded as necessary for each situation.

Enough knights were fief-holders, though, that in the eleventh century the knights' social status began to rise. In most of Europe, the knights' lowly origins were rapidly forgotten, except in Germany where a class of *ministeriales* – knights who legally remained serfs of their lord, no matter how much power and wealth

1028

Battle of Holy River (Helgaá), off the east coast of Skåne. King Cnut the Great leads an Anglo-Danish fleet against Olav of Norway and his ally Onund of Sweden, driving Olav into exile.

1027

Council of Toulouges. First declaration of the Truce of God, an attempt to limit warfare during holy days and seasons.

Sancho III the Great of Navarre and Aragón completes his conquest of Christian Spain. The kingdoms are redivided after his death.

Norman mercenaries in Italy are granted Aversa, the first permanent Norman settlement in Italy.

they gained – continued to exist throughout the Middle Ages. One of the greatest success stories of the Middle Ages is that of the *ministerial* Werner II of Bolanden, who in the twelfth century faithfully served Emperor Frederick I Barbarossa. At his height, Werner controlled 17 castles and was lord of 1100 knights.

It is usually very difficult to judge the proportions of heavy cavalry and infantry in armies, because the extant narrative accounts of battles concentrate on the glories of chivalric encounter rather than on the lowly footmen. In reality, almost all medieval armies had both cavalry and infantry, and infantry usually heavily outnumbered cavalry. But from the later tenth century until the end of the thirteenth, it was the cavalry that *won* battles – at least in the eyes of the chroniclers. Although in the late Middle Ages infantry forces proved that they could take on and defeat cavalry, it was a terrifyingly risky matter. Good commanders used the two types of soldier together.

Hastings

The Battle of Hastings, fought on 14 October 1066 between the English king Harold II (Harold Godwinsson) and William the Conqueror, illustrates the mixed tactics that won battles. To begin, Harold was caught at a serious disadvantage. His army had defeated the Norse invader Harald Hardrada at Stamford Bridge on 25 September. Only three days later, Duke William of Normandy landed in the south. Harold made the decision to rush southward to engage the second invader as soon as possible, perhaps because William was devastating Harold's own family estates. So he force-marched his army – at least, those elite soldiers (mostly mounted) who could keep up – some 304km (190 miles) south from York to London. He then halted in London for six days, calling up local levies to reinforce his weary troops, before continuing the further 80km (50 miles) to the site of the battle, 11.2km (7 miles) north of Hastings (the modern town of Battle).

There, Harold appears to have been surprised by the Normans as he waited for more troops to join him. The English army was caught on high ground, from which it could not retreat because of Norman cavalry. (Although modern military historians are coming around to the view that pre-conquest English armies included cavalry, there is no evidence of them at Hastings). Most desperately, Harold seems to have had few archers with him, probably because he had not had time to summon levies from the western shires that provided archers, and the northern ones had been left behind as Harold hurried south. So Harold's force of 7000 to 8000 fighters, without cavalry and without archers, was only able to defend rather than attack. The Norman army, by contrast, had between 1000 and 2000 cavalry and 5000 to 6000 infantry. Many of the infantrymen were archers. They proved so essential to the victory that the aristocratic designer of the Bayeaux Tapestry felt compelled to include a number of William's archers in the design – although they are depicted smaller than the knights.

Hastings was a desperately fought battle that lasted from dawn until dusk. The English formed a shield wall, lining the infantry up closely side by side so that they could defend themselves and their neighbours with battleaxes and shields. The front ranks were surely stiffened by the household troops of Harold and his nobles, men who knew there was no retreat from the Norman horsemen. And in fact,

1030

31 August Battle of Stiklestad, Norway. King St Olav of Norway is defeated and killed when he attempts to return from exile in Russia.

1031

Fall of the caliphate of Córdoba, leaving Muslim Spain divided among a number of rival successor states *(taifas)*.

1035

Civil war in northern Italy, caused by a revolt of the vavassour class.

William charged time and again, only to be repulsed by the well-armed Saxons. William himself was nearly killed as he led his knights. Finally, a combination of two elements brought the battle to an end. William saw how a group of Englishmen had broken formation to chase retreating Norman cavalrymen. So he tried his favoured ploy of a feigned retreat. As in France, a large number of the enemy started a pursuit, and were easily killed when the knights turned on them at the signal. Even such ploys would probably not have been enough to win the day, though, if it had not been for the devastation that was wrought by the Norman archers. They inflicted severe casualties on the English throughout the day, finally bringing down King Harold himself with an arrow in his eye, at which resistance crumbled.

The Cavalry Advantage

William the Conqueror rapidly settled knights in England after the conquest, creating a new military aristocracy of about 5000 men. This force, combined with the service of about 1000

Left: William the Conqueror surveying the battlefield after the Battle of Hastings (1066).

Right: Weapons being carried to the ships for the Norman invasion of England (1066), from the Bayeux Tapestry.

1038–1040

A Byzantine army under George Maniaces attempts to recover Sicily from Muslim control, taking Messina and Syracuse.

1039

Milan, Italy. First known use of a *carroccio*, a standard in the form of a banner on a pole mounted in a wheeled cart.

Bretislaus I of Bohemia invades Poland, conquering part of Silesia and sacking Gniezno.

dependable knights from Normandy, gave William by far the largest force of knights west of the Rhine. Nonetheless, William and his successors also depended heavily on mercenaries, especially infantrymen, recruiting them above all from Brittany.

Knights in their first great age of prominence did not yet fight as they did in the later Middle Ages, charging in a tight mass with lances firmly couched under their arms, so the power of both knight and horse lay behind the lance thrust. Instead, as can be seen in the Bayeux Tapestry, knights fought holding spears either overhand or underhand depending on the situation, often using the height of the horse (admittedly only about 12 hands on average in the eleventh century) to thrust downward at dismounted enemies.

Indeed, knights appear to have been regarded as useful in the eleventh century not for their shock tactics but for their mobility and training.

....

The Battle of Hastings has fascinated the English ever since 1066. This Victorian illustration depicts a Norman knight with reasonable accuracy, although Norman archers did not wear pantaloons.

1040

15 **August** Macbeth of Scotland kills his cousin King Duncan I in battle at Pitgaveny and seizes the throne.

1041

German emperor, Henry III, defeats the Bohemians.

4 **May** Battle of Monte Maggiore. The Normans in southern Italy defeat a Byzantine army, the most important of three victories in 1041.

1042-1043

Civil war in Milan between nobles and non-nobles.

This engraving suggests that William the Conqueror's coronation as king of England was a violent event; in reality, most of the English accepted him as their rightful ruler after the Battle of Hastings.

It is important to note that, while not professionals by modern definition, knights tended to be highly trained men who repeatedly showed their military discipline in engagements all over Europe and the Near East. We know nothing about the training of prospective knights in this period, although we can be certain that it included a great deal of muscle building, riding (often in the form of hunting) and exercises to improve hand-eye coordination. The popularity of tournaments allows us to gain a better look at how adult knights remained in fighting trim.

Tournaments – mock battles between opposed teams of knights – first became popular in the 1090s, and were well established in much of Europe by about 1130. Unlike the individual jousting of the later Middle Ages, the tournament in the central Middle Ages was a melée that could include over 100 knights on each side. The most successful tournament fighters were those who employed good teamwork, the same quality that won battles. There is no mention of using blunted weapons until the thirteenth century, and death and serious injury were frequent occurrences. Churchmen repeatedly tried to outlaw

Tournaments first became popular in the late eleventh century, but it was only much later that one-on-one combats became the norm.

1042–1044

German campaigns against the Hungarians, in response to a Hungarian attack on the German southern frontier.

tournaments, threatening excommunication and even denying Christian burial to those killed while participating. Like so many of the Church's proscriptions of medieval war, though, these admonitions passed unheeded. Tournaments were simply too useful. Besides providing training that would make knights more likely to survive and win glory in battle, a tournament was a great place to catch the eye of a wealthy lord and thus win position in a noble household or even a fief. Tournaments were also an important source of wealth for impoverished knights, because a knight fortunate enough to subdue and capture an enemy knight was able to claim his arms and horse.

The Age of Fortifications

Another important military trend that became omnipresent in the eleventh century was the building of castles, small fortresses intended for security and to hold a hostile countryside. Earlier medieval Europe had known a spate of town-wall building after the Vikings, Magyars and Saracens began their raids. Individual noble manors, however, remained for the mostly unfortified.

Clifford's Tower, York, was first built in wood in 1068 to help William the Conqueror control northern England.

One of Europe's first important castle-builders was Count Fulk Nerra of Anjou, who in the late tenth and early eleventh century was absolutely unrelenting in his effort to seize territory from his neighbours. He won a series of battles – but battles alone do not suffice to hold a land. So Fulk constructed lines of castles, gradually extending into enemy territory. The Normans who conquered southern Italy in the eleventh century followed a similar policy, expanding their control over a region castle by castle, using each castle as a base to terrorize the surrounding territory into submission. These fortresses offered security to small garrisons that could be left on the spot permanently. Enemy forces could not move freely in the vicinity of castles, for fear that the garrison would sally out in surprise attacks. And even a simple fortress was a formidable obstacle to the technological abilities of the day. Almost the sole option available to attackers was the construction of a counter-castle, using it as the base for a long blockade. Only at the end of the century, during the First Crusade, do we see the evolution of more complex techniques.

1043

Russian attack on Constantinople is halted by the Byzantine fleet.

Battle of Lysborg. A Wendish army invades Jutland, but is defeated by a Norwegian force led by King Magnus I Olafsson.

1044

Battle of Menfö. German emperor, Conrad II, decisively defeats the Hungarians, forcing the Hungarian king to become his vassal.

Battle of Aarhus. King Magnus of Norway and Denmark defeats his rival Earl Svein.

Byzantine emperor Constantine IX Monomachus disbands his native troops in Armenia, demanding tax payments instead of military service.

First mention of gunpowder, in a Chinese written work.

Arundel Castle, West Sussex. At the heart of the castle, the mound and circular building is a motte and bailey structure that dates back to the Norman period.

Most castles were simple indeed. The most common form is what is known as the 'motte and bailey' castle, which could be built in as little as a month by 100 to 200 men. The design was simple: the builders excavated a deep trench, heaping the dirt into a mound that could stand as high as 20m (66ft.). At the top of the artificial hill, which had a diameter of up to 30m (98ft) at its height, they then built a simple wooden palisade. Often another palisade enclosed a larger area at the foot of the mound – the bailey. For something more permanent, a lord could erect a keep, a simple square structure with thick walls of stone and its sole entrance well above ground level to help with defence.

The war-prone duchies of northwest France were soon filled with castles; one survey of a 20sq km (12.4 sq mile) area of Normandy found the remains of no fewer than 5 stone castles and 24 earthworks! William took the castle-building mania with him to England, constructing an estimated 500–550 castles in the country between 1066 and 1087. He had great stone castles erected at London (the White Tower of the Tower of London) and Colchester, but soon found such building projects too expensive and turned to more modest structures. Without such a building programme, William would never have been able to hold England.

The Great German Civil War

Castles were a means of control that naturally developed earliest in regions whose populace had cause to dislike their rulers. This was a

1047–1064

King Harald Hardrada of Norway fights Svein Estrithson in an ultimately unsuccessful attempt to bring Denmark back under Norwegian control.

1047

Battle of Val-ès-Dunes. Duke William of Normandy and his ally King Henry I of France defeat a coalition of rebel Norman nobles southeast of Caen.

1048–1069

Seljuk Turkish raids into Byzantine-held Asia Minor.

The imperial palace at Goslar, Saxony, built in the eleventh century. Its lack of fortifications suggests the strength of German rulers in the period.

peace between the end of the Magyar raids in 955 and the death of Emperor Henry III in 1056. Thus both kings and nobles normally lived in unfortified manor houses, such as the royal palace that still stands at Goslar.

That internal security began to crumble even in the time of Henry III, and the problem rapidly escalated in the reign of his son Henry IV (1056–1106). The problem was fourfold. The issue of longest standing was the growing discontent of the Saxons. The dukes of Saxony had been kings of Germany for most of the tenth century and had given their homeland many privileges. Ever since 1004, though, German kings had rarely visited Saxony – but still tried to assert personal rule without personal knowledge of the needs and personalities of the region. A second issue, catastrophic for royal control in Germany, was that Henry III had died prematurely, leaving a

matter for France in particular, a land of weak political organizations, and for the regions conquered by the Normans. Germany did not follow suit until the middle of the eleventh century. Under its Ottonian and Salian rulers, Germany had enjoyed a high degree of internal

1052

Summer The exiled Earl Godwin and his family invade England. King Edward the Confessor's army refuse to fight, and the king is forced to make terms.

1053

17 June Battle of Civitate. Pope Leo IX personally leads an army against the Normans of southern Italy led by Robert Guiscard. The papal army is heavily defeated; Pope Leo is captured and forced to acknowledge Norman control of southern Italy.

25 October Battle of St-Aubin-sur-Scie. Duke William of Normandy defeats Henry I of France, ending a French invasion of Normandy.

1054

Great East–West Schism of the Church begins.

Earl Siward raids Scotland in a major operation that includes a fleet as well as a land army.

Battle of Dunsinane, Scotland. Malcolm III Canmore, son of the murdered king, Duncan, defeats Macbeth.

six-year-old boy to take the throne and no strong figure to serve as regent. So the young Henry IV found himself at the centre of a power struggle, kidnapped several times by unscrupulous men who wanted to control Germany through him. The problem was only exacerbated when Henry IV came of age and began to reclaim his rights and take vengeance against those who had seized them – Henry had anything but a conciliatory personality. Adding a final assurance of chaos, Henry IV became embroiled in a fight with the papacy – the so-called 'Investiture Controversy', which led a series of popes to do everything in their power to undermine the king of Germany's power and authority.

By about 1060, German nobles were building castles in large numbers, anticipating troubled times to come. For example, the earliest reference to Zollerburg, the family castle of the Hohenzollern dynasty, dates from 1061.

Henry IV of Germany, begging Countess Matilda of Tuscany to help him in his quarrel with Pope Gregory VII. Henry IV reaped the consequences of his dynasty's strength – a strong reaction from the German nobility that tore Germany apart in civil war.

1055

Seljuk Turks capture Baghdad.

Battle of Hereford. The exiled Earl Aelfgar of Mercia invades England with an Irish and Welsh force. He defeats a royal army under Ralph the Timid of Hereford.

REX ROGAT ABBATEM. MATHILDIM SUPPLICAT ATQ;

Hohenzollern Castle, near Stuttgart, Germany. The castle was originally built in the eleventh century; the current structure was built between 1454 and 1461.

Frederick of Büren built Staufen, headquarters of the Hohenstaufen dynasty, in about 1077. And Henry IV built castles by the dozen, in the face of the Saxons' unrest. His castles only provoked *more* rebellion, initiating a downward spiral of social anarchy and the building of castles. Many of the castles that still attract tourists to Germany, Austria, Switzerland and Italy owe their start to the social dislocation of the Investiture Controversy and the German civil war that accompanied it. These castles tended to be located on natural defensible sites, so did not normally include the motte that was characteristic of castles further west.

An Age of Rebellion

The German civil war of the eleventh century is only the bloodiest example of another feature of warfare in the eleventh century: a surprising amount of military effort took the form of rebellion and putting down rebellion. Sometimes these conflicts were unequal, as lords and their

---

1057

15 August Battle of Lumphanan. King Macbeth of Scotland is defeated and killed by Malcolm III Canmore, his rival for the throne of Scotland.

August Battle of Varaville. William of Normandy routs a French/Angevin invasion led by Henry I of France and Count Geoffrey of Anjou.

1061–1091

Norman conquest of Sicily.

1062

9 August King Harald Hardrada of Norway defeats the Danish Svein Estrithsson in a nondecisive sea battle at Nisaa.

well equipped fighting forces suppressed peasant insurrections. More often, though, the battles were waged between similarly equipped opponents and thus tended to be drawn-out and inconclusive affairs.

Italy was particularly prone to rebellion. Northern Italians did not much like being ruled by the German emperors, and tended to revolt when they had the opportunity. The largely hands-off German government in that region also proved to be a fertile ground for urban development, and non-nobles sometimes took up arms against nobles, as in Milan's civil war of 1042–1043. In southern Italy, the Normans held tenaciously onto the land they had seized, but a series of popes encouraged the Normans' new subjects to rebel – not that they probably needed encouragement, since the Normans were demanding overlords.

Elsewhere, 'new' power was resented. In Normandy, the baronial class had returned to anarchy when their strong duke, Robert the

Now regarded as romantic, the many ruined castles of Germany attest to the land's violent history in the later Middle Ages.

1063

Norman conquest of Maine, France.

Earl Harold Godwinsson raids Wales, employing a fleet to reinforce his army.

Battle of Cerami. A Norman force under Roger I, the Great Count, defeats a much larger Muslim army in an all-day battle that gives the Normans a foothold in Sicily.

Sultan Alp Arslan unites the Seljuk empire.

1064

German 'Great Pilgrimage' to Jerusalem by a reported 7000 pilgrims, led by the bishop of Bamberg.

Conquest of Barbastro by an Aragonese and French force, in the first important success of the *reconquista*. (Barbastro is lost again within the year.)

Italian Normans led by Robert Guiscard and Roger I, the Great Count, attack Palermo with the assistance of a Pisan fleet, but are driven off.

Hereward the Wake led the most important Anglo-Saxon rebellion against Norman rule; this illustration shows his attack on Peterborough Abbey in 1070.

Magnificent, died in 1035. When Robert's illegitimate son William came of age, he had to fight for years to regain his rights. As was often the case when dealing with rebels, the young William could be savage in his reprisals: at the siege of Alençon in 1049, he mutilated all survivors of the garrison for mocking him as a lowborn bastard. As king of England after 1066, William proved to be similarly ruthless, most notably in the 'Harrying of the North' of 1070, when he put down rebellion in northern England with such massive punitive raids that much of the population starved. It should be noted, though, that many English soldiers helped William to suppress local uprisings, especially when confronted with the threat of being declared *nithing* – worthless cowards.

In other cases of supposed insurrection, no clear dynasty had yet been established. Eleventh-century Scandinavian claimants to the thrones of Norway and Denmark fought one another repeatedly in a process of state formation that is more reminiscent of rams competing for dominance than of an unquestioned king defending himself against clearly defined rebels. In Scotland, too, Macbeth's defeat and killing of King Duncan was a normal consequence of rapidly shifting political alliances (despite what Shakespeare says), as was Macbeth's own defeat and death at the hands of his rival Malcolm III Canmore at the Battle of Lumphanan on 15 August 1057.

The Rebellion Against Henry IV

The most shocking of eleventh-century rebellions was that against Henry IV of Germany, the heir of a long-established and strong royal authority that simply proved to be too strong for its subjects' taste. The Saxons broke out in revolt in 1073, after Henry IV tried to annex the duchy on the death of the old duke. Attacks on the king were directed especially against his hated new castles. This hatred went so deep that peasants destroyed Harzburg near Goslar in 1074, even razing the church and desecrating the graves of Henry IV's brother and infant son in the process. Such sacrilege lost the rebels support, and royal forces routed the rebels at the Battle of Langensalza in June 1075, but a second revolt soon broke out. While the second revolt did not enjoy the broad popular support of the first, it proved to be

1066

April Appearance of Halley's Comet.

20 September Battle of Gate Fulford. King Harald Hardrada of Norway invades England and defeats the army of the northern earls, Edwin and Morcar, at Gate Fulford (now a suburb of York). The earls make terms with Harald.

25 September Battle of Stamford Bridge. An English force led by King Harold Godwinsson surprises Harald Hardrada. The Norwegian force is decisively defeated, and both Hardrada and Harold Godwinsson's rebel brother Tostig are killed.

28 September Duke William of Normandy's invasion fleet lands at Pevensey, England.

14 October Battle of Hastings. In a hard-fought battle 11.2km (7 miles) north of Hastings, William of Normandy decisively defeats and kills Harold Godwinsson.

25 December William of Normandy (the Conqueror) is crowned king of England at Westminster.

1068

King Sancho I Ramirez of Aragón becomes a papal vassal, hoping for military support against the Muslims kingdoms of central Spain.

Ending the first phase of Germany's long civil war, the Saxon nobles submitted to King Henry IV at Speyer, 25 October 1075.

more dangerous because it consisted of nobles, the knightly class and a large number of churchmen. The situation was aggravated by Henry's major rift with Pope Gregory VII. The pope excommunicated Henry and encouraged rebellion. Henry averted deposition only by crossing the Alps in midwinter (evading the rebels who tried to prevent this move) and reaching the pope at Canossa in northern Italy, where Henry then pleaded so persistently for forgiveness that Gregory had to raise the excommunication. Nonetheless, the rebels soon elected Duke Rudolf of Swabia as anti-king and the fight continued. Over the years, two of Henry's sons joined the rebellion against him, and Henry V succeeded in deposing his father in 1105.

Most battles of the German civil war were indecisive, leaving such confused accounts that both sides could claim victory. These battles saw interesting experimentation on how to use

1068–1071

5 August 1068–16 April 1071 Siege of Bari. The Norman Robert Guiscard gains the last Byzantine stronghold on the peninsula.

1069

King Svein Estrithson of Denmark attacks England, making common cause with a general uprising in Yorkshire against Norman rule. King William bribes the Danes to leave.

1070

The 'Harrying of the North'. William the Conqueror's great punitive raids against northern England after the uprising of 1069.

Svein Estrithson of Denmark invades England, joining with the rebel Hereward 'the Wake' of Lincolnshire. The Danes are bribed to leave.

cavalry and infantry together. For example, at the Battle of Elster on 15 October 1080, the Saxons were short on infantry (which had been pursuing Henry IV, whose army had been ravaging the duchy), so they dismounted many of their cavalry to strengthen the line against Henry's cavalry. Although the anti-king Rudolf was killed in the battle, the advantage probably went to the rebels, especially as Henry IV had fled the field as soon as close fighting began. At Pleichfeld in August 1086, the Saxons again fought dismounted around their standard, and inflicted a serious defeat on the king.

The Expansion of Europe

The last major development of European warfare in the eleventh century was a decisive

....

Left: The tomb of Rudolf of Swabia (died 1080), who fought against Henry IV as anti-king until his death at the Battle of Elster.

Right: Entry of Rodrigo Díaz, the Cid, into Muslim Valencia. One of the greatest Christian generals of medieval Spain, the Cid became the subject of legend and song.

1071

Summer Siege of Ely. William the Conqueror defeats rebels led by Hereward at Ely. Hereward escapes.

5, 19, or 26 August Battle of Manzikert. A Seljuk army led by Sultan Alp Arslan annihilates a large Byzantine army commanded by Emperor Romanos IV Diogenes.

Seljuk conquest of Jerusalem from the Fatimids.

22 February Battle of Cassel. Robert the Frisian defeats and kills his nephew Arnulf III, claiming the county of Flanders.

turn in favour of expansion on a number of fronts. Except for the Ottonian rulers of Germany's ultimately unsuccessful efforts to establish lordship over Slavic territory, the tenth century had been a time when Europeans had been invaded instead of invading others. Times were changing, however. The governments of the eleventh century, whether local or at the level of states, were rapidly developing bureaucracies under which they could not only survive but expand. For a prime example of this phenomenon, look no further than the magnificent logistical effort behind the Norman conquest of England in 1066. States were getting ambitious, and had more money to invest in campaigning than Europeans had had at their command since ancient Rome. And thus began a series of enterprises that continued for centuries: the Spanish *reconquista*, the successful Italian claim to the Mediterranean, and the crusades.

The Reconquista
Since the Muslim conquest of most of Spain in the early eighth century, a number of small Christian kingdoms had held onto a bare

Muslim cavalrymen tended to rely more on speed and mobility than their Christian counterparts, armouring themselves or their horses less frequently than Western knights.

existence in the foothills of the Pyrenees. They suffered periodic raids from the forces of the Umayyad caliphate to their south, which could

muster a considerably greater military force than all the Christian Hispanic kingdoms combined. Ultimately, however, the caliphate proved to be

1072

10 January Muslim Palermo falls to Norman duke, Robert Guiscard, after a long blockade and naval victory over a Tunisian relieving fleet.

Great Raid of Scotland. William the Conqueror of England pillages the eastern coast of Scotland by land and sea, forcing Malcolm III Canmore of Scotland to accept William's overlordship.

1073–1074

Saxon siege of the royal castle of Harzburg, near Goslar, Germany. Henry agrees to dismantle the castle, but local peasants raze it themselves.

1073–1075

1073–1075 Saxon rebellion against German emperor Henry IV, provoked by Henry IV's aggressive castle-building policy.

unstable, and it dissolved under a variety of internal pressures in 1031. The Muslim successor states, the *taifas*, were much smaller, spent much of their time fighting each other, and had much less access to the slave-soldiers who had provided the core of Umayyad armies. At about the same time, French-style heavy cavalry was gradually being introduced into the Christian kingdoms.

The result was the beginning of what was proclaimed as a *reconquista* – a reconquest – of lands that belonged to the Christians by right (although ruled by Muslims for the past three centuries). The Christian kings began probing for weak spots among the *taifas*, demanding tribute and seizing outposts. In 1064 came the first important success, the conquest of Barbastro by a mixed Catalan and Aragonese

....

Left: Pope Alexander II (1061–1073), a reforming pope whose actions included blessing William the Conqueror's invasion of England and a move toward alliance with the Normans of southern Italy.

Right: Loarre Castle, in Huesca province, Spain. Much of the castle dates back to the later eleventh century.

1074

Pope Gregory VII campaigns unsuccessfully against the Norman Robert Guiscard in southern Italy.

1075

9 June Battle of Unstrut. Henry IV of Germany's army routs Saxon rebels.

1076

14 February Pope Gregory VII excommunicates Henry IV of Germany.

Rodrigo Díaz de Vivar, known as El Cid (1040–1099). Although regarded as the first great hero of the Spanish reconquista, El Cid frequently fought alongside Muslims and against Christians.

....

force. Pointing the way to the future, these Spanish troops had been joined by a force led by the duke of Aquitaine from southern France, to whom Pope Alexander II promised a remission of penance in return for participation in this godly endeavour. King Sancho I Ramírez of Aragón became a vassal of the pope in 1068, apparently hoping to gain more military support. The next great coup, however, went to Alfonso VI of Castile, who took the great Islamic city of Toledo in 1085.

These Christian successes provoked a reaction, however. The alarmed emirs of the taifas begged for assistance from a strong new dynasty of northern Africa, the Almoravids. The Almoravid ruler Yusuf ibn Tashufin did indeed come to Spain and decisively defeated Alfonso VI at Sagrajas on 23 October 1086. The Castilians tried to sweep the enemy before them with a large-scale cavalry charge. It failed,

1076–1088

Second Saxon rebellion. Unlike the first rebellion, this is a rising mostly of secular and ecclesiastical nobles, without broad popular support.

1077

26–28 January Henry IV begs the pope's forgiveness at Canossa, and is finally released from his excommunication.

March German rebels supported by Pope Gregory VII elect Duke Rudolf of Swabia as anti-king.

Pisa establishes control of Corsica.

1077–1122

Wars of Investiture. A confused and devastating civil war is fought in Germany and Italy between supporters of Henry IV and Pope Gregory VII.

The Almoravid dynasty of North Africa developed in a society still filled with reminders of the Roman past, such as this amphitheatre at El Jem, Tunisia.

though, because the Muslim infantry spearmen were well disciplined enough to maintain tight ranks before the threat (rather like the Englishmen at Hastings), and the Castilians were outnumbered. The arrival of the Almoravids for a time reversed the direction of reconquest, although before the end of the century Rodrigo Díaz of Valencia (famed in later legend as 'El Cid') proved in several battles that the new invaders were not invincible.

War in the Mediterranean

Also a sign that times were changing was the new aggression of several Italian cities in the Mediterranean. Trade had been limited for centuries because the early Muslim conquests had broken Byzantine domination of the main sailing routes. Piracy was endemic, seen in the tenth century in periodic raids on Italy and southern France as well as the seizure of ships.

1078

7 August Battle of Mellrichstadt. A long battle between Henry IV and Saxon rebels, in which both sides claim victory.

1080

27 January Battle of Flarchheim. A bloody but indecisive battle between Henry IV of Germany and his rival Rudolf of Swabia.

15 October Battle of Elster (Hohen–Mölsen). An indecisive battle between Henry IV and his rival Rudolf of Swabia, in which Rudolf is killed.

1081

Battle of Durazzo (modern Albania). The Italian Normans under Robert Guiscard invade Byzantine territory, only to be defeated by a Byzantine-Venetian fleet.

18 October Second Battle of Durazzo. Fighting on land, the Normans under Robert Guiscard defeat a Byzantine army.

By the second half of the eleventh century, several Italian port cities were ready to contest this state of affairs. They had won effective independence from the control of the German emperor, and wealthy merchants, who wanted to protect and expand their interests, dominated town councils. Thus in 1087 Pisa and Genoa agreed on a joint expedition against Mahdia in North Africa, a major pirate centre. They took the place and sacked it, a key step in gaining Latin ascendancy in the western Mediterranean.

The Turkish Threat

In the ninth and tenth centuries, the Byzantine Empire had done a good job protecting the eastern flank of Europe. Emperor Basil II was able to subdue the Bulgarians, thanks especially to his great victory at Belashita on 29 July 1014,

The Byzantine Empire suffered a steep decline during the reign of Empress Zoe (1028–1050) (right) and her husbands, including Constantine IX Monomachos (left), who was a good general but could make little headway against the political rivalries of his age. He is remembered mostly for undermining the system that had paid for the Byzantine army for centuries.

1084

Battle of Corfu. The Norman Robert Guiscard invades the Byzantine Empire with a large fleet, defeating a Greco-Venetian fleet off Corfu.

Seljuk Turks conquer Byzantine Antioch.

Henry IV of Germany sack Rome. Pope Gregory VII flees into exile with the Normans of southern Italy.

Henry IV of Germany is crowned emperor by the anti-pope he installed in Rome.

1085

In a battle off Syracuse, Robert Guiscard's southern Italian fleet defeat a large Muslim flotilla.

6 May Alfonso VI of Castile-Léon takes the major Muslim centre of Toledo after a short siege.

A massive military coalition is formed against William the Conqueror of England, including Denmark, Flanders, France, Scotland, Anjou, and William's son Robert. The invasion never takes place, thanks to the assassination of Cnut IV of Denmark.

when he captured almost all of Tsar Samuel's army – and blinded a reputed 15,000 prisoners to prevent further resistance. After Basil's death in 1025, however, the Byzantine military establishment suffered a rapid decline as bureaucrats and generals manoeuvred for power at court. By the 1040s, Emperor Constantine IX Monamachos was engaged in a ceaseless quest for money. He went so far as to disband the native troops in Armenia in 1044, ordering them to pay taxes instead of providing their traditional military service and instead relying on mercenaries. Unfortunately, this was precisely the period when the Byzantine Empire began to suffer raids from the Seljuk Turks.

Turkic peoples had been moving into the Islamic Middle East for centuries, many as slave-soldiers in the

King Baldwin I of Jerusalem (1100–1118) in battle with the Turks, from a fifteenth-century chronicle.

1086

The Muslim ruler al-Mu'tamid of Seville, worried at Christian successes, invites the Almoravid Dynasty of North Africa to Spain.

August Battle of Pleichfeld. Saxon rebels defeat the army of Emperor Henry IV.

23 October Battle of Sagrajas. An Almoravid force led by Yusuf ibn Tashufin decisively defeats the Castilian army under King Alfonso VI.

1087

9 September Death of William I, the Conqueror.

A joint Pisan/Genoese expedition seizes and sacks Mahdia (modern Tunisia), a major pirate centre, establishing Latin ascendancy in the western Mediterranean.

1090s

Tournaments first became popular in western Europe.

service of the caliph. The Turks fought in the manner of the steppe, mounted, without body armour, and carrying only a light shield and sword. They relied for the most part on strong composite bows. Under the Seljuk dynasty, the Turks launched significant raids into Byzantine lands from 1048 to 1069, also capturing Baghdad in 1055 and establishing a 'protectorate' over the Abbasid caliph.

By 1071 the Seljuks, welded into a strong state

....

Left: Byzantine emperor Alexios Komnenos, from a twelfth-century mosaic in Hagia Sofia.

Right: Emperor Romanos IV Diogenes (1068–1071) and Empress Eudocia.

1090–1097

German Emperor Henry IV campaigns unsuccessfully to subdue rebellion in Lombardy.

1091

29 April Battle of Mt Levunion. Byzantine emperor Alexios I Comnenos and Kuman allies annihilate a Pecheneg army, ending the Pecheneg threat to Byzantium.

by their sultan Alp Arslan, were a serious threat, and the Byzantine emperor, Romanos IV Diogenes, took the field against them in a major campaign intended to recover Armenia and restore his eastern frontier. Unfortunately, though, his army was low in morale and training, and included traitors among the commanders. These factors, added to the difficulty of coming to grips with the mounted Seljuks, led to a disastrous defeat at Manzikert. The emperor himself was captured and, although he was released soon after agreeing to Alp Arslan's quite moderate demands, he was murdered soon after his return to Constantinople.

The Battle of Manzikert was certainly a major defeat, but a

A fifteenth-century French artist's impression of one of the battles of the First Crusade.

1092–1105

After Sultan Malik-shah died in 1092, his sons fight for the throne in an extended succession crisis.

1093

13 November First Battle of Alnwick. King Malcolm III of Scotland invades England, but is defeated and killed.

German emperor Henry IV's son Conrad rebels, winning the allegiance of northern Italy and the papal party to his cause.

1094

Fatimid caliph al-Mustansir dies, after nearly 60 years of rule, sparking an extended succession crisis.

single battle could not completely destroy the centuries of Byzantine military infrastructure. A restoration of the army soon began under Emperor Alexios II Comnenos (1081–1118), who annihilated the Pechenegs in 1091 and prepared to regain the lands seized by the Seljuks in Asia Minor.

Calling the Crusade

At that point, the military agenda of eastern and western Europe converged in a fashion both startling and ultimately, for the Byzantine Empire, devastating. Alexios, short of troops, sent an embassy to Pope Urban II, asking for his help to raise mercenaries in the West. Urban was quite interested in sending western knights to the East, but for very different reasons. The pope was deeply concerned with the endemic warfare of Europe, and had joined in proclaiming the Truce of God in an effort to limit the devastation of Europe. Himself the son of a French knightly family, Urban saw

....

Godfrey of Bouillon storming the wall of Jerusalem (15 July 1099) in an illustration that depicts the defenders as savages, rather than the well-equipped soldiers they were.

Battle of Cuarte, Spain. Rodrigo Díaz (El Cid) routs an Almoravid army.

Battle of Bairén. Rodrigo Díaz (El Cid) heavily defeats an Almoravid army.

the destruction wrought by large numbers of younger sons who had no profession other than fighting and no security in society. And, most importantly, he was a product of Western spirituality in the eleventh century in his fascination with the earthly home of Jesus Christ, the Holy Land – which Christians regarded as territory now unjustly held by Muslims.

Therefore, Emperor Alexios did not get what he bargained for when he asked for Pope Urban's help. Instead, at a great council held at Clermont, France, in November 1095, Urban proclaimed what has become known as the First Crusade. The goal was no longer war against the Turks to preserve the Byzantine Empire, but war against all Muslims to regain Jerusalem for Christendom. And those who engaged in the war were not to be mercenaries but would receive a great spiritual reward – the remission of penalty for all the sins they had committed before that point.

....

Duke Robert of Normandy on the First Crusade. He mortgaged his duchy to his brother and never succeeded in reclaiming it on his return from the Holy Land.

1094

El Cid captures Valencia, Spain.

The proclamation of the First Crusade caught the imagination of Western Europe, especially France. Wandering preachers spread the word, and no fewer than five major armies eventually set out for the East. It is reckoned that anywhere between 30,000 and 70,000 fighters took part, along with about 30,000 non-combatants, presenting a logistical challenge unheard of since Roman times. Perhaps as many as nine-tenths of these men and women died or turned back before they reached their goal. Nonetheless, the first crusaders succeeded in taking Jerusalem on 14 July 1099, and established several small European colonies on the eastern coast of the Mediterranean. The struggle to hold onto these small states in the face of Islamic efforts at reconquest became a major theme in European warfare for centuries, as crusade after crusade set off to hold or regain the Holy Land.

The Lessons of the First Crusade

The First Crusade, falling as it did in the years 1096–1099, provides a handy primer of Europe's military capabilities at the end of the eleventh century. Close examination shows that

Crusaders at the city of Nicaea. The city made a negotiated surrender to Byzantine emperor Alexios.

1095	1096–1099	1096
		German crusaders led by Count Emicho of Leiningen attack and destroy Jewish communities in the Rhineland.
March Council of Piacenza, at which emissaries of Byzantine emperor Alexios Comnenos seek papal help against the Turks.	First Crusade.	
		August Count Emicho of Leiningen's crusader army is annihilated in Hungary.
27 November Pope Urban II proclaims the first crusade at the Council of Clermont.		**August** Battle of Nicaea. A Seljuk force slaughters much of the 'People's Crusade' led by Peter the Hermit.
		21 October Battle of Civetot. The remnant of the 'People's Crusade' is ambushed and destroyed by a Seljuk army.

1097–1102

War between Hungary and Venice. King Calomar I of Hungary wins control of the coast of Dalmatia.

1097

19 June Nicaea (Asia Minor) surrenders on terms after a short siege by the crusader army and a Byzantine fleet.

1 July Battle of Dorylaeum. Seljuks under Sultan Kilij Arslan attempt to ambush the main crusader army, but the crusaders win a major victory that ends the Seljuk threat to the First Crusade.

Rodrigo Díaz (El Cid) conquers Almenara, Spain.

1097–1098

October 1097–3 June 1098 Siege of Antioch. After a long and painful siege, the crusader army gains access to Antioch when a traitor opens a city gate.

1098

28 June Battle of Antioch. The crusaders break out of Antioch and defeat Kerbogha, governor of Mosul.

Rodrigo Díaz (El Cid) takes the seemingly impregnable Rock of Murviedro, confirming his reputation as one of the greatest commanders of the age.

This miniature by Jean Fouquet (dating from about 1450) depicts Pope Urban II's call for the First Crusade at the Council of Clermont, 1095.

....

the armies of the First Crusade, when well led by major nobles, were an astonishingly well trained and cohesive military force, with surprising sophistication in leadership and logistical support.

Without eleventh-century developments in transport, the crusade could never have succeeded. Some of the crusaders did indeed set out without making adequate provision: the so-called People's Crusade looted its way through Hungary, and German crusaders led by Emicho of Leiningen stole supplies while massacring much of the Jewish population of the Rhineland. By contrast, the great lords like Duke Godfrey of Lower Lotharingia, Duke Robert of Normandy, or the Italian Norman Prince Bohemund of Taranto, bought supplies beforehand, arranged for markets en route, and intelligently provided themselves with money and goods for an expedition that they knew would last several years. Indeed, it is a tribute

to their organizational skills that the crusaders did not suffer serious famine until the long siege of Antioch in 1097–1098, when a Turkish army blocked their supply route.

A second important lesson is that Europe's heavy cavalry, when well led by captains whom the men knew and trusted, could deal brilliantly with unexpected situations. The most telling example of this occurred at the Battle of Dorylaeum on 1 July 1097, when Seljuks ambushed the crusaders. The crusaders responded so rapidly and effectively that they turned catastrophe into a convincing victory, the Western knights and foot soldiers working in close coordination while under enemy fire. The discipline and capabilities of the western soldiers showed again at the Battle of Antioch on 28 June 1098, when, although starving and with most of their horses dead, they won a victory by manoeuvre against the vastly superior force of Kerboghah of Mosul. A third major victory, fought outside Ascalon on 12 August 1099, drove home the lesson that this was a trained, professional army, not a horde of barbarians. The crusaders also showed that Europeans had learnt a great deal in the past

century about fortifications – and how to overcome them. In their amphibious assault on Nicaea in 1097, they utilized a range of siege engines, some of which can admittedly be attributed to their Byzantine allies. At Antioch the walls were too imposing to assault, but the crusade leaders managed an effective blockade for over seven months. And at Jerusalem, we can see the full range of European siege expertise at the time, including machines that shot stones and large bolts, battering rams, and two enormous siege towers.

The Future of European Warfare

A final element of the First Crusade indicates what will characterize European warfare in the future: the presence of fleets. The Italian naval cities, especially Pisa, Venice and Genoa, provided logistical support at key times, a portent of much greater naval engagement in the future. And, in another sign of coming times, Venetian and Pisan seamen clashed in the harbour of Rhodes in 1099 while on their way to join the crusaders. Clearly, warfare in the eastern Mediterranean would not be waged only against Muslims.

1099–1102

Almoravid conquest of Valencia, Spain.

A Fatimid army under Wazir al-Afdal seizes Jerusalem from the Seljuks.

The Welsh Gruffudd ap Cynan launches naval raids on Anglesey and Gwynedd in alliance with the king of Mann, then defeats the earls of Chester and Shrewsbury in a sea battle off Anglesey.

Magnus III Bareleg of Norway conquers the Orkneys, Hebrides and Isle of Man.

1099

Death of Rodrigo Díaz (El Cid).

15 July Fall of Jerusalem to crusaders of the First Crusade and massacre of its inhabitants.

12 August Battle of Ascalon. Crusaders surprise and rout a large Egyptian army under Wazir al-Afdal.

The Twelfth Century: Castles and Crusaders

The twelfth century witnessed the 'coming of age' of several trends in European warfare. By now, Europe was thoroughly fortified. Nobles and rulers constructed castles of increasing complexity; towns were fortified with impressive walls. And while it has been argued that town walls in particular were built out of civic pride more than because of military need, many towns, especially in the twelfth century, did indeed need to defend themselves.

In large part because of the special challenges of siege warfare, it became increasingly common in the twelfth century to hire trained infantry, rather than summoning a general levy of men who were often poorly equipped and only available for limited service. This practice, of course, put further strains on governmental systems that had never been intended to bear such costs. Fortunately, warfare within the bounds of Europe was becoming even more

Left: Pope Alexander III blessing Doge Sebastiano Ziani as he sets out with the Venetian fleet.
Right: The city walls of Avila, Spain (1090) are among the most impressive medieval walls surviving in Europe.

rare, monarchs no longer conducting annual campaigns as a matter of course. But although there were thus fewer opportunities at home for the military class, crusading flourished in the twelfth century. Nearly every year in the twelfth century, contingents of warriors made their way to the Holy Land; the concept of the crusade also spread to non-Christians on the frontiers of Europe.

The Knights
In the twelfth century, Europeans learned how to use heavy cavalry, effectively the elite branch of later medieval armies. The status of knights rose in most regions, although Germany continued to have large numbers of 'servant knights' (*ministeriales*) and Spain even had

A European's impression of the Turkish incursion into Anatolia, one of the factors that sparked the First Crusade.

numbers of peasant knights, equipped as military retainers by their lords but still regarded as members of the lower class. In France, though, knighthood had for the most part become an inherited status, a practice that England increasingly emulated. And throughout Europe, knights can be seen by the end of the century consciously creating a 'noble' self-identity, whether in literary romances of knightly quests or in the religious ceremonies to 'make' a knight that were introduced in the course of the century.

Iron production increased in the twelfth century, thanks to better furnaces and the introduction of bellows driven by water power (hammer mills also came into use by the thirteenth century). This meant it was more financially possible for a knight to equip himself with the best armour and weapons possible. Knights already wore a chain-mail hauberk. To that they added mail leggings (*chausses*) by about 1150, and foot armour shortly thereafter.

1100–1101

The 'Crusade of 1101', led by Duke Welf IV of Bavaria, Count Stephen of Blois, Duke William IX of Aquitaine, Count William II of Nevers and Count Hugh of Vermandois.

1101

August Battle of Merzifon. Dashminid Turks annihilate a Lombard, German and French crusader army in Asia Minor.

20 August Battle of Heraclea (Asia Minor). Turks ambush and mostly destroy an army of Bavarian and Aquitanian crusaders.

26 August Second Battle of Heraclea. Turks crush William of Nevers' crusading army.

6 September Battle of Ramla. King Baldwin I of Jerusalem defeats a large Fatimid army in a dawn surprise attack.

1102

17 May Second Battle of Ramla. A Fatimid army under Saraf destroys a mixed force of settlers and crusaders led by Baldwin I of Jerusalem. Baldwin is almost the only survivor.

Left: The Teutonic Knight of this illustration is fully equipped with typical armour of the late twelfth century, including mailed protection for both hands and feet.
Right: A thirteenth-century French manuscript page depicting trade and industry.

By the end of the twelfth century, the sleeves of the hauberk were even sometimes extended into full mail mittens. Better helmets were also developed, with round-topped helms appearing in the middle of the century, soon with the addition of face guards; by the early thirteenth century, a flat-topped helm had evolved and this completely enclosed the knight's head. By the end of the century, it was hard work indeed to kill a knight.

But what to do with the knights on the battlefield remained a matter for experiment. We tend to think today that a knight was inseparable from his horse, but such was not the attitude of twelfth-century commanders, who often deployed dismounted knights to strengthen an infantry line. Such a tactic could win major battles, such as the victory of Henry I of England over his brother Duke

1103	1105	1105-1106	1106
Norwegian king Magnus III Bareleg is killed while campaigning in Ireland.	**20 April** Battle of Artah. Prince Tancred of Antioch defeats Ridwan of Aleppo.	German emperor Henry IV's son Henry rebels, forcing his father from power.	**28 September** Battle of Tinchebrai. King Henry of England defeats and captures his brother, Duke Robert of Normandy, reuniting England with Normandy.

Robert of Normandy at Tinchebrai in 1106, or the English triumph over King David of Scotland in the Battle of the Standard of 1138.

Left: At the Battle of the Standard (1138), the English force rallied to a carroccio, a wagon with a massive standard mounted on a ship's mast, a device common on the Continent but otherwise unheard-of in England.

....

Over the course of the century, though, the massed cavalry charge increasingly became the norm.

The Mercenary Curse

Commanders responded to the rising cavalry threat with infantry that was more highly trained and equipped with bows or spears. This in turn helps to explain why twelfth-century rulers increasingly employed mercenary foot soldiers. Rulers had a right to military service from their nobles, just as the nobles had a right to demand service from the knights who held land for them. But often the military service that arrived was not what a commander actually needed in a given fighting situation. Knights came with attendant squires and sergeants, less heavily armed but usually mounted. Trained archers, especially archers able to fight as a team, were not included in feudal levies, yet all

XIIᵉ SIÈCLE.

N.º 49.

PIETON, Arbalétrier.

1107–1110	1108	1109–1111	1109
German-Polish war.	German invasion of Hungary is repelled.	Bohemond of Antioch's 'crusade' against the Byzantine Empire. Bohemond besieges the town of Durazzo, but Emperor Alexios Comnenos destroys Bohemond's fleet. Bohemond is trapped and forced to agree to a humiliating treaty.	Latin conquest of Tripoli.
	King Sigurd of Norway's crusader fleet of 60 ships defeats a Muslim fleet off the coast of Portugal.		**14 August** Battle of Glogau (Hundsfeld). A Polish army led by Boleslav III defeats a German invasion of Silesia.
			Battle of Naklo. Boleslav III of Poland retakes Pomerania.

Left: Crossbows became a standard part of European warfare in the twelfth century.

....

twelfth-century armies needed archers and infantry spearmen to work with the knights. Even when the feudal levy was summoned, its usefulness was diminished by limited terms of service that could be demanded, which was most often 40 days per year.

There had probably been some mercenaries on battlefields since the dawn of the Middle Ages, but by the second half of the twelfth century rulers relied on mercenary companies for much of their military force. The best foot soldiers came from towns, in the form of military confraternities of townsmen. Thus the English kings, for example, focused their recruitment efforts on the towns of Flanders.

Their employers could usually control paid, actively engaged mercenaries. However, during the slack season or when their employers ran out of money (a frequent occurrence), mercenaries were a menace. Their employers were often unable to control their unruly employees, and mercenary companies roamed

the countryside of Europe, looting and raping at will. Surprising local initiatives appear, such as the private force mustered by the abbot of St Martial's, Limoges, in 1177 to fight the Brabançon mercenaries who were devastating the region. In a five-hour battle at Malemort, the abbot's army won a notable victory, killing a reputed 2000 Brabançon men and women, a figure that emphasizes the scale of the problem. The Third Lateran Council in 1179 excommunicated both mercenaries and their employers – with little effect. Mercenaries had by now become necessary to the waging of war, and the opinion of churchmen mattered not one bit.

Battles in an Age of Transition

The Battle of Brémule, fought between Henry I of England and Louis VI of France in 1119, demonstrates well the tactics of this age of transition. King Louis had invaded Normandy, supporting the claim to the duchy made by William Clito, son of the defeated and imprisoned Robert of Normandy. Louis decided on a cavalry charge against Henry's force, but his knights had apparently not quite mastered

The Battle of Brémule (1119) was one of many confrontations between England and France in the twelfth century.

1110	1111	1111–1112	1113–1115
A Norwegian crusade fleet commanded by King Sigurd conquers Sidon for the Kingdom of Jerusalem.	**26 October** Battle of Sepúlveda. King Alfonso, 'the Battler' of Aragón, defeats the supporters of his repudiated wife Urraca and claims her inheritance of Castile for himself.	King Baldwin of Jerusalem besieges Tyre, but is forced to raise the siege for lack of a fleet.	Crusade to the Balearic Islands. A combined Pisan, French and Catalonian fleet assisted by Catalan and southern French crusaders conquers the Balearic Islands from their Muslim ruler.
Crusader conquest of Beirut.			

Some cities by the twelfth century were so strong that enemy forces could only sit outside the walls and wait for starvation to take its toll of the defenders.

the knack of the mass charge. The first French charge against the Anglo-Norman infantry was brave but undisciplined, and was repelled. A second charge broke through the first rank of the enemy's infantry, only to be stopped by Henry's second infantry line, which had been reinforced by dismounted knights – more highly trained fighters with much better armour than the typical infantryman's. Then, taking advantage of the disorder in the French ranks, Henry launched his cavalry in an effective charge that broke the French ranks and even captured King Louis' standard.

The type of tactics employed was, of course, important, but as the case of Brémule shows, a commander's ability to command the obedience of his men and use them intelligently was the crucial factor in this era without a clear superiority of one tactical approach over another. A sense of the land was crucial, as in 1128, when William Clito defeated Count Dietrich of Alsace at the Battle of Thielt by hiding his reserve behind a hill. And sometimes who won or lost a battle was a matter of luck. For instance, Prince Roger of Antioch was an intelligent and skilful commander, but was killed with most of his army at the 'Field of Blood' in 1119, when wind blew dust into the Christians' faces. Supernatural aid should also be taken into account, as in 1097, when the first crusaders credited their victory at Antioch to the Holy Lance that they had discovered or even the personal intervention of St George or another of the warlike saints.

The two keys to a successful cavalry charge were the ability to train men to act as a group and the development of a heavier lance that could be 'couched' – stretched out horizontally under the knight's arm and resting on the horse's neck for greater stability. The lance that evolved was made of hard wood, about 4m

1115–1116	**1115**	**1116**	**1118**
The North African Almoravids conquer the Balearic Islands, returning them to Muslim control.	**February** Battle of Welfesholz. Lothar of Supplinburg, duke of Saxony, defeats Emperor Henry V of Germany.	**Autumn** Battle of Philomelion. Byzantine emperor Alexios Comnenos defeats the Seljuk Turks and regains the coast of Anatolia.	**November** Battle of Alençon, France. Count Fulk V of Anjou routs an Anglo-Norman army commanded by King Henry I.
	24 July Death of Countess Matilda of Tuscany. Matilda's death leaves possession of the so-called 'Matildine lands' as a new bone of contention between emperor and pope.		

Left: This image shows the high, supportive cavalry saddles that had developed by the twelfth century.

Right: In the twelfth century horse armour, called barding, became increasingly common.

(13ft) long, whose leaf-shaped metal head had a wing attachment behind the lance head to prevent deep penetration. As the cavalry charge became important, it also became more common to equip horses with armour, at least in the form of a quilted cloth or leather blanket (called a *caprison* or *bard*). After all, horses remained the most expensive part of a knight's equipment.

The rest of knightly effectiveness was, to a large extent, a matter of training. Horses have a strong herd instinct, which could make a mass charge easier – but also made it very hard for knights to keep their chargers under control during retreats. Knightly spurs were not just symbolic; they were utterly vital equipment for horse control, especially since stallions were used almost exclusively in battle. Training a team of knights and horses to act together in close order apparently started with small groups of 10–12 men. And the place to practise was at tournaments.

Tournaments and War

To be effective, organized cavalry charges required large-scale organized practice. Throughout Europe, lords encouraged formal

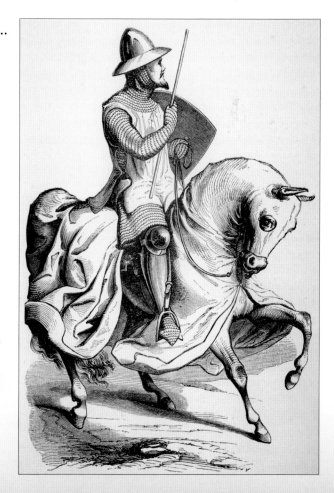

1119

28 June Battle of the Field of Blood. A force led by Atabeg Ilghazi of Aleppo defeats and kills Prince Roger of Antioch with most of his army.

14 August King Baldwin II of Jerusalem marches to save Antioch with a force of 700 knights and several thousand infantry, defeating the army of Ilghazi of Aleppo at Hab, southwest of Aleppo.

20 August Battle of Brémule. Henry I of England defeats Louis VI of France, halting a French invasion of Normandy.

c. 1120

Foundation of the Order of the Poor Knights of the Temple of Solomon (Knights Templars) by Hugh de Payens.

The Berber Muhammad ibn Tumart founds the Almohad Dynasty in northern Africa.

1120–1121

Byzantine emperor John II Comnenos recovers most of Anatolia from the Seljuk Turks.

Left: Charles the Good, count of Flanders (c. 1084–1127), who was murdered when he tried to take rights from a powerful family of ministeriales.

participate in the competitions of others. For example, Count Charles the Good of Flanders (d. 1127) travelled to tournaments all over France and Normandy with an entourage of 200 knights, which suggests the scale of some of these events. Heraldry, marking the banners, surcoats, or shields of knights with distinctive family emblems, probably had its start at the tournaments of the early twelfth century, because winning public recognition was such an important part of the undertaking. Although the competitors did not fight to kill, these mock battles were very dangerous even to those equipped with the best possible armour. For example, in 1186 Henry II of England's son Geoffrey was trampled to death at a tournament.

Great tournament champions won fame and very concrete rewards. The greatest champion of the twelfth century, William Marshal of England (1144–1219), was said

competitions, the *tournaments*, in which teams of knights fought each other in simulated battles. Such contests became a central element of knightly culture. By the early twelfth century, it had already become common for important nobles to hold their own tournaments and to

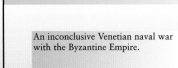

1121

7 May The army of Duke Lothar of Saxony storms the imperial city of Münster, Germany, burning the cathedral and most of the town.

1122–1128

An inconclusive Venetian naval war with the Byzantine Empire.

1122

Byzantine emperor John III Comnenos crushes the Pechenegs in the Battle of Beroia (modern Bulgaria).

1123

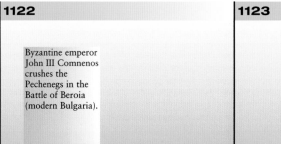

May A Venetian crusader fleet of about 40 ships commanded by Doge Domenico Michiel completely defeats the Fatimid (Egyptian) fleet outside the port of Ascalon.

to have defeated 500 knights in tournaments (often working in partnership with a fellow knight). Besides the wealth he gained from his many victories, William parlayed his fame into an honourable position in King Henry II's service and, in time, received the ultimate reward: marriage to an heiress and, as a result, the earldom of Pembroke.

Like many aspects of medieval warfare, though, the tournaments attracted strong opposition from churchmen, who persistently condemned these mock battles as suicidal violence. Charles of Flanders had to expiate his love of tournaments with heavy penances. St Bernard of Clairvaux simply proclaimed that anyone killed in a tournament would

....

Left: Effigy of William Marshal (c. 1146–1219), Temple Church, London.

Right: St. Bernard of Clairvaux (1090–1153), the incredibly charismatic Cistercian abbot who popularized the Knights Templars and preached the Second Crusade.

go to hell. And the First Lateran Council of 1139 denied Christian burial to men killed in the events.

Further Church councils forbade tournaments in 1148, 1157, 1179, 1215, 1245 – showing how ineffective such condemnation was. Tournaments were useful to lords and exciting and profitable for knights, who had fewer and fewer opportunities to display their skills, at least within the core lands of Europe.

Thanks to a modern numbering scheme, we are accustomed to think of crusades as specific, circumscribed wars, such as the First Crusade of 1096–1099, the Second Crusade of 1147–1149, and so on. In reality, though, crusades to the Holy Land were a massive

1124

16 February–7 July Second crusader siege of Tyre by the army of the Kingdom of Jerusalem and a Venetian fleet. Tyre surrenders.

March Battle of Bourgthéroulde. The army of Henry I of England defeats Norman rebels who supported William Clito, son of Duke Robert of Normandy.

1125–1135

Civil war for the throne of Germany between the Welf (Guelf) Frederick of Swabia and the Waiblingen (Ghibelline) Lothar II.

1125

Alfonso I of Aragón attacks Granada.

1127

2 March Murder of Count Charles the Good of Flanders by *ministeriales* in his service. Civil war for control of Flanders.

1128

21 June Battle of Thielt. William Clito's army defeats the force of Count Dietrich of Alsace, his rival claimant to the county of Flanders.

1130–1208

Norwegian civil war for control of the throne.

1130–1135

Byzantine war against the Danishmend Turks.

ongoing process that is better visualized as a fluctuating line with occasional peaks when a ruler or magnate went to the East to fight the Muslims, but with crusaders (and Latin settlers in the Kingdom of Jerusalem) engaging in military operations nearly every year.

The 'Crusade of 1101' was at least as large an expedition as the First Crusade, as those who had taken crusading vows but broken them were forced eastward to reinforce the fragile conquest of Jerusalem in 1099. It proved to be such a failure that few Western chroniclers were even willing to write about it. It is useful, however, to consider the events of 1101 to keep from feeling too smug about any supposed Western military superiority. The truth of the matter was that the first crusaders had won a relatively easy victory in large part because of the disunion of their enemies. When the second wave of crusaders arrived in the East, they met much more organized resistance.

....

Left: The coronation of Count Baldwin of Flanders and Hainaut as first emperor of the Latin Empire of Constantinople, 1204.

The Seljuk Turks adopted a scorched-earth policy. Disagreements between the crusade leaders and tactical errors completed the tragedy, and in several battles almost the entire crusader force was annihilated. The West's heavier cavalry proved ineffective when it was not well led.

Those who had settled in the small Latin kingdom, however, were able to take advantage of a limited superiority in equipment over their Muslim opponents when conditions were right. Thus King Baldwin I of Jerusalem won an impressive victory over the Egyptian army at Ramlah on 6 September 1101. Although he had a much smaller force than the Fatimid Egyptian commander (probably only about 260 knights and 900 foot soldiers), he used them well in a surprise attack at dawn on the Fatimid camp. The inexperienced Fatimid army dissolved into flight, suffering particulary heavy losses among the 21,000 infantrymen said to have been present, who could not escape the Latin knights. Muslim equipment was lighter, even horsemen usually wearing little body armour and riding much lighter horses. Such disparity could only do so much, though. The following

year, King Baldwin suffered a serious defeat, also at Ramlah. A large Fatimid force surprised the king, on a reconnaissance with only about 500 cavalrymen. Baldwin attempted a charge against the Muslims, which only he and a few of his knights survived. Baldwin escaped, but came back 10 days later, reinforced by a band of crusaders, and in this second encounter he routed the Fatimids.

Winning the Latin Kingdom

King Baldwin's experience at Ramlah in 1102 is typical of crusading warfare in the twelfth century. The kings and great lords of the Kingdom of Jerusalem often had a good understanding of rational military goals and of how to fight Muslim forces. But they would not have had enough manpower for major military expeditions if they had not been able to count on a steady stream of reinforcements from the West, men eager to prove their valour, fight the enemies of God, and find wealth. The kings were usually able to control the smaller bands of crusaders, but the more important crusaders, ignorant of the military situation, could make the situation in the Holy Land worse rather

---

1130

Roger II unites the Norman conquests of southern Italy and Sicily into a single kingdom with a strong central government.

1132

24 July Battle of Nocera. Apuleian rebels defeat King Roger II of Sicily.

1134

4 June Battle of Fotevik, Skåne. King Niels of Denmark defeats his rival Erik, winning control of Denmark.

17 July Battle of Fraga. Alfonso I of Aragón launches a major advance into the Ebro Valley, but is defeated at Fraga by a large Almoravid force.

1135

Militarization of the Order of the Hospital of St John of Jerusalem (Knights Hospitallers).

Pope Innocent II offers a crusading indulgence for anyone who fights against King Roger II of Sicily.

King Roger II of Sicily's fleet attacks and captures the island of Djerba, a major pirate centre.

The departure of King Louis VII of France on the Second Crusade (1148), from a fifteenth-century chronicle.

than better. Such was the case with the wretchedly mismanaged crusade of King Louis VII of France and Emperor Conrad III of Germany, usually known as the Second Crusade, which culminated in a futile and strategically indefensible attack on Damascus.

Working together, settlers and crusaders succeeded in creating and maintaining several viable Western European colonies in the Holy Land in the twelfth century. The kings of Jerusalem with their allies gradually took the Muslim-held ports of the coast. They fought off periodic attacks from their Muslim neighbours. They even tried to expand their territory into Egypt, as with the failed joint attack on Damietta, Egypt, by the military force of the Latin kingdom and its Byzantine allies in 1169. As was often the case, the main reason for failure in this venture was that the allies did not cooperate well together. During their repeated wars with the Muslim states on their borders, the western settlers adapted when it was militarily expedient to do so. For example, the kings of Jerusalem made increasing use of light cavalry *(turcopoles)* through the twelfth century, although they did not abandon their own knights. The Muslims for their part introduced a heavier cavalry to supplement their own light riders. The Westerners even adopted the Palestinian Muslim use of carrier pigeons. But other distinctive elements of the Holy Land's military establishment were fundamentally European: the erection of large numbers of castles to hold the land, and the introduction of the military religious orders.

The Fighting Monks
The Latin Kingdom of Jerusalem had a manpower problem, not so much in its efforts at expansion but to hold the land year in and year out against hostile neighbours. Although the conquests were parcelled out as knights' fiefs,

1136	**1136–1153**	**1137**	**1137–1138**
Battle of Crug Mawr. A force of Welsh rebels led by Owain Gwynedd defeat an Anglo-Norman force.	English Civil War between rival claimants to the throne Count Stephen of Blois and the Dowager Empress Matilda (daughter of King Henry I).	Emperor Lothar III of Germany leads an expedition against King Roger II of Sicily, at the pope's invitation.	Byzantine Emperor John III Comnenos attacks the crusader principality of Antioch.
		30 October Battle of Rignano. Duke Ranulf of Apuleia defeats Roger II of Sicily in a struggle for control of Apulia.	

A woodcut showing the army of the Second Crusade finding the remains of the People's Crusade, destroyed at Civetot in 1096.

....

the reserve fighting force thus provided was not large enough for the settlers' needs, while crusaders usually went home after a short campaign. The answer proved to be the military religious orders, whose members made permanent monastic-style vows, but, unlike monks, bore arms. This new phenomenon was born in the wake of the First Crusade, when a group of knights vowed to remain in the Holy Land, guarding the roads to outlying pilgrimage sites. By about 1120, this group was incorporated as the Order of the Poor Fellow-Soldiers of Christ and of the Temple of Solomon (the Knights Templars). The Templars proved to be only the first example of an immensely popular vocation that spread across Europe and the Near East.

The Templars were soon followed by the Knights Hospitallers, a number of orders in Spain, and several orders in the Baltic that were eventually absorbed into the Teutonic Knights. All provided a solution to two great military problems of the twelfth and thirteenth centuries: how to produce a thoroughly professional permanent military force and how to finance it. The key was the strong religious motivation behind the organizations. Although a haven for younger sons of the noble and knightly classes, the military orders *were* a religious form of life, with a strict prayer regimen and a moral system upheld by punishments, which were, in some cases, draconian. The rules included harsh military discipline, with heavy penalties for turning from the enemy, letting a standard sink or fall, or getting ahead of the line during a cavalry charge. They were a means to win salvation while still retaining the honour and

1138

22 **August** Battle of the Standard (Northallerton). A northern English army raised by Archbishop Thurstan of York decisively defeats an invading Scottish army commanded by King David I.

1139

25 **July** Battle of Ourique. A Christian Portuguese army defeats a much larger invading Almoravid force.

Portuguese prince Afonso Enriques declares himself king of Portugal as Afonso I.

The Second Lateran Council bans tournaments and the use of crossbows against Christians.

prestige of knighthood. The organization of the orders was modelled on that of monasteries, in which individual members vowed absolute obedience to their leader – a valuable trait on the battlefield. And those Europeans who could not join the orders themselves could at least win merit by supporting such a holy enterprise. All the orders soon gained a complex infrastructure of lands and privileges given to them by faithful Christians, which they administered to funnel money and supplies to the fighting men of the orders, on the borders of Christendom.

In the twelfth century, kings supported the military orders both

A Knight of Malta. The Knights Hospitallers survived the Middle Ages, moving to Rhodes and then Malta to carry on war against the Turks in the Mediterranean.

in the Holy Land and on the Iberian Peninsula. The fighting men of the orders – infantry and lightly armed sergeants as well as knights – could stay in the field longer than local levies, and were much better trained. They also learned local conditions in a way that few transitory crusaders did. For example, the military orders in the Holy Land won many enemies because

Left: A meeting of the general chapter of the Knights Templar, under Grand Master Robert de Craon (1147).

Right: The Teutonic Knights, last of the great military religious orders, gradually moved their operations from the Holy Land to the Baltic.

c. 1140

King Afonso I of Portugal and about 70 crusader ships unsuccessfully besiege Lisbon.

1141

3 February Battle of Lincoln. A Matildine force led by Robert of Gloucester comes to relieve Lincoln Castle, under siege by King Stephen; in the ensuing battle Stephen's force is defeated and the king is captured.

14 September Battle of Winchester. Empress Matilda's force besieging Wolvesey Castle are trapped and defeated by King Stephen's army. Matilda's half-brother Robert of Gloucester is captured and later traded for the captive King Stephen.

21 December Weinsberg Castle, Saxony, held by Welf rebels, surrenders to Emperor Conrad III after a long siege.

Krak des Chevaliers, Syria, constructed by the Knights Hospitallers. Frequently expanded between 1150 and 1250, it could house a garrison of up to 2000 men.

they refused to help crusaders conquer land that could not be held. But the orders themselves accepted frontier lands from monarchs, defending them by means of massive castle constructions that no monarch of the era would have been able to afford. To mention just one example, the greatest order castle, the Hospitaller fortress Krak des Chevaliers in southern Syria, was a massive bulwark on the flank of the Kingdom of Jerusalem, which can be seen in something approaching its former glory thanks to a major French restoration project in the 1930s. It occupied a space of nearly 140 x 210m (460 x 689ft) on an easily defensible hilltop in mountainous terrain, with an elaborate double set of defences. At times of need, the castle could hold over 2000 soldiers. Krak survived attacks in 1125, 1163, 1167, 1188, 1207, 1208, 1229, 1252, 1267 and 1270, falling only after it had been almost completely evacuated in 1271. The Latin kingdom would

1142

1 July Battle of Wilton. Robert of Gloucester besieges King Stephen at Wilton. Stephen's army is defeated when he breaks out of the city, but the king escapes.

September–December King Stephen besieges Matilda in Oxford, taking the town and blockading the castle. Matilda escapes, after which the garrison surrenders.

1142–1143

Byzantine emperor, John III Comnenos, attacks the crusader principality of Antioch.

1144

Emperor Manuel Comnenos' Byzantine army defeats Prince Raymond of Antioch.

28 November–24 December Imad ad-Din Zengi of Mosul besieges and conquers Edessa, the first crusader principality to be regained by Islam.

1145–1150

The Almohad 'Abd al-Mu'min ibn 'Ali conquers and united the small states of Muslim Spain.

Sigurd I Magnusson of Norway (1103–1130) was the first Scandinavian king to go on crusade. In his later years he was mentally unbalanced; legend tells that only a child dared reproach him for his bad behavior.

not have survived long without such defences and the members of the military orders who manned them. By 1187, the Templars and Hospitallers could muster about 600 knights on active duty in the East, about half of the entire number of knights available to the kings of Jerusalem, besides large numbers of more lightly armed sergeants and foot soldiers.

Winning Control of the Sea

The role of the military religious orders in taking and holding land in Palestine, the Iberian Peninsula and the Baltic is well known; the role of naval powers in the expansion of Europe, by contrast, is often ignored. Yet the twelfth century is the first great century of medieval navies, both Italian and northern. From their small start in the First Crusade, the fleets of Italian cities in particular came to be an essential element of war in the lands bordering the Mediterranean. As early as 1107, Sigurd of Norway, the crusader king, defeated Muslim fleets off both Portugal and Palestine, and helped King Baldwin I take the port city of Sidon in 1110. A crusader fleet of 116 ships from England, Norway, the Netherlands and the

King Afonso I Henriques of Portugal (1139–1185), who became the first king of Portugal after his victory over the Muslims at Ourique (1139).

Rhineland also joined Afonso I of Portugal to take Lisbon in 1147. The Mediterranean campaigns were, however, dominated by the fleets of Italian cities, notably Genoa, Pisa and Venice. These fleets included both merchant

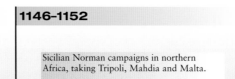

1145

December Pope Eugenius III proclaims the Second Crusade.

1145–1149

Second Crusade.

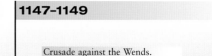

1146–1152

Sicilian Norman campaigns in northern Africa, taking Tripoli, Mahdia and Malta.

1147–1149

Crusade against the Wends.

ships and oared galleys. Free citizens of these largely independent towns, whose governments usually negotiated important trading privileges in return for naval assistance, manned them. The dynamic between the Italian fleets and their cities created a new level of aggressive, entrepreneurial warfare that can be seen in the twelfth century especially in the crusading movement. From 1100 on, they also ferried a majority of crusaders to the East.

The Pisans and Genoese had already shown their naval initiative in the late eleventh century. To some extent, they continued to engage in joint expeditions with other fleets, as in 1113–1115, when Pisan, French and Catalonian fleets joined with crusaders to take the Balearic Islands. As the century progressed, though, it became the norm for only one city to join with crusaders at a time, in return winning major concessions. The best example of this

···

The Venetian fleet victorious over that of Emperor Frederick Barbarossa, painted in 1407 as part of a series of paintings commemorating Pope Alexander III.

1147

26 June The Wendish prince Nyklot launches a pre-emptive strike against Lübeck, where troops are preparing for the Wendish crusade. The attack destroys ships and kills 300 men.

In North Africa, the Almoravid dynasty is overthrown by Almohad leader 'Abd al-Mu'min ibn 'Ali.

King Roger II of Sicily conducts a great raid against Greece, sacking Thebes, Corinth and Athens and conquering the island of Corfu.

28 June–24 October A Northern European crusader fleet of 116 vessels joins with Afonso I of Portugal to take Lisbon from its Muslim ruler. First clear evidence of a traction-driven trebuchet in Western Europe.

17 October The Muslim-held city of Almería, Spain, falls to a largely Genoese crusader fleet and land forces commanded by Alfonso VII of León-Castile.

25 October Second Battle of Dorylaeum. A large Turkish army ambushes and routs German crusaders.

1148

The Council of Rheims bans tournaments.

January Battle of Cadmus. French crusaders are defeated by a Turkish army in Asia Minor.

A Byzantine–Venetian fleet defeats the navy of Roger II of Sicily.

Battle of Adalia. The French crusading infantry is ambushed and mostly destroyed in Asia Minor, while King Louis VII and most of the cavalry go to the Kingdom of Jerusalem by sea.

24–28 July Siege of Damascus, Syria. A crusader army under Louis VII of France and Conrad III of Germany attempt a siege of Damascus, but are soon forced to withdraw.

December Fall of Tortosa. The city falls to Ramon Berenguer IV of Barcelona in alliance with a Genoese crusading fleet.

The Venetian capture of Tyre in 1124, as shown in one of the many Renaissance Venetian paintings that depict the city's medieval greatness.

phenomenon is the Venetian Crusade of 1123–1124. The city committed major resources to this venture, about 40 ships commanded by Doge Domenico Michiel. The force certainly included four large merchant ships, as well as galleys, some carrying adapted catapults. The presence of merchant ships confused the commander of the Fatimid fleet, who left the safety of Ascalon's harbour in May 1123 to attack them. The Venetians proceeded to rout the Egyptian fleet, then went on to cruise along the Palestinian coast, seizing Muslim merchant ships as they went. The Venetian Crusade culminated in the siege of Tyre, a nearly impenetrable island port bound to the mainland only by a narrow causeway, from 16 February to 7 July 1124. The Venetians blockaded the city by sea while the king of Jerusalem attacked by land. When Tyre finally fell, the Venetians were granted major trading concessions. Similarly, when a Genoese fleet helped King

Alfonso VII of León-Castile take Almería in 1147, Genoa received a privileged trade status.

The kings of Sicily also took advantage of sea power in their relentless quest for territory and glory. Although attacks against Greece failed in face of the Byzantine Empire's continued military and naval prowess, King Roger II of Sicily enjoyed considerable success in attacks on northern Africa. In 1135, he captured Djerba, going on to capture territory along the African coast.

Naval Failure

On the whole, Muslim rulers could not muster effective naval resistance to western attacks. This should probably be regarded as a failure of will rather than a sign that western ships were better than those of the Islamic world. True, the Europeans had improved their ships by adopting Arabic rigging and sail techniques, and by the late twelfth century were replacing steering oars with a sternpost rudder (an innovation brought to the Mediterranean from northern Europe). It is unlikely, though, that European ships enjoyed technological superiority. But the Italian fleets in particular appear to have enjoyed high morale,

---

1149

28 June Battle of Inab. An Antiochene force under Prince Raymond of Antioch comes to relieve Nur ad-Din's siege of Inab, but suffers a crushing defeat. Prince Raymond is killed.

Byzantine reconquest of Corfu from the Normans.

c. 1150

First known use of the cog, an improved roundship.

Introduction of mail chausses (leggings).

c. 1150–1300

German *Drang nach Osten* ('Drive to the East') – expansion and settlement in the Slavic lands of Eastern Europe.

1151

First known use of Greek fire in Western Europe (by Count Geoffrey V of Anjou at the siege of Montreuil-Bellay).

Conquest of the southern Italian town of Ancona by a Byzantine force.

fighting for the good of their cities and often led by their civic leaders. By contrast, it was a rare Muslim ruler who invested in sea power in the twelfth century. It has been suggested that, by this time, Muslims disliked and feared the sea and were simply unwilling to wage naval war. Certainly, between 1100 and 1160 no Muslim leader made a concerted effort to attack the Christian port cities of the Holy Land, thus allowing crusaders unhindered access. After Ascalon fell to King Baldwin III in 1153, the Fatimid fleet had no watering point along the coast, making Muslim naval aggression even less likely. Sultan Saladin attempted to rebuild the Fatimid fleet in the 1170s, but it did not repay his investment, the untrained and unwilling rowers fighting poorly. By that stage, Christian Mediterranean fleets had worked out means to protect their rowers from the arrows and other missiles that dominated the early stages of sea battles. And by the end of the century, Christians had learned to mount siege towers and ladders on ships, launching daring assaults even on heavily fortified walls.

Left: Christ crowns King Roger II of Sicily (1130), from a mosaic in Palermo, Sicily.

Below: Sultan Saladin (1174–1193), who conquered most of the Latin Kingdom of Jerusalem and fought the Third Crusade to a stalemate.

1151–1153	1153	1154	1155–1168
Byzantine war with Hungary.	King Baldwin II of Jerusalem conquers Ascalon. **November** Treaty of Winchester. The end of the English civil war, making Empress Matilda's son, Henry, the heir to King Stephen.	The first expedition of Emperor Frederick I (Barbarossa) against northern Italy, attempting to force the Lombards to recognize the emperor as their overlord. Henry II becomes king of England. Beginning of a campaign to reduce the number of baronial castles and increase the number of royal ones.	Byzantine war with Hungary.

Right: The capture of King William the Lion at the Battle of Alnwick (1174), a confused encounter in which both sides were hindered by heavy fog.

Below: King David I of Scotland (1124–1153), who attempted to conquer Northumbria during the chaos of the English civil war.

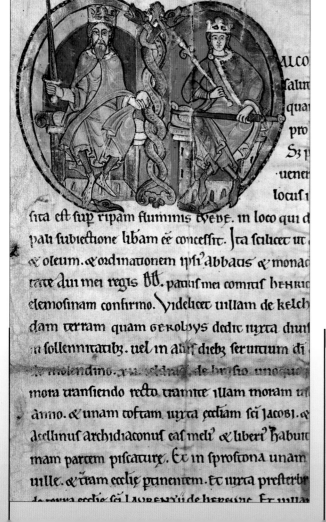

1155

Pope Hadrian IV makes an ally of the Byzantine emperor, Manuel I Comnenos, against King William I the Bad of Sicily.

Battle of Apulia. The Byzantine navy defeats William I of Sicily.

1155-1157

Byzantine invasion of southern Italy in a failed attempt to reclaim the region from the Normans.

1156

Battle of Brindisi. The Normans under William I of Sicily decisively defeat Byzantine invaders and expel them from Italy.

The European Frontiers

Europe's core lands – the metal-rich regions that were able to equip heavy cavalry and arm their troops with a weight of metal that peripheral lands could only dream of – tended to expand in the twelfth century. Poland, Bohemia, Hungary and Scandinavia all made at least a partial transition to the fighting style of Western Europe, creating numbers of heavy cavalry to fight side by side with more lightly armed troops. Rulers who could afford to do so kept up with military innovations, both to prevent other monarchs from absorbing them and because of the advantage it gave them over their subjects. One can trace the military transformation particularly well in Scandinavia, as when the Danish throne claimant Erik decisively defeated King Niels of Denmark at Fotevik in 1134. With a striking force of only about 60 knights, though they were well deployed, Erik shattered a large traditional infantry levy, winning himself the crown. Scandinavia also saw major developments in castle building in the twelfth century. The Scandinavian situation is in some ways comparable to that of Scotland, whose kings

encouraged Norman settlement in the twelfth century, but which never had a heavy cavalry corps comparable to that of England, France or Germany. The Scots raided northern England frequently, pillaging and enslaving captives, but could not fight a pitched battle on equal terms. For example, at the Battle of the Standard (or Northallerton) in 1138, Archbishop Thurstan of York had raised a northern army to confront David I of Scotland, who had invaded with a much larger army. King David had a good plan of battle, but lacked firm control over his men. He gave way when his 'Galwegians' (Scots from south of the Forth) demanded the right to launch the first assault against the English, who had taken a defensive position on a slope, mixing archers with dismounted knights and holding cavalry in reserve. The ill-disciplined and poorly armed Galwegians charged on foot, only to be shot full of arrows ('like porcupines', says a contemporary report) and driven off in disarray. In the only other major pitched battle

An Almohad cup. The Almohad dynasty of North Africa (1130–1269) took control of Muslim Spain in the twelfth century.

1157

23 October Waldemar I defeats and kills his rival Swein III to become king of Denmark.

Crusade to Finland led by King Erik III Eriksson of Sweden.

21 August Battle of Muradel. Alfonso VII of Castile-León invades Muslim Spain, but is defeated and killed by an Almohad army.

1158

6 August–7 September The city of Milan surrenders to Emperor Frederick I Barbarossa after a short siege.

1158–1166 Duke Henry the Lion of Saxony campaigns against the Slavic Wends and Abodrites.

1158–1164 Henry II of England conquers Wales.

1159

First mention of a mercenary army in Italy (raised by Pope Alexander III to fight Emperor Frederick I Barbarossa).

1159–1160

7 July 1159–27 January 1160 Crema surrenders to Frederick I Barbarossa after a long siege. The town is sacked and razed.

between Scots and English in the twelfth century, fought at Alnwick on 13 July 1174, a Yorkshire force took advantage of a thick fog to surprise the Scots under their king, William the Lion, defeating them decisively and capturing the king.

Christians fighting to expand their holdings in Spain confronted rather different problems, since the North African Almoravid dynasty was probably their equal in terms of military equipment and ability. Still, the kings of Aragón, Castile and Portugal made significant advances during the twelfth century, thanks in large part to regular infusions of crusaders, who were promised the same spiritual rewards as their counterparts fighting for Jerusalem (at much lower cost). By 1139, the Christians had already won a victory over the Almoravids at Ourique, Portugal, suggesting that Almoravid military power was on the wane. Afonso I of Portugal went on to besiege Lisbon twice (with the help

King Henry II of England (1154–1189), who pacified England after the civil war between Stephen and Matilda, only to end his reign in civil strife.

of large crusader fleets), taking the city in 1147.

In 1147, however, a new foe appeared on the Iberian Peninsula: the Almohads, a new militaristic dynasty of northern Africa. They took Seville almost immediately and soon halted Christian advances. The situation was complicated by rivalries between the Christian kings of the north. In 1195, León and Navarre went so far as to ally with the Almohads against Castile, despite strong papal protests and threats, especially after the Almohad caliph al-Nasir heavily defeated Alfonso VIII of Castile at Alarcos on 17 July 1195.

Core Lands and Unarmed Savages

Only in two regions, the Slavic lands of eastern Europe and the Celtic fringe (Ireland and Wales), did the technological superiority of the core lands prove to be decisive. The most straightforward case is that of Ireland. By the early twelfth century, the more important Irish kings employed some cavalry, but few had the heavy armour of core-land knights. Infantry, too, was sufficient for fights against other Irish kingdoms but not much use against the better-equipped knights of France or England. Too

---

1160

Foundation of the Hanseatic League, a trade alliance of Northern European towns.

9 August Battle of Carcano, Italy. Frederick I Barbarossa tries to raise the Milanese siege of Carcano, but his army is driven off.

1162

1 March Milan surrenders to Frederick I Barbarossa after a nine-month siege. The population is dispersed to villages and the city is then systematically destroyed.

1163

Duke Henry, the Lion of Saxony, takes Werle, a major Wendish centre.

1164

Foundation of the military religious order of Calatrava in Spain.

Battle of Demmin (Verchen). Duke Henry, the Lion of Saxony, defeats the Abodrites.

many were *kerns*, lower-class warriors without armour, who fought with swords and javelins.

The Irish received a rude awakening to contemporary military developments in the year 1169, when King Dermot McMurrough of Leinster recruited the Anglo-Norman earl Richard de Clare (nicknamed 'Strongbow') to help fight the rival king of Ossory. The native Irish forces proved incapable of dealing with Anglo-Norman knights and their archers, and Strongbow defeated several superior forces, as in 1170 when 10 knights and 70 archers proved sufficient to defeat 3000 Waterford men. Strongbow soon claimed the kingship of Leinster. His overlord, Henry II of England, was alarmed at the growing power of his vassal – and keen to make a show of reforming the Irish Church to appease the pope, outraged by the recent murder of Thomas Becket. So, in 1171, Henry invaded Ireland, with a force of about 4000, including 500 knights. The Irish did not even attempt military resistance, and kings and nobles from most of the island swore

King Louis VII taking the Oriflamme at St-Denis in 1147, before his departure on the Second Crusade.

1165

Establishment of the margravate and bishopric of Schwerin in Abodrite territory.

Massive Welsh revolt against English overlordship.

English expedition against Wales, led by King Henry II. The expedition fails because of bad weather.

Anti-pope Paschal III canonizes Charlemagne in an effort to increase support for Emperor Frederick I Barbarossa.

1166

Great Assize of knight service owed in England, held at the order of King Henry II.

1167

19 March King Amalric of Jerusalem in alliance with Wizar Shawar of Egypt invades Egypt, but is defeated by Shirkuh, commander for Nur al-Din, at al-Babein, 320km (200 miles) south of Cairo. Amalric has to withdraw.

June–July Emperor Frederick I Barbarossa attacks Rome. He takes the Leonine City and St Peter's, enthroning his anti-pope. The next day an epidemic (maybe malaria) breaks out, virtually destroying Frederick's army.

1 December Formation of the Lombard League.

fealty to Henry, beginning an English military presence in Ireland that continues to the present. The English who were granted fiefs in Ireland soon began construction of castles to help them hold the land, such as the impressive Trim Castle, the keep of which dates to about 1173.

The Welsh, too, were unable to offer pitched battle to the English in the twelfth century, despite resentment at the king of England's claim of lordship over them. The year 1164 saw a massive Welsh revolt, and the following year, the response – a massive punitive expedition that included soldiers from all over Henry II's Angevin empire. The Welsh survived only thanks to rainstorms, which bogged down the expedition and prevented Henry's army from forcing the Welsh into a pitched battle.

On the eastern frontier of Europe, the Slavic Bohemians and Poles had coalesced into states in the tenth century, but a large number of Slavs remained, their tribes sometimes joined into loose confederacies. Otto I of Germany had

....

The 'coronation' of Duke Henry the Lion and Princess Matilda of England, from the Evangeliary of Henry the Lion (1188).

1168

In an amphibious attack, Danish forces under King Waldemar I capture Arkona on the isle of Rügen, main stronghold of the Wends.

Waldemar I of Denmark attempts to invade Norway, but fails because defenders block an important strait with catapults.

Battle of Semlin (Zeumun). Byzantine emperor, Manuel I Comnenos, defeats the Hungarians and annex Dalmatia.

King Stephen's queen pleads for his release from his rival for the throne of England, Queen Matilda.

subjected a number of these tribes in the middle of the tenth century, but they had regained their political liberty in the great Slav revolt of 982. In the twelfth century, though, the Germans returned to the offensive, conquering and colonizing two-fifths of the territory that is now Germany during the years 1125–1346.

A crusade proclaimed against the Wends in 1107–8 had little success, and the same was true of the so-called 'Wendish Crusade' of 1147–1149. In both cases, the crusaders from the core lands, while enjoying a great technological superiority over their enemies, found themselves unable to bring those enemies to open battle. The Slavs fought with pre-emptive strikes, such as Prince Nyklot's attack on Lübeck before the crusade set out, or relied on ambush and guerrilla tactics. The configuration of Western European armies, based on heavy cavalry and depending on a willingness of the enemy to come out and fight, was not very effective under the circumstances. Duke Henry, the Lion of Saxony, proved more successful in a series of

1169

Saladin becomes wizar of Egypt.

A joint siege of Damietta, Egypt, by armies from the Byzantine Empire and the Kingdom of Jerusalem, fails due to a lack of co-operation.

Battle of Gowran Pass, Ireland. King Diarmuid McMurrough of Leinster and his Norman ally Earl Richard of Pembroke ('Strongbow') defeat King MacGillipatric of Ossory's superior force.

1170–1171

Earl Richard of Pembroke ('Strongbow') conquers Leinster, Ireland.

1171

September Battle of Castleknock, Ireland. Strongbow routs the army of High King Rory O'Connor.

King Henry II of England invades Ireland with a force of about 4000 men and receives the homage of the Irish kings.

Venetian conquest of Chios and Ragusa from the Byzantine Empire.

1172

Ayyubid sultan Saladin begins a systematic shipbuilding campaign to create a navy for use against the Kingdom of Jerusalem.

King Stephen of England (1135–1154), most of whose reign was spent in a civil war with his cousin Matilda for the throne of England.

campaigns against the Wends and Abodrites in the years 1158–1166. He adapted his tactics to those of the enemy, waging a war of ambush and reprisal. The Abodrite fortresses, such as Werle, proved unable to stand against western siege machines. Then, when he did succeed in bringing the Abodrites to battle, near Demmin in 1164, he was able to defeat them handily. The Danes also got in on the act, King Valdemar I conquering Rügen in 1168, and Archbishop Absalon destroying the Pomeranian fleet in 1184. By the end of the century, both Germans and Danes, eager to expand their trading networks and to gain new lands, were looking towards the Baltic territories that lay beyond the Slavs.

The First English Civil War

Although the highest concentration of warfare had shifted from Europe's core lands to the frontiers, twelfth-century Europe was by no means a haven of peace. England saw two major rebellions in the course of the century: a civil war between followers of Stephen and Matilda for control of the English throne, 1138–1153; and a major rebellion against Henry II in 1173–1174. The Stephen/Matilda war, which broke out after Henry I's daughter and nephew both claimed the throne of England, illustrates particularly well the military situation in Europe within the first half of the twelfth century.

In 1066, it had been possible for William the Conqueror to take England with one decisive battle. Such a scenario was impossible for Matilda when her half-brother, Robert of Gloucester, raised the flag of rebellion on her behalf in 1138. The problem was the hundreds of castles that dotted the English countryside. Some were simple motte and bailey affairs with wooden stockades, but even such a structure could fatally delay an attacking army. Many other castles were stout stone keeps, from which a small garrison could repel attackers for weeks, if not months. The castles had been designed to keep enemies from taking the land, and they proved how well they could do the job time after time.

1173–1174

Great revolt against King Henry II of England. Louis VII of France, William the Lion of Scotland, the counts of Flanders, Boulogne and Blois, four English earls and Henry's own sons join in the revolt.

1173

Battle of Fornham. A force loyal to Henry II defeat the rebel earl, Robert of Leicester, near Bury St Edmund.

3–28 July Henry II takes the rebel-held town of Leicester after a short siege. The keep continues to resist until 22 September

9 August Battle of Verneuil. Louis VII of France besieges Verneuil in Normandy, but Henry II of England arrives with a relieving force on the day the defenders had promised to surrender if not relieved. Louis' army flees in disorder, losing its rearguard.

1174

Saladin became ruler of Damascus.

13 July Second Battle of Alnwick. King William the Lion of Scotland invades England. While besieging Alnwick in Yorkshire, his force is surprised in a thick fog by supporters of Henry II. In the confused fighting, King William is captured.

It is often said that pitched battles became much more rare in the twelfth and thirteenth centuries, commanders being unwilling to risk all in a single decisive encounter. Historians have represented battles as almost accidental, usually developing when a force came to relieve a besieged garrison. But such a battle was anything but accidental, and was very common. A relieving force came with the expectation of a fight, and the besieging force was usually prepared to engage them. Such was certainly the case in the war between Stephen and Matilda.

To give an example, King Stephen came to besiege Lincoln at Christmastide 1140. The citizens let him into the town, but the castle within the town held out. When Robert of Gloucester appeared with a larger army to relieve the castle in February 1141, he must have expected a decisive engagement. Stephen could not, in fact, retreat easily in the winter countryside, with Robert's army nearby. So the king chose to stay and fight, coming out to meet

···

Frederick I Barbarossa in Aachen, where he was crowned as king of Germany on 4 March 1152, in a nineteenth-century painting by Albert Bauer.

1174–1176	**c. 1175**	**1175–1176**
Emperor Frederick I Barbarossa campaigns against the Lombard League of northern Italy.	Niort, France. The earliest known use of machicolation – a projecting stone gallery on a fortress wall, with openings for defenders to drop projectiles on the attackers.	Papal approval of the Order of Santiago and the organization soon called the Order of Alcántara, Spain.

the enemy army instead of forcing Robert to besiege him in turn. And, in fact, Stephen was defeated and imprisoned. The civil war would have been over if Matilda had not alienated the citizens of London, who prevented her coronation as reigning queen. Matilda was forced to release Stephen

several months later, after she had suffered a fate similar to Stephen's at Lincoln. In September 1141, Matilda's army was besieging Wolvesey Castle near Winchester, but a relief force loyal to Stephen defeated the Matildines. Her troops were then

besieged, and defeated when they tried to break out. In the process, Matilda's commander, Robert of Gloucester, was captured. Without his leadership skills, Matilda's cause would have failed completely, so she agreed to trade Stephen for Robert.

A number of English civil war battles were similarly fought under the walls of towns or castles, or even within towns. This is hardly surprising, since sieges were a slow and difficult matter, pinning the besieging army down and exposing it to supply problems, disease (especially dysentery) and enemy attack. The English made some attempts to employ siege equipment; for example, Stephen built a siege tower at his second siege of Lincoln Castle in 1144, but abandoned the siege when the tower collapsed killing 80 men. On the Continent, Matilda's husband, Count Geoffrey of Anjou, appears to have been more innovative, including the first known use of Greek fire in the West.

A simple ballista. Although the counterweight trebuchet had developed by the twelfth century, there was still a place for smaller catapults.

Right: Emperor Frederick Barbarossa's defeat at Legnano (1176), in a painting by Massimo Taparelli d'Azeglio (1798–1866).

1176

29 May Battle of Legnano. The allied army of the Lombard League, Venice, and the papacy defeat Emperor Frederick I Barbarossa.

First mention of the Portuguese military religious order of Évora.

17 September Battle of Myriocephalon (near modern Denizli, Turkey). Byzantine emperor, Manuel I Comnenos, invades Seljuk territory with a large army, but is catastrophically defeated by Sultan Kilij Arslan II, fatally weakening the Byzantine Empire.

1177

17 April (Palm Sunday) Battle of Malemort, France. The abbot of St Martial's, Limoges, leads local forces to a major victory against Brabançon mercenaries who are looting the region.

25 November Battle of Montgisard. King Baldwin IV of Jerusalem heavily defeats the invading sultan Saladin, assisted by an apparition of St George to the Christian force.

1179

The Third Lateran Council bans tournaments and condemns mercenaries.

Duke Henry, the Lion of Saxony, is outlawed for refusing military service to Frederick I Barbarossa. Henry attempts resistance, but Lübeck, his last stronghold, falls in August 1181, after which Henry surrenders and accepts exile.

10 June Saladin defeats the army of the Kingdom of Jerusalem, but cannot exploit his victory because new crusaders arrive, led by Count Henry of Champagne.

1180–1190

Dover Castle built, at a cost of £7000.

1180–1196

Led by Stephen Nemanya, the Serbians successfully rebel against the Byzantine Empire.

1181

Assize of Arms, England. King Henry II orders that all free men of England must bear arms in the king's service on demand. The edict lays out the arms and armour required of each rank.

2. The German vanguard retreats before the Milanese cavalry.

3. Frederick Barbarossa directs a cavalry charge that plunges deep into the Milanese lines.

1. The Milanese cavalry surprise the German vanguard in the first phase of the battle.

5. The Milanese cavalry, having regrouped behind their infantry lines, attack the Germans on their left flank, leading to a rout of the imperial troops.

4. The Milanese cavalry flees, leaving the Italian infantry to successfully take the brunt of the German charge.

Battle of Legnano, 1176

1182

Peace of Constance. The Lombard League recognizes Emperor Frederick I Barbarossa's overlordship of northern Italy in principle. In return, Frederick abandons his claim to imperial lands in the region, and authorizes the continued existence of the Lombard League.

Saladin invades Galilee, but is stopped at the castle of Saffuriyah.

1183

Saladin invades Galilee, but is again stopped at the castle of Saffuriyah.

1184

Massacre of Western Europeans, mostly merchants, in Constantinople.

Pentecost Battle of Stralsund. Danish archbishop Absalon destroys a Pomeranian fleet that is attacking Rügen.

1185

Battle of Berrhoe. The Bulgarians defeat a Byzantine army in Thrace.

King William II of Sicily storms the city of Thessalonica, Greece.

7 November Battle of Strymon (Struma), Thessaly. King William II of Sicily's army is routed in battle and the Thessalonians damage much of the Sicilian invasion fleet.

The civil war eventually ended in compromise in 1153: Stephen agreed to accept Matilda's son Henry (the future Henry II) as his heir, and Henry duly inherited the throne in 1154. Much of his energy was then directed at reducing the number of baronial castles in England and increasing royal control of those vital and troublesome resources.

Frederick Barbarossa in Italy

Exceeding even the English civil war in ferocity and duration was Emperor Frederick I of Germany's long effort to reclaim the Italian lands that had fallen from imperial control in the long wars of the Investiture Contest. Called 'Barbarossa' for his red beard, Frederick seems to have had a fiery temper and a strong streak of stubbornness. He desperately longed for the resources of Italy, hoping to restore the German monarchy to its former strength. And thus began his Italian expeditions, the centrepiece of European warfare from 1154 until the re-establishment of a grudging peace at Constance in 1182. The Italian city-states of northern Italy had enjoyed half a century of freedom from imperial lordship when Frederick began his

effort to bring them to heel. The cities had established strong oligarchies and encouraged a strong civic sense among the citizens, and they were not prepared to accept imperial rule meekly.

This was especially true of Milan, the greatest city of the north, which guarded the road from Germany into Italy. In the years 1156–1158, the citizens of Milan, fearing Frederick's intentions, built a 5km (3 mile) earthen rampart, the *Terraggio*, to reinforce the city's old Roman walls, surrounding the structure with a moat. By the middle of the twelfth century, though, siege warfare on the Continent had advanced well beyond merely sitting outside the walls and waiting for the inhabitants to starve. When Barbarossa invested the city, he

....

Gustave Doré's moving woodcut of the dead of the Kingdom of Jerusalem in the aftermath of the Battle of Hattin, 1187.

1186	1186–1187	1187	1187–1189
August Geoffrey of Brittany, son of Henry II and Eleanor of Aquitaine, is killed in a tournament.	Bulgarians rebel against Byzantine control and found an independent empire under Ivan Asen I.	Saladin invades Galilee, but is stopped at the castle of Saffuriyah. **4 July** Battle of Hattin. A 30,000–strong Muslim army under Saladin decisively defeats the army of the Kingdom of Jerusalem commanded by King Guy of Lusignan (about 20,000 men). **2 October** Jerusalem surrenders to Saladin after a 12-day siege.	All major fortresses of the Kingdom of Jerusalem except Tyre fall to Saladin.

undermined weak sections of the wall and bombarded the walls with engines that perhaps included early counterweight trebuchets, which could throw a heavy stone with enough force to damage walls. In fact, the city soon surrendered, apparently because it had not been provisioned adequately for a siege.

Frederick's war bogged down in a long series of slow, painful sieges that illustrate every possible method of breaking into fortified places known at the time. Frederick's siege engineers contrived ever more elaborate means to break in, while the Lombards constructed ever more elaborate defences to hold them out, such as at the key castle of Alessandria, which Frederick never managed to take. At the siege of Crema in 1159, for example, a city protected by double walls with a moat between, the emperor was not content to sit and wait for surrender. In his first assault, his men constructed a causeway and rolled a siege tower to the wall, protecting the siege tower from enemy bombardment by

chaining Cremascan prisoners to it. That assault failed, and when Frederick did manage to breach the wall the defenders rapidly constructed another wall behind it. The imperial army succeeded only after Frederick's main siege engineer built an armoured siege tower that stood 45m (150ft) high, with a great bridge from which the attackers could cross into the city. When it was in position, the citizens surrendered, but Frederick's angry troops still sacked and razed the town. Similarly, when Milan surrendered to the emperor a second time in 1162 after a nine-month siege, the citizens were forced to leave and the city, including even the churches, was then destroyed.

The destruction of Milan had an adverse effect: the Lombard cities formed a league of 16 cities against Barbarossa, able to field 20,000 men. Clearly, war was becoming a bigger business. Fighting continued at intervals,

King Philip II Augustus of France (1180–1223), who won Normandy from King John of England and defeated Emperor Otto IV at the Battle of Bouvines (1214).

1188

Levy of the 'Saladin Tithe' to raise money in England and France for the reconquest of Jerusalem.

1189–1192

Third Crusade.

1189–1191

August 1189–12 July 1191 Siege of Acre by King Guy of Jerusalem, his force augmented by crusaders as they arrive in the East. Acre finally surrenders, after which most of the French crusaders under Philip II Augustus go home.

although Frederick found it ever harder to convince German nobles and knights to cross the Alps for him, as the men died like flies from enemy attack and disease. Finally, on 29 May 1176, the Lombard League's forces defeated the emperor – the German cavalry charge at Legnano was unable to penetrate the League's close infantry formation. Frederick blamed his defeat on the refusal of Duke Henry, the Lion of Saxony, to support him on campaign. Barbarossa returned to Germany with blood in his eye, and charged Duke Henry with failure in his feudal duties. The duke was outlawed in 1179, although it took a largely mercenary army nearly two years of devastating Saxony to drive him into exile.

Richard Lionheart and a State at War

The only Christian commander in the twelfth century who could compare to Frederick Barbarossa in the total commitment of his state to military objectives was Richard I of England (1189–1199), nicknamed 'the Lionheart'. Richard's reign was so heavily devoted to war, both in France and on crusade, that he spent a scant ten months of his reign in England – and

then only to raise money for further warfare. Richard had good reasons to fight. Before coming to the throne, he joined in a major rebellion against his father Henry II, who had denied his sons any meaningful role as they grew to adulthood. But his first great challenge was the Third Crusade, called after Sultan Saladin had annihilated the army of the Kingdom of Jerusalem at the Battle of Hattin had taken most of the kingdom, including the holy city of Jerusalem, in 1187. Three rulers – Richard, Philip II Augustus of France and the ageing emperor Frederick Barbarossa – all took the cross. But Frederick drowned in a Turkish river before reaching Palestine, and Philip lacked the resources and will to win back the Holy Land. This left the initiative in the hands of Richard and his astonishingly well-equipped and expensive army, which numbered perhaps as many as 17,000 troops and seamen, a huge force for the twelfth century. That Richard

Legend tells that, in the First Crusade, Godfrey of Bouillon's companion Gerard of Avesnes was captured by Muslims and crucified on the walls of Asur, one of many atrocities by both sides in the crusades.

1190

18 May Battle of Iconium (Asia Minor). The German contingent of the Third Crusade, led by Emperor Frederick I Barbarossa, win a major victory over the Seljuk Turks.

10 June Frederick I Barbarossa drowns while crossing the small River Salef in Asia Minor. The German crusade army disintegrates, most of the crusaders returning to Europe.

1191

6 May Battle of Kolossi, Cyprus. King Richard I of England's crusader force defeats Isaac Comnenos, Byzantine governor of Cyprus, after Isaac detains English crusaders. Richard takes control of Cyprus.

August Battle of Jaffa. A small battle, in which a crusader force commanded by Richard I beats off an attack by Saladin's light cavalry.

7 September Battle of Arsuf, Kingdom of Jerusalem. The crusader army defeats Saladin's force.

1192–1194

Captivity of Richard I the Lionheart, held for ransom in Germany after being shipwrecked while returning from crusade.

1193

Pope Celestine III orders the Spanish kings to stop warring against each other and terminate their truces with Muslims.

1193

4 March Death of the Ayyubid
sultan Saladin.

1193–1196

Spring 1193–1196 Philip II Augustus of France
attempts to seize Normandy, taking advantage
of Richard I's imprisonment in Germany.

1194

Battle of Fréteval. Philip II of France tries to avoid
a pitched battle with Richard I, but Philip's rear
guard is attacked and his baggage train captured.

Richard I creates the first English royal dockyard
at Portsmouth.

Emperor Henry VI of Germany seizes the kingdom
of Sicily in the name of his wife Constance.

1195

18 July Battle of Alarcos. A large Almohad
army under Caliph al-Mansur heavily
defeats the army of Alfonso VIII of Castile.

The ruins of Château Gaillard, Richard the Lionheart's 'saucy castle' intended to defend Normandy from French invasion.

....

fought Saladin to a stalemate is an extraordinary tribute to what a Western European army could perform when well commanded. All the advantage lay on the Muslim side, including access to supplies and a string of victories to boost morale, as well as a charismatic leader who had created great enthusiasm for a holy war against the Christians. Richard completed the conquest of Acre, which had been besieged for over two years, using the latest in siege technology, perhaps in emulation of Frederick's campaigns in Italy.

Richard's Victory over Saladin

Military capability at the end of the twelfth century can best be seen, though, in Richard's victory over Saladin at Arsuf on 7 September 1191. A large majority of the Christian troops were Richard's subjects, but the crusade army also included members of the religious orders and an assortment of crusaders from other regions. After taking Acre, the army set out for Jaffa, in what turned into a fighting march down the coast road of Palestine. In contrast to the disorder of Louis VII's march under similar circumstances on the Second Crusade, the men led by Richard were clearly expected to hold to their formations – and they did. The king positioned his infantry and archers on the left, where they kept the Turkish mounted archers out of range and guarded the baggage.

On 7 September, when Saladin's attacks reached their height, the English archers held the enemy off until they were close to exhaustion, at which point Richard was ready with a massed cavalry charge. He even believed his troops to be so disciplined that the knights would charge at the signal of six trumpets, although in fact two knights charged before the signal and the rest followed. The premature but orderly charge caught the Muslims by surprise, although Richard did not attain the decisive victory for which he must have hoped. Ultimately Richard had to leave the Holy Land without taking Jerusalem, but he left the remnant of the Latin kingdom far better able to defend itself. Richard was shipwrecked and held for an enormous ransom on his way home. Philip Augustus of France took advantage of his enemy's extended absence to overrun several of Richard's continental possessions. After his eventual return, Richard spent the rest of his reign embroiled in a long war with France, a war that continued to demand more resources than ever before. To give just the most notorious example, Richard spent more than his annual revenue for Normandy to construct the great fortress of Château Gaillard, the 'Saucy Castle', intended to protect a major route into Normandy.

Cavalry Charge and Castles

By the time Richard died ingloriously of gangrene, after being wounded by a crossbow bolt while besieging a small castle, he had confirmed several central military lessons of the twelfth century. The cavalry charge and castles would have a long future, although the fact that even Richard's military genius was not enough to recover Jerusalem dampened ardour for future crusades.

1196	1196–1198	1198	1199
Pope Celestine III excommunicates Alfonso IX of León and encourages his subjects to rebel, after Alfonso makes allies with the Muslim Almohads against Castile.	Richard I constructs Château Gaillard in Normandy about 32km (20 miles) up the Seine from Rouen, at a cost of £11,500.	Militarization of the Hospitallers of St Mary of the Germans in Jerusalem (Teutonic Knights).	Crusade against Markward of Anweiler in Romagna and the March of Ancona, the first crusade waged against a Christian ruler.
		First crusade against the Livonians.	**6 April** Death of Richard I the Lionheart at the siege of Châlus, Aquitaine.
		Battle of Gisor. Richard I of England defeats a French army.	
		Germans found Riga, Livonia.	

The Thirteenth Century: An Age of Wars

The thirteenth century is remarkable in the history of medieval European warfare by an increase in the scale of military engagements. The size of armies had been on the rise throughout the twelfth century, a century that had also witnessed several longer wars, most notably several large crusades. In the thirteenth century, however, multi-year wars became much more common.

Before this time, such wars would simply have been beyond the financial and military resources of European states. But Europe's economy was flourishing, and thanks to developing bureaucracies, kings were increasingly able to siphon off funds for their own projects – with war at the top of their list of interests. Indeed, at the beginning of the century we can already see protests at kings' expensive warmongering in the most politically precocious state of Europe, England. By the end

of the century, revolts against royal exactions were becoming endemic, as war's expenses far surpassed the ability of kings to pay. Individuals could still make their fortunes on the battlefield, but the high cost of war meant that it was very rare for a government to profit.

Byzantine Decline

One of the few regions where a bold ruler could still hope to gain wealth as well as fame was the Byzantine Empire, whose government and military capability had weakened significantly in the course of the twelfth century. The Byzantines had started the century strong, Emperor John III Comnenos (1118–1143)

Left: Harlech Castle, Wales, constructed in 1283–1290 for King Edward I of England.
Right: A gold hyperperon of Emperor Manuel I Komnenos, known as 'the great' (1143–1180).

King William II of Sicily (1166–1189), being crowned by Christ, a mosaic from the cathedral William constructed at Monreale, near Palermo.

continuing his father's efforts to revive Byzantium's military capability. John waged successful wars against the Venetians, the Danishmend Turks and the Latin Christian Principality of Antioch, while also crushing the Pecheneg threat against his borders. His successor Manuel I Comnenos (1143–1180) was too ambitious, though. He launched an expedition against the Norman state of Sicily and southern Italy in 1155–1157, only to be driven off with heavy losses. That defeat, however, paled in significance compared to the disaster the Byzantine army suffered at Myriocephalon on 17 September 1176. Emperor Manuel invaded Seljuk territory with a large army and siege train, plainly intent on regaining lost territory. While marching near the Tzibritze Pass, however, Sultan Kilij Arslan II launched a surprise attack. The Byzantines, unable to deploy, were annihilated, fatally weakening their empire.

c. 1200

Hungary seizes Bosnia with papal support as the country contained heretics. Hungary also attempts to conquer Orthodox Serbia.

1201

Almohad conquest of the Balearic Islands.

1201–1204

Fourth Crusade, which is diverted to conquer Christian Constantinople.

1202

The military religious order of Sword Brothers is established at Riga, Livonia.

1 August Battle of Mirebeau. Arthur of Brittany, a claimant for the crown of England, had been besieging his grandmother Eleanor of Aquitaine at Mirebeau. King John of England relieves the siege, decisively defeating Arthur and his allies.

November Conquest of Zara, Dalmatia. The army of the Fourth Crusade takes Christian Zara.

Having lost much of their army, Byzantine officials were now desperate for money and increasingly resentful of the major trade concessions granted to Italian cities, which were impoverishing the empire's cities and diverting funds that would otherwise have gone to the emperor. A massacre of Western residents in Constantinople in 1183 increased European hatred and suspicion of the Byzantines, a situation made worse by the religious divide between the two branches of Christendom. King William II of Sicily invaded the empire in 1185, one of many Norman attacks in the course of the century, both from Italy and from Antioch. He was defeated at Strymon on 7 November 1185, but distrust between East and West rose to an even higher pitch. In fact, when Frederick I Barbarossa decided to take the land route on setting out on the Third Crusade in 1189, the Byzantine emperor was so suspicious of Frederick's intentions that he

The Conquest of Constantinople, 1204, by Domenico Tintoretto (1560–1635), a historically inaccurate but moving depiction of the confusion of the assault and Venetian pride in their accomplishment.

1203–1204

August 1203–6 March 1204 Siege of Château Gaillard (Normandy). King Philip II Augustus of France takes this supposedly invincible castle after a long siege.

1203

17 July Assault on Constantinople by French crusaders and a Venetian fleet. The crusaders succeed in taking a section of wall, after which the city accept the crusader-sponsored Alexius IV as emperor.

1204

12 April Conquest of Constantinople by French crusaders and a Venetian crusader fleet led by Doge Enrico Dandalo.

Installation of Count Baldwin of Flanders as the first Latin emperor of Constantinople.

1204–1261

Latin Empire of Constantinople.

renewed his alliance with Saladin, the crusaders' great enemy.

The Fourth Crusade

The Third Crusade had failed to retake Jerusalem, so it was inevitable that a new crusade would be proclaimed. A number of important French nobles took the cross. They arranged transport with the naval city Venice, upon which the Venetians devoted all their resources for a year to provide transport for 33,500 men and 4500 horses, along with 50 war galleys. But only about 12,000 crusaders turned up at the rendezvous in the summer of 1202.

The Venetians proceeded to divert the crusade to their own benefit, in an effort to recoup their heavy losses. First they convinced the crusaders to help retake the city of Zara on the eastern shore of the Adriatic, which Venice had lost a few years before. Then a perfect opportunity seemed to present itself: the son of a deposed Byzantine emperor begged the crusaders for help to recover his throne. In return, he promised to pay the crusader debt to Venice and to join in a campaign to liberate Jerusalem. Ignorant of the Byzantine political

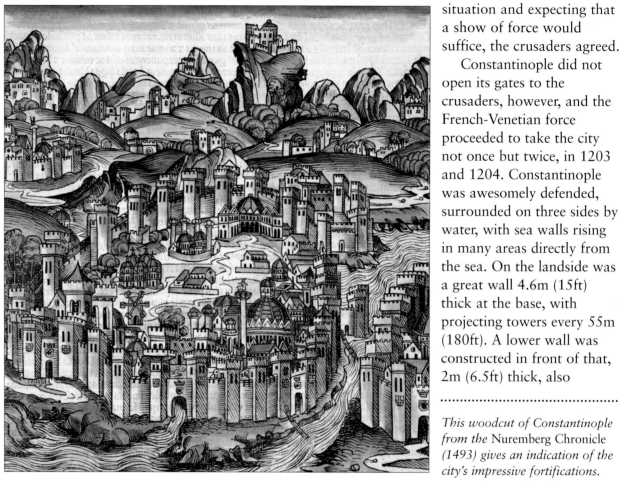

situation and expecting that a show of force would suffice, the crusaders agreed.

Constantinople did not open its gates to the crusaders, however, and the French-Venetian force proceeded to take the city not once but twice, in 1203 and 1204. Constantinople was awesomely defended, surrounded on three sides by water, with sea walls rising in many areas directly from the sea. On the landside was a great wall 4.6m (15ft) thick at the base, with projecting towers every 55m (180ft). A lower wall was constructed in front of that, 2m (6.5ft) thick, also

....

This woodcut of Constantinople from the Nuremberg Chronicle *(1493) gives an indication of the city's impressive fortifications.*

1205

5 April Battle of Adrianople. The Bulgars under Czar Kalojan disastrously defeat a Latin force, capturing King Baldwin of Constantinople. A relief force led by Doge Enrico Dandalo of Venice rescues the remnants of the army.

1206

Unification of the Mongols under the leadership of Genghis Khan (c. 1162–1227).

1207

Pope Innocent III places England under an interdict in an effort to force King John to accept his choice of Stephen Langton as archbishop of Canterbury.

1208

Henry I of Constantinople defeats the Bulgarians under czar Boril at the Battle of Plovdiv (Philippopolis).

protected by towers, and a moat dug in front of all. The French crusaders attacked the land walls, while the Venetians, who had broken into the Golden Horn (Constantinople's great harbour), attacked the sea wall by landing men with ladders where there were narrow beaches and by lowering bridges from the masts of their ships. When they had already taken part of the wall, the Byzantine usurper fled and the citizens opened their gates to welcome their deposed lord. But the restored emperor found himself unable to keep his promises to the crusaders. So in 1204 they took the city again, sacking it and installing a Latin Christian as emperor.

The Latin Byzantine Empire lasted until 1261, fighting Bulgars, combating Byzantines who wanted to restore Greek rule, and finally being forced out when a Byzantine force broke through an unguarded gate. The restored Byzantine Empire, though, never really recovered. It proved less able to protect the eastern flank of Europe from the new Turkish threat that soon appeared.

Ongoing Crusades

Despite the failure of the Third Crusade and the odd diversion of the Fourth Crusade, the

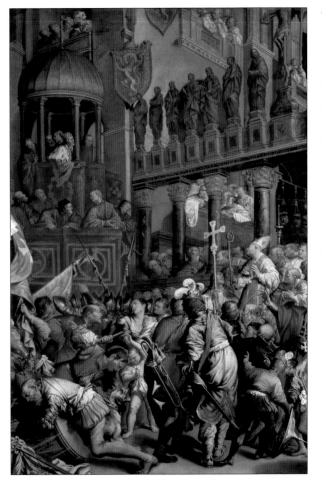

crusading movement was too central to medieval religious and military belief to simply stop. Popular enthusiasm can be seen in the 'Children's Crusade' of 1212, a mass exodus of the young and poor, who hoped that their prayers would free Jerusalem. This effort broke up when the Mediterranean failed to open so that the crusaders could walk across it, but a new crusade was soon preached. It was meticulously prepared, with an elaborate system of papal fundraising to help pay the heavy expenses of well over 10,000 troops (including about 1200 knights). These crusaders advanced against Egypt, deciding that the only way to take and hold Jerusalem was to attack the heart of Muslim power. They eventually captured the great port city of Damietta in 1219 – but it was soon lost again, when the advancing army was trapped and surrendered to the enemy at al-Mansurah on the Nile. In 1229, Emperor Frederick II won Jerusalem by treaty, in the

Doge Enrico Dandolo of Venice recruiting for the Fourth Crusade, by Jean Leclerc (1621). Geoffrey Villehardouin's contemporary account makes it plain that this was an emotion-laden event.

1209–1229	1209	1210	1211
Albigensian Crusades against the Cathar heretics of southern France.	**22 July** Fall of Béziers, France, to crusaders. The inhabitants are massacred.	**3 June–22 July** Siege of Minerve in the Albigensian Crusade. The castle surrenders to crusaders when their water supply fails. The defenders are promised their lives, but 140 Cathars are burned.	Battle of Castelnaudary. Albigensian crusaders led by Simon de Montfort defeat an alliance of southern French nobles.
	August Fall of Carcassonne, France, to crusaders under papal legate Arnold Aimery and Simon de Montfort.		
	Pope Innocent III excommunicates King John of England.		

course of a bizarre crusade with almost no troops, led by a ruler who had been excommunicated precisely for not fulfilling his vow to go on crusade. But the Kingdom of Jerusalem was then torn from 1229 to 1243 by rebellion against Frederick's administration. The internal struggle only really ended with the savage Muslim reconquest of the city on 11 July 1244. The Muslim Khwarasmians, allies of the 'Ayyubid ruler of Syria, proceeded to annihilate the army of the Latin kingdom at La Forbie.

The stream of crusaders who continued to travel to fight in the East did, however, delay the doom of the Latin kingdom. Louis IX led a crusade 1248–1254 that, like the Fifth Crusade, ended up attacking Egypt. Louis' crusade is more notable for the resources he was able to muster for the expedition than for its limited successes. He led an army of at least 15,000, providing about half the troops himself. He and his army ended up surrendering to the enemy, and Louis had to pay a literal king's ransom to win his freedom. Even after that, Louis remained in Palestine for over a year restoring fortifications. A staggering sum of money was raised and expended on the enterprise,

The army of King Louis IX of France capturing Damietta, 6 June 1249. The city put up little resistance; Louis soon lost it again after he and his army were captured.

1212

Children's Crusade. Thousands of adolescents and poor people set out to free Jerusalem. Many are dispersed while still in France and Germany; others reach Italy but turn back when the sea does not open for them to walk to the Holy Land, as promised. A late legend tells that some were promised transport by merchants but sold into slavery in Egypt.

16 July Battle of Las Navas de Tolosa. Pedro II of Aragón leads an allied Spanish force to win a major victory against the Almohad caliph al-Nasir.

1213

Pope Innocent III threatens to depose King John of England and calls on Philip II of France to lead a crusade against him.

May John of England submits to the pope.

31 May An English navy of 500 ships surprise a French fleet preparing for an invasion of England under Prince Louis at Damme (the port of Bruges) and destroy it.

12 September Battle of Muret. Pedro II of Aragón brings an army to Toulouse to support his ally Count Raymond against the Albigensian crusaders, only to be defeated by crusaders under Simon de Montfort. Pedro is killed.

1214

27 July Battle of Bouvines, France. In a hard-fought battle, Philip II Augustus of France decisively defeats the invading army of emperor Otto IV of Germany.

Left: The most unusual crusade was that of Emperor Frederick II Hohenstaufen, who was excommunicated at the time and did not fight any battles.

Right: Attackers could expect bloodshed when assaulting a breach, which explains the massacres after a successful assault.

demonstrating magnificently the resources that could be invested in a war which, even if successful, could never have yielded much by way of tangible gain, though it might have reaped spiritual rewards and enhanced the honour of participants. Louis' second crusade, in 1270, diverted to northern Africa by Louis' ambitious brother the king of Sicily, ended with nothing accomplished and the king's death from dysentery.

The Mongol Interlude
The Latin foothold in the eastern Mediterranean survived as long as it did

1215–1217	1215	1216
Barons' War in England, a major rebellion against King John.	**15 June** King John of England is issued Magna Carta.	**15 January** King John of England takes the town of Berwick by storm, then raids further into Scotland to punish King Alexander II for his alliance with the rebellious barons of England.
	30 November Rebel-held Rochester surrender to a besieging force commanded by King John when their food supplies are exhausted.	**May** At the invitation of rebellious barons, Prince Louis of France invades England. The English fleet, mauled by a storm, fails to intercept the invasion fleet.
	The Fourth Lateran Council bans tournaments.	Scottish invasion of England, led by King Alexander II in alliance with English rebels.

A fanciful image of Genghis Khan by the French artist Pierre Duflos (1780). In reality, the Mongol leader prided himself on dressing and living like his warriors.

only thanks to the unification of the Mongols under Genghis Khan (c. 1162–1227) and their devastation of much of the Islamic world. Only the periphery of Europe suffered direct Mongol onslaught. In all cases, Western military power proved unable to deal with the Mongol style of fighting – a completely cavalry force, mostly archers, who specialized in ambush, feigned flight and attack from a distance.

The Mongols first assaulted Russia in 1223, winning a significant victory at the River Kalka, but then withdrew. They came again from 1237–1240, defeating the armies of several Russian princes and taking a number of Russian towns, most notably Kiev, by storm. They crushed a

....

Mongols at the gates of Leignitz in 1241, after defeating the army of Duke Henry II of Silesia. They are carrying Henry's head on a lance.

German/Polish force of about 20,000 men under Duke Henry II of Silesia at Liegnitz on 9 April 1241, and a mere two days later annihilated the Hungarian army under Béla IV at Mohi. And then the steppe warriors withdrew, continuing to rule parts of Russia for centuries but otherwise leaving Europe untroubled.

1217

King Alexander II's second invasion of England, in support of the barons rebelling against King John.

Second Siege and Battle of Lincoln. Rebellious barons besiege Lincoln. The regent William Marshal comes to relieve the royalists. The rebels refuse battle and shelter in the city while continuing the siege of the castle, but William Marshal breaks in, achieving complete surprise and capturing a large number of rebel nobles in street fighting.

24 August Battle of Sandwich (Dover). A French fleet sent to England with reinforcements for Prince Louis is met and defeated by an English fleet under Hubert de Burgh.

Battle of Alcácer do Sol. A Portuguese-crusader force led by Afonso II of Portugal defeats the Almohads.

1217–1221

Fifth Crusade (Crusade of Damietta).

1218–1215

November 1219 Siege and conquest of Damietta, Egypt, by forces of the Fifth Crusade, led by Duke Leopold of Austria.

Left: The ruins of a crusader castle, one of the many taken by the Egyptian sultan Baibars (1260–1277).

The Fall of the Kingdom of Jerusalem

Perhaps the Mongols' greatest importance for the history of European war is that a new military elite, the Mamluks, came to prominence in Egypt in the wake of their defeat of a Mongol invasion at 'Ain Jalut in 1260. The Mamluk sultan Baybars proceeded to carry out a long and careful plan to rid Palestine of crusaders once and for all. One by one, he took the Kingdom of Jerusalem's castles by siege, assault or treachery. He employed heavy siege equipment, including the counterweight trebuchets that were capable of breaching walls. At the siege of Beaufort in 1268, for example, Baybars had 26 such machines.

Several more small crusades reached the Holy Land, buying a little time for the Western outposts but not ending the threat. Finally, in 1291, the Mamluk sultan al-Asraf Halil moved against Acre, the last great crusade foothold. He took the city on 18 May 1291 after a short siege, killing all the male defenders who could not escape by ship and enslaving the women

In 1265, the Mamluk sultan Baibars captured the crusader-held cities of Haifa, Arsuf and Caesarea. His massacres of civilians helped provoke a crusade in 1267.

and children. Although efforts to regain Jerusalem continued to be planned for the rest of the Middle Ages, the age of the Holy Land crusade had effectively come to an end.

The Conquest of Prussia

The thirteenth century also saw the development of a major crusade front in the Baltic. German

---

1219

14 May Death of William Marshal, earl of Pembroke and regent of England.

15 June Battle of Reval (Tallin). A major Danish victory over the pagan Estonians, aided by a miraculous standard that fell from heaven – the Danebrog (a white cross on red background).

1221

29 August The army of the Fifth Crusade, trapped at al-Mansurah on the Nile while marching into Egypt, surrenders to the Ayyubid sultan al-Kamil. They give up Damietta as ransom for their release.

1222

The military religious order of Knights of Dobrin is established in Prussia.

Boleslav V of Poland and his successor, Leszek the Black. Boleslav, known as 'the chaste', was the leading prince in a fragmented Polish state. He rebuilt Cracow, destroyed in 1241 by the Mongols, but suffered another devastating raid in 1259.

merchants had founded Riga in the late twelfth century, and the initiative of a German bishop established a military religious order, the Sword Brothers, to protect settlers and missionaries, in about 1202. Another small order, the Knights of Dobrin, was established on the fringe of Prussia about 20 years later. The Danes enjoyed some success over the non-Christian Estonians, as at the Battle of Reval in 1219, a victory blessed by a holy banner (the *Danebrog*, still copied on the modern Danish flag) that was said to have fallen from heaven. The frontier, however, proved to be highly unstable. Livonians, Estonians, Prussians and other Baltic peoples were naturally reluctant to admit foreign colonists who stole their land and tried to impose an alien religion upon them. A native rising in Estonia killed hundreds of Germans, including nearly half of the Sword Brothers. Border defence, not to mention expansion, required organized forces that could hold the territory as well as win battles.

In 1230, Duke Conrad of Masovia, unable to stop Prussian raiding, invited one of the Holy Land military orders, the Teutonic Knights, to Prussia. Like the Templars and Hospitallers, the Teutonic Order had a substantial infrastructure of estates (mostly in Germany) to pay for military adventures, as well as larger numbers than their niche in the Holy Land could justify. So the master of the order, Hermann von Salza, established a second front for the order in Prussia. Emperor Frederick II promised that the order could have all the Prussian territory it succeeded in occupying, and a series of popes was happy to grant crusading indulgences to Europeans who offered assistance to the Teutonic Knights in their war against the non-Christian Baltic peoples.

Between 1230 and 1285, the order, supplemented by regular crusading expeditions,

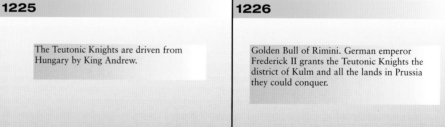

1223

May Battle of the Kalka River. Invading Mongols commanded by Subutai rout an army of the Russian princes.

Uprising of Estonians against Christian rule.

1224

Distraint of Knighthood in England. An edict orders that all Englishmen with the necessary financial resources must be knighted.

John of Nicaea defeats the military force of the Latin Empire of Constantinople at the Battle of Poimanenon.

Battle of Serres. Theodore of Epirus defeats an army of the Latin Empire of Constantinople.

1225

The Teutonic Knights are driven from Hungary by King Andrew.

1226

Golden Bull of Rimini. German emperor Frederick II grants the Teutonic Knights the district of Kulm and all the lands in Prussia they could conquer.

conquered Prussia and established an independent church-state there. Initially, the task must have seemed easy. The native Prussian nobility were light cavalry, while the poor fought on foot, often armed only with stones and clubs. The emphasis was on independent

....

Below: Ottokar I, the first king of Bohemia (1198–1230), a title granted by Frederick II Hohenstaufen in return for military assistance.

Above: Teutonic Knights, as portrayed in the classic Russian film Alexander Nevsky *(1938), which celebrates the prince of Novgorod's victory over the Teutonic Order at the Battle of Lake Peipus.*

1227

Battle of Bornhöved. King Waldemar II of Denmark is defeated and forced out of Estonia.

Pope Gregory IX excommunicates Emperor Frederick II for the failure to perform his crusading vow because of serious illness.

1227–1229

Duke Jaroslav of Novgorod seizes eastern Finland.

Crusade of Emperor Frederick II (who was excommunicated at the time).

1228–1230

Conquest of Majorca by King Jaume I of Aragón-Catalonia.

heroism rather than teamwork. Yet the Western knights and their better-armed and trained infantry were, in fact, ill suited to the conquest. The Prussians waged guerrilla war, rather than accepting pitched battles that they would inevitably have lost. The Teutonic Knights and their allies were forced to take the land mile by

mile, 'pacifying' each region with castles that had to be garrisoned year round.

Bohemians and Scandinavians also devoted considerable resources to the land-grab in the Baltic, and also found it a long hard fight. For example, the king of Bohemia launched a major attack on Samland in 1256. In 1257, the

Minerve in the Languedoc was an important Cathar refuge. It surrendered to crusaders after a siege in 1210; between 150 and 180 Cathars were then burned alive.

....

Samogitians asked for a two-year truce to consider their options, then decided to fight

1229–1239	1229	1229–1243	1230
Aragonese conquest of the Balearic Islands.	**18 February** Treaty of Jaffa. An agreement reached between Frederick II and the Ayyubid sultan al-Kamil grants Jerusalem to the Christians for ten years.	Rebellion against Hohenstaufen rule in the Kingdom of Jerusalem.	Duke Conrad of Masovia invited the Teutonic Knights to Prussia, to defend his territory against pagan raiders.
	12 April Treaty of Meaux-Paris ends the Albigensian Crusades and gives the king of France control over the eastern portion of Languedoc.		**9 March** Bulgar czar Ivan Asen II, defeats and captures Theodore of Epirus in the Battle of Klokotnitsa.

for their native religion and customs. They defeated several forces sent against them, and instigated a series of anti-Christian revolts in lands that had supposedly already been subdued. And the Westerners found it hard to prevail against ambushes and raids. In 1260, the Samogitians successfully ambushed a strong force of Teutonic Knights at Durben, starting a 30-year war just when the order thought it had succeeded in claiming the region. The Sudovians, the last of the Baltic peoples in Prussian territory, surrendered in 1283 – the same year that the Teutonic Order began a major new war with Lithuania that would last for nearly two centuries.

Crusades Against Christians

Technically defined, a crusade is any war summoned by a pope, for which an indulgence – a release from performing the penance for sins – is granted. The first crusades were against Muslims, but by the early twelfth century the term had already been expanded to include wars against non-Christians on the frontiers of Europe. At the very end of the twelfth century, in 1199, the term was expanded yet again to

This eighteenth-century artist's impression of Simon de Montfort the Elder (1160–1218) suggests the crusader's charismatic leadership. (The armour is an unfortunate fifteenth-century anachronism.)

include wars against Christians who had proved in some way to be enemies of the faith.

The Albigensian Crusades, fought against the Cathar heretics of southern France between 1209 and 1229, proved to be a devastating military enterprise that combined religious goals with a knightly lust for land. Most Provençal nobles who took arms against them were not, in fact, heretics; at the most, they had sometimes protected the Cathars. The early stages of the war were marked by a number of successful crusader sieges, such as Béziers and Carcassonne in the summer of 1209. In both cases, when the crusaders took the cities they killed the inhabitants indiscriminately – a treatment usually reserved for non-Christian enemies – and burned large numbers of Cathar prisoners. As was typical in Europe by the thirteenth century, the process was greatly

---

1230–1283

Conquest of Prussia by the Teutonic Knights and crusaders.

1234

27 May Battle of Altenesch. The peasants of Stedingen (northwest of Bremen) refuse to pay tithes and taxes to the archbishop of Hamburg-Bremen. A crusade called against them in 1233 fails, but a large crusade army annihilates the peasants at Altenesch.

The fleet of the Hanseatic city Lübeck defeats a Danish flotilla.

1234–1235

Prince Henry of Germany rebels against his father Emperor Frederick II, in alliance with Milan and other Lombard towns. The rebellion collapses when Frederick marches on Germany, and Henry is captured. Imprisoned, he commits suicide years later.

slowed by the large number of castles dotting the landscape, which had to be besieged individually (although at least the crusaders did not usually have to fear attack by a relieving force). One of the most notable sieges was that of Minerve in 1210, a castle perched on an inaccessible peak. The castle's only weakness was the water supply, and the crusaders bombarded defenders who tried to reach the well with high-powered and accurate trebuchets. The defenders eventually surrendered on condition that their lives were spared – which did not, however, prevent the crusaders from burning 140 Cathars.

The Albigensian Crusade included several pitched battles, won by the leadership of the noble Simon de Montfort, who had taken command of the crusade forces and planned to win for himself the county of Toulouse. His most notable victory was at Muret on 13 September 1213. Count Raymond of Toulouse and his ally Pedro II of Aragón were besieging the crusader-held town of Muret when Simon de Montfort came to break the siege. He had only a small force of about 800 knights and 1400–1500 other cavalry, along with infantry

who were apparently not engaged in the battle. Simon won a tactical victory over the overconfident Spaniards. He sent two squadrons directly against King Pedro's force, while he himself led a third squadron in an oblique move that crossed a marsh and took the enemy on the left flank. The flank attack caused a panic that worsened when Pedro (who had entered the battle dressed as a common knight) was killed.

The Extinction of the Hohenstaufen

Increasingly, the popes also called crusades against their political enemies, in the belief that any enemy of the institutional Church was undeniably a heretic. Most notorious were the repeated crusades summoned by the popes against Emperor

Frederick II Hohenstaufen (died 1250) was dubbed 'the Antichrist' by the popes who opposed him. He was suspected because he was on friendly terms with Muslims, in his kingdom of Sicily and in the Holy Land.

1236

22 September Battle of River Saule, Livonia. A force of Livonians and their allies annihilate the Order of Sword Brothers and hundreds of crusaders.

Fall of Almohad-held Córdoba, Spain, to Ferdinand III of Castile-León.

Conquest of Valencia, Spain, by King Jaume I of Aragón-Catalonia.

1237

Opening of the St Gotthard Pass over the Alps.

27 November Battle of Cortenuova. Emperor Frederick II decisively defeats the Lombard League.

Fall of Ryazan, Russia, to the Mongols after a five-day siege.

December Battle of Kolomna. The Mongols annihilate a force led by Grand Prince Yuri II of Vladimir, which had marched to relieve the town of Ryazan.

1237–1239

Mongol invasion of Russia.

Frederick II Hohenstaufen (who died in 1250) and his heirs. The Hohenstaufen ruled both Germany and the kingdom of Sicily (southern Italy and Sicily) thanks to a dynastic alliance. In short, they encircled the papal state, and a free-thinking and independent ruler like Frederick II inspired hysterical fear at the papal court. Frederick II had already suffered papal excommunication in the 1220s, when he waited too long to depart on his promised crusade, and papal efforts to seize Frederick's southern Italian realm in his absence suggest both the strength of papal fears and the lengths to which they were willing to go to lift the Hohenstaufen threat. It is not surprising that, when Frederick II followed in his grandfather Barbarossa's footsteps by attempting to bring Lombard back into the imperial fold, Pope Gregory IX regarded this as a danger to the papacy.

The emperor took an army of about 20,000 men to northern Italy, against a renewed Lombard League that took the field against him. He won a major pitched battle at Cortenuova in November 1237, a victory that the Classicist emperor celebrated with an ancient Roman

Pope Gregory IX (1227–1241), whose unremitting strife with Emperor Frederick II helped to weaken both the German empire and the papacy.

triumph. Although Cortenuova broke the Lombard League and many towns yielded to Frederick, the pope engineered a new anti-imperial alliance, and in 1239 he excommunicated Frederick again, encouraging his vassals to rise against him. After years of confused fighting, the papacy went even further, arranging that the Council of Lyons in 1245 excommunicate and depose the Hohenstaufen ruler, declaring him to be the Antichrist.

Frederick ended his reign on a low note, severely defeated while besieging Parma in a battle that saw the capture of the imperial regalia and treasury; he died, probably of dysentery, in December 1250. The papal vendetta against the Hohenstaufen extended to Frederick's offspring, however. Papal ambassadors offered the crown of Sicily (which had in the meantime been assumed by Frederick's son Manfred) to a number of

---

1238

7 February Fall of Vladimir, Russia, to the Mongols.

Jaime I of Aragón conquers Valencia.

1239

A naval force from Lübeck defeats a Danish fleet.

18 October Fall of Cherigov, Russia, to the Mongols after a short siege.

6 December Mongols storm and destroy the city of Kiev.

Pope Gregory IX excommunicates Emperor Frederick II for a second time, releasing the emperor's vassals from their oaths of fealty.

1239–1241

Crusades of Thibault of Champagne and Richard of Cornwall.

European rulers, on condition of a very large payment to the papacy and military intervention to defeat the Hohenstaufen and their supporters.

Left: Charles of Anjou, who won the throne of Sicily from the Hohenstaufen, only to face the threat of Aragón in the War of the Sicilian Vespers.

....

Below: Manfred's death at the Battle of Benevento, 1266.

In 1254, Henry III of England accepted the offer on behalf of his younger son Edmund, but could not raise the necessary money and troops in face of baronial opposition. So, after Manfred had won a major victory over papal troops at Foggia late in 1254, the pope turned to crusade proclamations, diverting crusaders in 1264 and 1265 from fighting the Mamluks in Palestine to fighting the Hohenstaufen in southern Italy.

The papacy finally sold Sicily to Charles of Anjou, younger brother of Louis IX of France. Charles invaded Italy with a sizeable force, defeating and killing Manfred at the Battle of Benevento on 26 February 1266. This encounter shows how complex battles were becoming by the second half of the thirteenth century. Charles had assumed a position behind the flooded River Calore. Manfred crossed to meet him, placing his Muslim archers in front (Sicily had a substantial Muslim population), followed by German cavalry and then Italian cavalry. The groups, however, became separated during the advance. Manfred's archers were scattered by a charge made by Charles' cavalry – moving infantrymen offered easy targets for a massed cavalry charge. Manfred's German knights counter-charged, but were surrounded by the enemy cavalry. Manfred's reserve had been posted too far in the rear to provide assistance.

1240

15 July Battle of the River Neva. Prince Alexander of Novgorod defeats a Swedish invasion in a major victory that wins him the honorary title 'Nevsky'.

Haakon IV of Norway suppresses a revolt led by Jarl Skuli.

1241

9 April Battle of Leignitz. An invading Mongol army defeats a German-Polish force under the command of Duke Henry II of Silesia.

11 April Battle of Mohi. Invading Mongols crush the army of King Béla IV of Hungary. The Mongols may have used rudimentary firearms in the battle.

Distraint of Knighthood in England. Henry III orders all gentlemen with land worth £20 per year or more to be knighted.

A Venetian fleet defeats a larger Byzantine force in the Sea of Marmara.

Battle of Montecristo. The Pisan allies of Emperor Frederick II defeat a Genoese fleet carrying bishops to Rome for a council intended to condemn the emperor. Over 100 council members are captured and imprisoned.

1242

21 or 22 July Louis VIII of France defeats Henry III and his allies, the counts of La Marche and Toulouse, at the Battle of Taillebourg.

5 April Battle of Lake Peipus. The army of Novgorod under Prince Alexander Nevsky defeat a German and Danish invading army commanded by Bishop Hermann of Dorpat.

After the Battle of Benevento, Manfred's children were imprisoned for life, but Charles was still not in a position to enjoy his conquest because Frederick II's grandson Conradin then attempted to claim the kingdom of Sicily. But Conradin, who was only 16 years old at the time, was defeated at Tagliacozzo in 1268, a battle that was lost when his troops dispersed prematurely to plunder Charles of Anjou's camp, leaving them unprepared when the French rallied. Conradin was captured and executed shortly thereafter.

The War of the Sicilian Vespers

After Tagliacozzo, Charles of Anjou was able to claim the kingdom of Sicily, but his rule was deeply resented, and a major rebellion broke out in 1282. It developed into a full-scale war between Charles (and his heirs) and Aragón for control of Sicily. It is called the War of the Sicilian Vespers from the rebels' use of a vespers bell as the signal to attack their French lords on Easter Monday 1282. The war, waged above all at sea, shows how far European powers were able to reach militarily, equipping a series of expensive fleets on an unheard-of scale.

The great rebellion against Angevin rule in Sicily, known as the Sicilian Vespers, broke out when an Angevin soldier insulted a woman.

King Pedro III of Aragón claimed Sicily through his wife, Manfred's daughter Constance. He was quick to take advantage of the rebellion, and had the resources to do so. Pedro III's father, Jaime I 'the Conqueror' (1213–1276), had established Aragón as the dominant power of the western Mediterranean, conquering the Balearic Islands and Valencia and especially building up the Aragonese fleet. When the War of the Sicilian Vespers broke out, the French pope Martin IV had offered the crown of Aragón to Philip III of France's younger son, thus encouraging a French invasion of Aragón.

Statue of Roger de Lauria, Aragón's great admiral in the War of the Sicilian Vespers.

1244

11 July Conquest of Jerusalem by the Khorezmians, central Asian nomads who are confederates of the Ayyubid sultans of Egypt.

17 October Battle of La Forbie (Gaza). An Egyptian-Khorezmian army crushes the army of the Kingdom of Jerusalem, under the command of Walter of Jaffa, and his Syrian allies.

Battle of Rensen. Duke Swantopulk of Pomerania defeats the Teutonic Knights.

March The last Cathar-held fortress of Languedoc, Montségur, falls after a 10-month siege; 255 captured Cathars are burned.

Treaty between Alexander II of Scotland and Henry III of England, leading to 50 years of peace between the two countries.

1245

Council of Lyons excommunicates and declares the deposition of Emperor Frederick II. The council also bans tournaments.

Battle of Krücken. Duke Swantopulk of Pomerania defeats the Teutonic Knights.

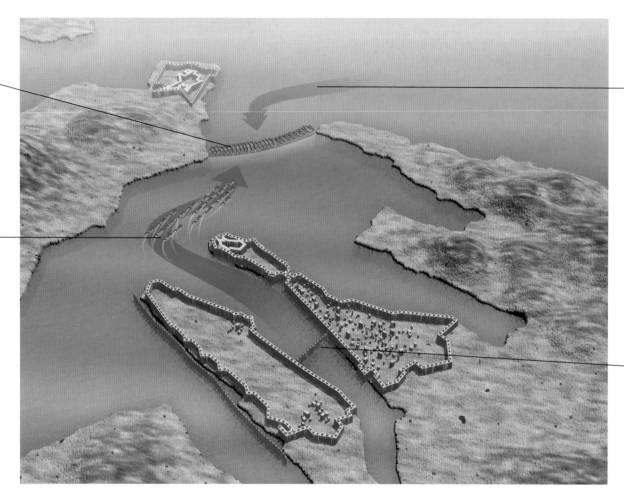

4. After waiting until the Angevin crews exhaust their supply of missile weapons, the Aragonese engage in hand-to-hand combat with the Angevins.

2. The Aragonese fleet, commanded by Roger de Lauria, enters the Grand Harbour of Malta, drawing up in line abreast to block the harbour entrance.

3. The Angevin fleet leaves its safe position on the beach to engage the attacking Aragonese.

1. Dockyard Creek, a highly defensible position where the Angevin fleet docked for safety.

The Battle of Malta, 1283

1246

Ferdinand II of Castile captures Jaén from the Muslims.

John of Nicaea conqueres Macedonia and Thrace.

1247

Mamluk conquest of Ascalon.

1248

18 February Battle of Parma. Emperor Frederick II besieges Parma during the winter, but the Parmesans break out and severely defeat Frederick. Frederick himself barely escapes, and the imperial regalia and treasury are captured.

Fall of Seville to Ferdinand III of Castile–León. Northern ships blockade the River Guadalquivir, keeping a Muslim fleet from relieving the city.

1248–1254

First Crusade of Louis IX of France.

The expedition proved to be a very expensive failure, though, the Catalan fleet destroying Philip III's support ships and Philip III himself dying during his retreat. In 1283 arrangements were actually made for a duel between King Charles and his rival King Pedro, but the event never took place. Henceforth, most battles of the war were fought at sea. The war ended in a compromise in 1302, with Aragón gaining control of the island of Sicily while the Angevins kept southern Italy. For nearly two centuries more, though, war flared up between the two inveterate enemies.

Pedro III was fortunate in possessing a brilliant admiral, Roger de Lauria, a Sicilian ex-patriot. Medieval naval warfare was far more than shiploads of men throwing missiles at each other as they lumbered closer, and then boarding for hand-to-hand struggle with the enemy, as Roger de Lauria's impressive string of victories shows. He won six major sea battles for Aragón, from the Battle of Malta in 1283 to the Battle of Ponza in 1300. In all of the engagements, he demonstrated that he and his Aragonese crews simply understood the sea better than the Angevins.

Roger used a variety of tricks, including throwing pots of soap on enemy decks so that the defenders lost their balance. He had galleys constructed with higher gunwales, protecting his men during the initial bombardment as enemy ships approached. Above all, though, the Aragonese fleet had specialized light troops, who were much better in a sea fight than the conventional land forces employed on Charles of Anjou's ships. The heavy armour of knights was a serious disadvantage in a battle at sea, as was the more modest armament of infantry. Instead, Roger employed Aragonese

Crossbows were a slow weapon but highly effective at sieges and in naval battles.

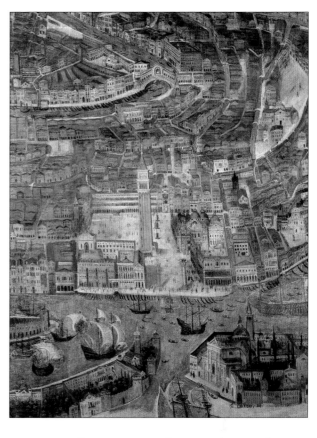

A seventeenth-century view of Venice, showing the seaborne traffic that had made the city wealthy in the twelfth and thirteenth centuries.

1249

A Hanseatic League fleet attacks Copenhagen, Denmark.

6 June Louis IX of France's crusade army conquers Damietta, Egypt, after a two-day siege.

1250

8 February Battle of al-Mansurah. An Egyptian force defeats the crusade army of Louis IX of France.

6 April Louis IX's army, riddled with disease, surrenders to the Egyptians.

Four-wheeled wagons with a front axle are introduced to western Europe.

1250–1273

Interregnum in the German empire, ends with the election of Rudolf I of Habsburg.

mountaineers, lightly armed troops who fought with javelins. Above all, he utilized large numbers of crossbowmen in an age when Aragón was famed for this military skill. Crossbows had been used since Roman times and were especially popular at sieges (despite clerical attempts to outlaw their use in wars against Christians). They were especially effective at sea, where the crossbowmen could stand still to load and the ship could do the work of approaching the enemy.

The Struggle for the Mediterranean

It was not only the Aragonese and the Angevins who waged war on the Mediterranean. By the thirteenth century, northern and central Italy consisted of more than 200 independent states, which fought each other constantly. Most omnipresent was competition for trade among the great port cities – Venice, Genoa and Pisa – which sometimes fought against each other and sometimes against the Byzantine fleet. Venice and Genoa in particular waged a series of four bitter wars that ranged over the eastern Mediterranean in the period 1253–1381. Battles on the Mediterranean were won or lost above all by the skill of admirals, depending on whether they could hold together their fleet during an attack, when further direct communication with the ships' captains was impossible. Thus a Venetian fleet commanded by Jacopo Dandolo destroyed the whole Genoese fleet off Trapani in 1266, probably because the Genoese admiral insisted on defensive tactics despite the advice of his captains.

The preferred ship type for Mediterranean war was the galley, a relatively long and narrow ship with one or two banks of rowers. Unlike ancient ships, these medieval models were not equipped with rams; their purpose was to capture, rather than sink, the enemy. Galley battles were particularly vicious because, after

A typical Mediterranean galley of the thirteenth century, relying on oars rather than sail in battle.

1253–1299	1254	1256	1257
War between Venice and Genoa.	Battle of Foggia. Manfred, the heir of Frederick II, wins a major victory over a papal army.	Count William of Holland defeats a Flemish army at the Battle of Westkapelle, Zeeland.	A Venetian fleet drives Genoese shipping from the harbour of Acre.
	King Ottokar II of Bohemia founds Königsberg while crusading with the Teutonic Knights.		
	Hungarian conquest of Bosnia and Herzegovina from the Serbs.		

Ships transporting soldiers, from the Codex Benito de Santa Mora *(fourteenth century).*

successful fleet action could create thousands of casualties, more than any but the very deadliest land battles. War at sea was also horribly expensive by the standards of the thirteenth century. States operated on relatively limited resources, so special taxes had to be levied for the cost of ships and payments for their crews. Usually it was only a desperate state that built large numbers of new galleys. For example, Genoa started creating a massive fleet of 120 galleys in 1282, 50 of the ships newly built by the commune – but the Genoese were desperate by that time, after a series of defeats at the hands of Venice and Pisa.

Genoa's investment paid off in the short run, most notably in their utter defeat of the Pisan fleet at Meloria in July 1284, a victory so complete that Pisa never recovered. The Genoese fleet also defeated a Venetian fleet off the coast of Cilicia in 1294. But Genoa ended up defeating its own purposes. In 1295, the city pulled together a 165-ship fleet and challenged Venice to battle, but Venice flatly refused the challenge. After that, the Italian cities returned to smaller, more manageable fleets that did not place such a great strain on their resources. Still,

successfully boarding an enemy ship, there was really nothing to do with the enemies except kill them directly or throw them overboard. Thus a

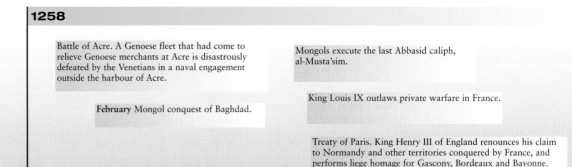

1257–1259

War of St Sabas between Genoese and Venetians in the Kingdom of Jerusalem.

1258

Battle of Acre. A Genoese fleet that had come to relieve Genoese merchants at Acre is disastrously defeated by the Venetians in a naval engagement outside the harbour of Acre.

February Mongol conquest of Baghdad.

Mongols execute the last Abbasid caliph, al-Musta'sim.

King Louis IX outlaws private warfare in France.

Treaty of Paris. King Henry III of England renounces his claim to Normandy and other territories conquered by France, and performs liege homage for Gascony, Bordeaux and Bayonne.

Genoa won a major victory over a larger Venetian fleet off Curzola Island in September 1298. Less than a dozen of the 96 Venetian galleys escaped. The 77 Genoese ships, a new model of trireme galley that soon came to dominate Mediterranean war, were larger and better equipped.

The Northern Seas

The thirteenth century also saw improvements in the naval capabilities of northern Europe. While both France and England used some galleys, they were badly adapted to the rougher waters of the Atlantic and cost more than the governments of the North could really afford (although the French created a galley dockyard, the Clos des Galées, at Rouen in 1294). It was more common to force merchant ships, cogs, into temporary royal service,

adding wooden castles fore and aft and sometimes fighting tops above the sails. John of England established an enormous galley

Left: Wax seals attached to the Document of Confederation of the Hanseatic League.

Right: King John of England (1199–1216), a bad king who suffered the inevitable reaction against his predecessors' expensive and unsuccessful wars.

1259

The Samogitians defeat the armies of Prussia and Livonia, prompting major anti-Christian revolts in both regions.

Mongols of the Golden Horde raid Silesia, sacking Cracow and Sandomir.

October Battle of Pelagonia. Michael Palaeologos of Nicaea defeats Michael Doukas of Epirus and his Latin allies, opening the door to re-establishment of Greek rule in Constantinople.

A Byzantine force takes the Latin-held fortress of Mistra in the Peloponnese.

October Provisions of Westminster. Henry III of England is forced to accept baronial oversight of his administration.

1260

July Battle of Kressenbrunn. King Ottokar II of Bohemia defeats Béla IV of Hungary and seizes Styria.

July Battle of Durben (Livonia). The Baltic Samogitians and Ottokar II of Bohemia defeat an allied Danish-Swedish-German-Teutonic Knight army, starting a 30-year war.

September Battle of 'Ain Jalut. The Mamluk sultan Qutuz of Egypt defeats a Mongol army led by Khan Hülegu's general Kitbuqa, ending Mongol westward expansion.

force, amounting to as many as 65 ships by 1212, but invested so heavily in war that he sparked a major rebellion by his overburdened and threatened subjects. Other rulers were more prudent.

John's fleet proved effective in 1213 when, in a daring raid on Damme, it crippled the French fleet, preventing a planned invasion of England. An English fleet stopped another French invasion in 1217, in a battle off Sandwich. In general, though, it was a risky matter to try to stop an invading army at sea in an age of poor communications and fragile ships. In 1216, the English fleet had, in fact, been mauled by a storm and thus unable to halt a French invading flotilla. Besides its partial effectiveness, the English fleet proved too expensive to maintain. Merchant ships returned to their trade, and the galleys were allowed to rot. Further north, sailing ships, the cogs, were standard for naval use, as when the Hanseatic League blockaded Norway in 1284.

....

King John signs Magna Carta, on 15 June 1215, promising to curb his exactions against England's nobles. Soon afterward, England dissolved in civil war.

1260–1290

A long Teutonic Knight war to establish control over the Samogitians, Livonians and Prussians.

1261

Summer Pope Alexander IV absolves Henry III of England of his oath to keep the Provisions of Westminster.

25 July Greek recovery of Constantinople. Byzantine emperor Michael VIII Palaeologos regains Constantinople when a force passing by the city breaks through an undefended gate. The Latin emperor Baldwin flees without a fight.

1262

Battle of Prinitza. The Frankish rulers of the Morea defeat a Byzantine army attempting to regain the Greek Peloponnese.

Reactions to the High Cost of War

The first half of the thirteenth century saw the ambitions of the English kings whittled down to size. Drawing on the resources of a large empire that included over half of France as well as England, Richard I had equipped one of the most magnificent crusading armies ever seen – but only by selling everything he could command (including the liberty of Scotland, which his father Henry II had reduced to vassalage). Like his father, Richard had also paid for overly ambitious wars by wringing every penny he could from his subjects.

The inevitable reaction came in the reign of King John (1199–1216), exacerbated by the king's own personality, a conflict with Pope Innocent III, and the unfortunate fact that the king of France finally found a legal pretext to seize Normandy, supporting John's nephew as heir after Richard's death instead of John himself. John won a major victory over his nephew Arthur of Brittany at Mirebeau on

Left: Simon de Montfort the Younger became the leader of a baronial resistance movement that defeated and captured Henry III.

1 August 1202, showing that he did indeed have some of his brother Richard's military skill. But when Arthur disappeared after being imprisoned by John, Philip II Augustus of France declared John to be a 'contumacious vassal' and his territories in France to be forfeit. Many

The fall of Simon de Montfort at the Battle of Evesham. This victory by Prince Edward of England was the first battle to display Edward I's skills as a general.

1263

Battle of Makoy Plagi. The Franks of the Morea defeat a second Byzantine attack.

Murder of Alexander Nevsky of Novgorod while on a visit to the Mongol khan of the Golden Horde.

3 October Battle of Largs (the Hebrides). King Haakon IV of Norway attempts to conquer the Hebrides, but a storm forces some of his ships to land, where Alexander III of Scotland attacked them. The battle is indecisive, and Haakon withdraws.

Battle of Settepozzi (Spetsai). A fleet of Genoese galleys encounter a Venetian crusader fleet and attack it, but are driven off with heavy losses.

1264

14 May Battle of Lewes, England. Rebellious barons under the command of Simon de Montfort the Younger defeat and capture King Henry III and his son Prince Edward.

14 August Genoa defeats a Venetian flotilla in the Otranto Channel near Durazzo (modern Albania).

Great revolt of the Spanish Muslims under Christian rule in Castile.

Battle of Trapani (Sicily). Venice defeat the Genoese fleet.

Normans welcomed the king of France, and his conquest of the duchy was completed in 1204 with the successful siege of Richard's mighty Château Gaillard, which John failed to relieve in time.

For the sake of his honour and revenues, John desperately needed to recover Normandy. He planned a great two-pronged invasion in 1205, but the English barons refused to go, so the expedition disbanded before it got underway. After a series of wasted efforts, John finally created a massive, and massively expensive, strategy to recover Normandy in 1214. He enlisted a large number of northern allies headed by Emperor Otto IV, paying them the vast sum of 40,000 marks. English troops under John invaded from Poitou, while the allies were to attack from the north, squeezing King Philip in the middle. The plan failed in the dust of Bouvines, when Philip won a decisive victory over Emperor Otto.

....

A thirteenth-century knight. Note the mail coif that protects the neck and throat. Most knights used open-faced helmets in battle, finding that the ability to see and hear outweighed the greater protection of a great helm.

1264–1266

First Genoese-Venetian War.

5. The allied left wing is defeated and flees, soon followed by other allied divisions.

3. The infantry of the French right wing, not needed to engage the Flemish cavalry, move to reinforce Philip Augustus' centre division.

1. The French army, arriving early on the battlefield, forms up in three divisions of both cavalry and infantry.

2. As the Flemish and German troops arrive on the battlefield, they immediately engage the French line.

4. The English and Boulognese troops attack the French left wing, only to be driven off in disorder.

The Battle of Bouvines, 1214.

1264–1267

English Barons' War. Rebel barons led by Simon de Montfort the Younger fight to secure their right to oversight of King Henry III's government.

1265

2 August Battle of Kenilworth. Prince Edward attacks the rebel army camped outside Kenilworth Castle in a surprise dawn attack, capturing many rebel leaders.

4 August Battle of Evesham. Prince Edward of England leads a royal force to victory over rebellious barons. Death of Simon de Montfort the Younger.

1266

26 February Battle of Benevento. Charles of Anjou defeats and kills Manfred in a battle for control of the Kingdom of Sicily.

Battle of Trapani (Sicily). A Venetian fleet under the command of Jacopo Dandalo destroys the entire Genoese war fleet.

1267

First known Western European recipe for gunpowder, in a treatise by Roger Bacon.

The Battle of Dürnkrut (Marchfeld), 26 August 1278, at which Emperor Rudolf I of Habsburg defeated his rival Otakar II to secure Habsburg rule over the Holy Roman Empire.

After Bouvines, a large number of John's barons defied him. John signed Magna Carta in June 1215, a charter of liberties that promised an end to excessive royal exactions and the removal of mercenaries from England. The king almost immediately broke his word, though, getting the pope to release him from his commitments. The result was England's first Barons' War, waged from 1215 to 1217, as many of England's magnates rose against their king. John enjoyed a number of successes, including the siege of Rochester, which surrendered in November 1215 after he had successfully undermined the wall. The king vindictively wanted to hang the whole garrison, but was persuaded to string up only some mercenary crossbowmen. He went on to wage a very effective campaign against rebels and Scottish invaders in northern England in January and February 1216. But the rebels

1268

18 May Mamluk conquest of Antioch. The city was razed and its population killed or enslaved.

23 August Battle of Tagliacozzo. Charles of Anjou defeats and captures Conradin, the last heir of the Hohenstaufen Dynasty.

29 October Execution of the 16-year-old Conradin, ending the Hohenstaufen Dynasty.

1269

Aragonese crusade to the Holy Land.

1270

25 August Death of Louis IX of France during the siege of Tunis.

Second Crusade of Louis IX of France (invasion of Tunis).

1271

8 April The Mamluk sultan Baibars captures the great Hospitaller fortress of Krak-des-Chevaliers.

Construction of Caerphilly Castle, Wales.

invited the French king's participation, offering the throne of England to his son Louis. Louis invaded with a large army and enjoyed some success. But when John died and his underage son inherited, the rebels no longer had an object against which to fight. One of the baronial leaders, the elderly William Marshal, became regent for the young Henry III and soon drove the French from the country.

The barons of England rebelled again in 1264–1267 against the feckless and fiscally irresponsible Henry III. The rebels, led by Henry's brother-in-law Simon de Montfort the Younger (son of the Albigensian Crusade leader), won a major pitched battle at Lewes in 1264, mostly because the royalist cavalry got out of hand and spent so long chasing some of the enemy from the field that the battle was lost in their absence. Prince Edward proved to be a better commander than his father, though, defeating and killing Simon at Evesham on 4 August 1265.

The Cavalry Moment

Heavy cavalry was important in European warfare from the tenth century until the end of the Middle Ages. It was only in the thirteenth century, however, that the massed cavalry charge came to be regarded as the truly decisive force that won battles. As we have seen, such a belief was overly simplistic, even in the thirteenth century. Nonetheless, the century is marked by a number of decisive pitched battles in which massed cavalry did indeed dominate the battlefield, creating a brief cavalry 'moment' even as military forces became more diversified and skilled infantry became more important.

The knight's equipment continued to develop during the thirteenth century. The typical warhorse of the later Middle Ages stood at 14–15 hands; a 15-hand horse is 152cm (60in) from the ground to the top of the withers. For battle, he was equipped with armour of leather and plates of metal at the chest, crupper, flanks and head. His rider was also better protected, beginning in the thirteenth century to wear plate armour, especially at joints to reinforce the chain-mail hauberk. By this century, shields

....

King Edward I of England (1272–1307), a warrior king who spent most of his reign fighting the Welsh, Scots and French.

1271–1272

Crusade of the Lord Edward (the future Edward I of England).

1272

Last French feudal summons for military service.

Prince Edward of England arranges an 11-year truce with the Mamluk sultan Baibars.

1274

Council of Lyons. Byzantine emperor Michael VIII Palaeologos accepts a reunion of the Eastern and Western Churches to prevent a crusade against him, led by Charles of Anjou. The union lasts only eight years.

were flat-topped and had become smaller, the better to manoeuvre from horseback. The 'great helm', a flat-topped helmet that covered the entire head, replaced conical helmets, although these may have been used more at tournaments than on battlefields because of the way they interfered with seeing, hearing and breathing. These developments were probably a response to increased crossbow use, since a crossbow bolt can penetrate mail with relative ease. In the thirteenth century, very large two-handed swords also appeared, probably to counter these improvements in armour.

The first of the great cavalry engagements of the thirteenth century was the Battle of Bouvines, fought on 27 July 1214 between the armies of Philip II Augustus of France and the German emperor Otto IV and his allies. Interestingly, Philip was present on the battlefield, but gave the command to Bishop Guérin of Liège, a former Knight Hospitaller who had much greater battle experience. At

The English parade with the head of Welsh prince Llywelyn ap Gruffud after he is killed at the Battle of Irfon Bridge, 1282.

Bouvines, Philip had at least 1300 knights and perhaps the same number of mounted sergeants, besides 4000–6000 foot soldiers. Otto's force probably included more knights and definitely more infantry.

The battle took place when Philip had decided to retreat westward before the invading Germans, but the enemy intercepted him at a key bridge at Bouvines. The French force was able to form a battle line behind a cavalry screen. Then the French commander Guérin launched each unit of the cavalry in turn, the small-scale repeated charges sapping the strength of the allied cavalry. When the Germans charged in turn, they were disordered – both because of the earlier French actions and because they lacked clear leadership and cohesion. A massive mêlée followed, before the Germans broke and fled. Philip allowed the pursuit to continue for only a mile before summoning his force back with trumpets, since the sun was setting – that they obeyed shows a higher degree of cavalry discipline than many battles both before and after. Interestingly, although this decisive battle destroyed the career of Otto IV and nearly ruined his ally John of

c. 1275	1277–1295	1277	1278
The earliest extant sea chart, a Pisan manuscript with a detailed drawing of the Mediterranean coast.	Edward I of England's conquest of Wales.	A Bulgarian peasant revolt placed Ivailo the Swineherd on the throne of Bulgaria. The rising is soon defeated by the Bulgarian boyars, with Byzantine assistance.	**26 August** Battle of Dürnkrut (Marchfeld). Emperor Rudolf I of Habsburg defeats and kills his rival Otakar II of Bohemia in one of the largest cavalry battles of the Middle Ages.
			Edward I of England opens the supposed tomb of Arthur and Guinevere at Glastonbury, re-interring the bones before the high altar of the abbey church.

Above: Caernarvon Castle, Wales. The castle was begun in 1283 by Edward I and never completed.

England, the casualties (at least among the knights) were very low, with only two French knights killed outright and perhaps 200 Germans. Armour had become so good that it took serious effort to kill a knight.

Similar cavalry dominance can be seen at other thirteenth-century battles, such as Las Navas de Tolosa in 1212, when Alfonso VIII of Castile and Pedro II of Aragón won a decisive victory over the Almohads, or Muret in 1213, when Pedro was in turn defeated and killed by Simon de Montfort's force of crusaders in southern France. One of the largest cavalry battles of the Middle Ages was not fought until later in the century: the Battle of Marchfeld (or Dürnkrut) in 1278. In this engagement, at which Emperor Rudolf I and King Otakar of Bohemia each had an army about 20,000 strong, Rudolf's force included not just heavy cavalry but allied Hungarian

Right: King John Balliol of Scotland (1250–1313). Although chosen as king by Edward I of England, John soon rebelled against English interference.

c. 1280	1281	1282	1282–1302
The compass is introduced to the Mediterranean, encouraging the shift to a year-round sailing season.	Battle of Homs. Mamluk sultan Kala'un defeats an army of Ilkhan Mongols, ending the latter's invasion of Syria.	**30 March** The Sicilian Vespers. An uprising breaks out against Charles of Anjou in Sicily when a Frenchman insults a married woman.	War of the Sicilian Vespers. Outraged by the harsh rule of Charles of Anjou, the people of the Kingdom of Sicily rebel and call on King Pedro III of Aragón for assistance.
Charles of Anjou, king of Sicily, defeats a Tunisian army in the Battle of Carthage.	Spring Siege of Berat (modern Albania). Byzantine forces inflict a heavy defeat on King Charles of Sicily, who is attempting to establish a foothold in the Byzantine Empire.	**11 December** Battle of Irfon Bridge. Welsh prince Llywelyn ap Gruffudd is killed in a small battle against the English.	

The Battle of Stirling Bridge (1297), a major tactical victory by Scottish rebel forces led by William Wallace.

mounted archers. The battle, fought north of Vienna, opened with these mounted archers devastating Otakar's right flank. The Bohemian left wing then charged Rudolf, who was himself unhorsed but saved by his armour. Rudolf had a strong reserve, however, which broke Otakar's line, retreat soon turning into a rout. The battle secured the Habsburg Rudolf's claim to the imperial throne.

Pleasant though it may be to imagine that noble knights fought for both their lords and their honour in these engagements, the reality is that armies of the thirteenth century relied less and less on feudal levies. Even in 1202–1203, Philip Augustus maintained a year-round non-feudal army, and most feudal service was

1283–1410

Teutonic Order war against Lithuania.

1283

8 June Battle of Malta. An Aragonese fleet under Roger de Lauria defeated a Sicilian-French fleet.

11 October Battle of Messina. An Aragonese-Catalan fleet commanded by Roger de Lauria defeats the Sicilian fleet, forcing King Charles of Sicily to raise his siege of the rebel-held town of Messina.

1284

5 June Battle of the Bay of Naples. The Aragonese admiral Roger de Lauria wins a major victory over a Sicilian-French fleet, capturing 48 enemy galleys.

June Battle of Meloria. A Genoese fleet of 93 galleys tricks a Pisan force of 72 galleys into battle. The Pisan fleet is completely destroyed, ending Pisan sea power.

The Hanseatic League in alliance with Denmark successfully blockades Norway.

Foundation of the royal navy shipyard at Barcelona for the combined Aragonese-Catalonian state.

2–3 September Battle of the Bay of Roses, Catalonia. Admiral Roger de Lauria leads an Aragonese-Catalonian fleet to destroy the French invasion fleet, cutting King Philip III of France's supply route.

commuted to a military tax. The last French feudal summons was in 1272, and proved to be ineffective. In England, royal edicts in 1224 and 1241 ordered that all fief-holders and significant landowners be knighted, but this appears to have been to assure the manpower for local administration rather than on the battlefield. By the end of the thirteenth century the term 'man-at-arms' had emerged for a heavy cavalryman, whether aristocratic or not.

The Campaigns of Edward I

The state of European warfare in the later thirteenth century can best be summed up by a consideration of the campaigns fought by King Edward I of England (1272–1307). His extensive wars to conquer Wales and Scotland – and to prevent France from seizing the duchy of Aquitaine on the Continent – pushed the military capability of his realm as far as it could go. Indeed, his exactions at one point drove the

At the Battle of Falkirk (1298), English archers broke up Scottish formations before the English cavalry arrived to crush the mostly-infantry Scottish army.

barons of England to near revolt. Edward, however, dealt with the situation with a much greater grasp of practical realities than had his father Henry III or his grandfather John. Thus, out of his military ambitions evolved a practice whereby the king's important subjects were regularly consulted, and were granted the right to approve taxation – the English Parliament.

King Edward's conquest of Wales between 1277 and 1295 began on a small scale. Prince Llywelyn ap Gruffydd of Gwynedd had won *de facto* independence from English overlordship in the reign of the weak Henry III. Edward reminded Llywelyn of his vassalage in a small campaign. But in 1282 Llywelyn and other Welsh noble rebelled, a surprise move that allowed them to take a number of English castles. Edward responded with a massive expedition, intended to subject his Celtic neighbours once and for all. Pacification seemed a simple matter, especially after Llywelyn was killed in a small engagement at Irfon Bridge in December 1282. As in the twelfth century, the Welsh were incapable of meeting an English army in a major battle. But they rebelled again in 1287 and 1294. The campaigns are most

notable for Edward I's use of huge fleets to supply his armies, showing a level of logistical engagement that Europe (and he himself) had learned on the crusades.

To hold the land, Edward engaged in a highly ambitious project of building castles, beginning an outer ring of fortresses in 1277 and an inner ring after 1283. All were designed to be supplied by sea, and were the work of a Savoyard master mason, James of St George. They were manned by garrisons of 30–40 men during peacetime, but could hold much larger numbers if rebellion broke out. Magnificent though these edifices are, it must be said that they were probably not worth the cost: more than £80,000, about four times the annual income of the English crown in this period. Like other rulers of his time, Edward's concept of what could and should be done militarily far outran his purse.

When it came to the conquest of Scotland, Edward scaled back his castle building, but his armies were larger and more expensive than ever before. In 1291, Edward was invited to adjudicate the Scottish succession, after a succession crisis was created by the death of

1284–1285	1287	1288	1289
Philip III of France invades Aragón, after the pope offers the crown of Aragón to Philip's son Charles of Valois. The invasion fails and Philip dies during the retreat.	Aragonese conquest of Minorca.	**5 June** Battle of Worringen. The city of Cologne rebels against Archbishop Siegfried von Westerburg, defeating him in a major battle during which more than 2000 men are killed.	**2 April** Fall of Tripoli to the Mamluks. Massacre of the city's entire male population.
	23 June Battle of the Counts. Roger de Lauria defeats the Sicilian-French fleet in a naval battle noted for the number of French nobles who participate and are captured.		Battle of Campaldino. The Guelf League (led by Florence) defeats the Ghibellines (led by Arezzo) in a battle that demonstrates the growing importance of crossbows.

This romantic painting of Stirling Castle from the River Forth (1857) gives a good impression of the site's strategic importance.

Margaret, the child queen of Norway. All parties agreed to accept Edward's overlordship, and when the king of England's choice fell on John Balliol, John paid homage to Edward. Edward had a much more intrusive notion of overlordship than the Scots had bargained for, however, and King John soon rebelled against him. Edward's response was to invade with a large army in 1296, capturing Berwick and routing the Scots at Dunbar; King John soon surrendered and spent the rest of his life imprisoned in England as a disloyal vassal.

John Balliol's steward, however, a knight named William Wallace, soon raised the flag of rebellion in the south, as did the earl of Murray in the north. The Scots, by the standards of the day, were not the equals of Englishmen on the battlefield. They had few heavy cavalry and still relied mainly on peasant levies instead of the trained infantry Edward could command. Nonetheless, William Wallace defeated an

1291

18 May Fall of Acre, the last major Christian outpost of the Kingdom of Jerusalem, to Mamluk sultan al-Asfraf Halil. All male defenders who cannot escape by ship are killed; women and children are enslaved.

Mutual assistance pact between three Swiss cantons mark the beginning of the Swiss struggle for independence from the Habsburgs.

Scottish succession crisis on the death of Margaret of Norway. King Edward I adjudicates the dispute.

1294

Battle of Alexandretta, off the coast of Cilicia. A Genoese fleet defeats the Venetians.

Battle of Lajazzo. Venice sends 14 galleys to drive the Genoese from Famagusta and Lajazzo. The Genoese arm merchant galleys and fight back, inflicting a heavy defeat on Venice.

5 March Battle of Maes Moydog (Wales). The earl of Warwick marches an army to relieve King Edward I at Conway Castle. He annihilates a rebel force under Madog at Maes Moydog.

1294–1298

War between France and England begins when Philip IV of France attempts to confiscate the duchy of Aquitaine.

1296–1306

English conquest of Scotland, after Edward I of England condemned John Balliol of Scotland as a disloyal vassal.

Capture of Berwick (Scotland) by King Edward I. Massacre of the inhabitants.

Battle of Dunbar. An English army led by John de Warenne, earl of Surrey, defeats King John Balliol of Scotland, who soon surrenders and is imprisoned in England.

English army led by Earl Warenne and Hugh de Cressingham at Stirling Bridge on 11 September 1297, taking advantage of the disarray of the English troops as they crossed the narrow bridge.

Edward responded with overwhelming force, fielding an army of as many as 30,000 men – at that point, the largest army ever to have been raised in England. The Scots defended themselves outside Falkirk on 22 July 1298 by forming four great schiltrons. These consisted of pikemen tightly concentrated into defensive circles with archers placed between them. They did not, however, hold out long against Edward, who first broke the formations with archers and then completed the job with a massed cavalry charge. The pikemen did manage to prove their worth, killing about 2000 English fighters, but still the victory went to Edward. From then on, Scottish resistance was reduced to small-scale guerrilla war. By the time of his death in 1307, Edward had effectively become ruler of Scotland.

Edward's war with France, which lasted from 1294 to 1297 (officially ended by treaty in 1303), was a much smaller affair, but very expensive. Edward could commit small numbers of troops only because of his commitments in Scotland and Wales. He did, however, succeed in recovering his duchy of Aquitaine from the large French army of occupation that King Philip IV had imposed after Edward refused to accept an overlordship as harsh as his own had been against John Balliol.

Multi-year wars, ambitious fortifications and larger and more professional armies than ever before in the Middle Ages are the hallmarks of Edward's campaigns. Perhaps most notable of all, Edward's armies were *his* armies in a much more direct sense than the loose amalgamations of troops that were typical of warfare before (and sometimes during) the thirteenth century. A staggering number of the men whom Edward took with him on campaign were his own household troops, paid directly by the king – nearly 800 of them on the Falkirk campaign of 1298, forming a whole division of the army. The rest of his armies were for the most part recruited, rather than summoned as part of a feudal call to arms. Much of his cavalry was recruited by contracts that included promises of compensation for loss of horses. And his recruitment of infantry was massive: in Wales, Edward's army at its largest included over 15,000 foot soldiers, while almost 26,000 took part in the Scottish campaign of 1298.

The High Cost of War

The wars of the thirteenth century strained states throughout Europe to the breaking point. By the end of the century, it is reasonable to describe the situation as a European arms race. States had to keep up with their neighbours in the scale and quality of their army, castle-building techniques, ships and siege engines – or suffer the consequences. Commanders were quick to adopt military innovations, such as building state-of-the-art castles with curtain walls and round towers, as Edward did in Wales. Meanwhile, his siege equipment became ever more impressive: at the siege of Stirling Castle in 1304, one of Edward's trebuchets, fondly named 'Warwolf', fired 135kg (300lb) stones that brought down a large stretch of wall. The siege of Stirling Castle may also have seen the first use of gunpowder in Western Europe, a Chinese invention that would have a long future in European war.

1297

Aragonese conquest of Sardinia (although the Muslims soon regain the island).

Edward I of England removes the Scottish regalia and Stone of Scone to Westminster.

20 August A French army commanded by Count Robert of Artois defeats the Flemings at the Battle of Furnes.

11 September Battle of Stirling Bridge. Scottish rebels under William Wallace defeat an English army led by John de Warenne and Hugh de Cressingham.

5 November King Edward I of England reissues Magna Carta and cancels a highly unpopular tax to fund his war with France, acknowledging the need for parliamentary approval of taxes.

1298

2 July Battle of Göllheim. The German princes who had deposed Emperor Adolf of Nassau defeat and kill Adolf in a battle near Worms.

22 July Battle of Falkirk. A large English army commanded by King Edward I defeat Scottish rebels under William Wallace.

8 September Battle of Curzola. The Genoese defeat the Venetians in an Adriatic fleet engagement.

1299

Battle of Cape Orlando. The Aragonese fleet under Roger de Lauria defeat yet another Sicilian-French fleet.

The Fourteenth Century: An Infantry Revolution?

European warfare experienced rapid change in the fourteenth century. In particular, the Hundred Years War between France and England proved to be a hothouse for military innovation, as the two countries struggled for a pre-eminence that neither could really finance.

The fourteenth century has been acclaimed as the era of an 'infantry revolution', as common foot soldiers adopted new techniques that made it possible for them to master heavy cavalry – when conditions were exactly right. For the most part, what we can see in this century is a greater degree of integration between infantry and cavalry on the battlefield. War also became bloodier. Nobles appear to have enjoyed killing commoners who tried to withstand them, while the reverse was also true.

Left: The Battle of Poitiers, 1356. Archery played an important part in the victory, although the artist had little idea of how archers were actually used.
Right: Statue of Jacob van Artevelde (c. 1295–1345).

It is not surprising that Flanders (roughly the territory of the modern Netherlands and parts of Belgium) should have led the way in creating infantry forces that could defeat heavily armed and mounted men-at-arms. Flanders had urbanized to a surprising extent, and its cities had won considerable rights of self-government. To protect those rights, towns like Bruges and Ghent formed citizen militias, mostly infantry, but effective nonetheless. The urban militiamen were well equipped, were organized by craft and district, and even wore uniforms, encouraging a high *esprit de corps*.

King Philip IV ('the Fair') of France attempted a direct annexation of Flanders in 1297, but Flemish townsmen and nobles alike resented his interference in their affairs. They

rose in a major rebellion at the end of the thirteenth century. It seemed likely that they would be exterminated by Philip's army, because infantry had rarely stood up to massed cavalry charges, and when they had it was because they had been reinforced by dismounted knights. The Battle of Courtrai on 11 July 1302, also known as the Battle of the Golden Spurs from the 700 pairs of spurs taken from dead French knights on the battlefield, overthrew the notion that cavalry always wins over infantry. It demonstrates well the changing face of battle.

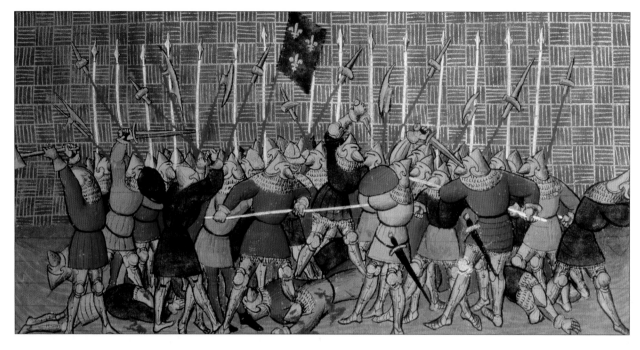

Above: The Battle of Courtrai, 1302. A battle of French cavalry against well-sited Flemish infantry, Courtrai was the first great infantry victory of the fourteenth century.

Left: King Philip IV, 'the Fair', of France (1285–1314), whose reign was devoted to strengthening the monarchy's power at the expense of regional interests.

The Flemish force consisted almost entirely of Flemish militiamen, armed with pikes (elongated spears, 5.5m/18ft long with a 25cm/10in steel head) and wooden maces called *goedendags* – 'good-days' – in joking reference to their impact. The Flemish leaders, Guy de Namur and William of Jülich, both fought

c. 1300

Development of the moveable visor for helmets.

Development of the halberd.

Battle of Ponza. The culminating sea battle of the War of the Sicilian Vespers, in which Roger de Lauria leads Aragón to victory against a Sicilian-French fleet.

Development of prise (later called purveyance) in England, a system of compulsory food sales for the army.

dismounted in the front rank along with their bodyguards. Count Guy knighted more than 30 leaders of the commoners before the battle, to stiffen morale (a fairly common proceeding). They deployed eight deep in a carefully chosen position that was defended by canals and a river at their backs, so the militiamen couldn't break and flee even if they wanted to do so.

The French commander Robert of Artois was simply over-confident, apparently contemptuous of the non-professional force before him. The ground, dug with pits and trenches, was not suitable for a massed cavalry charge, but that is exactly what he ordered. Compounding his error, Robert did not order the large number of crossbowmen in his army to 'soften up' the Flemish pikemen, as Edward I had done with

....

Left: Statue of Count Robert III of Artois (1287–1342), in the palace of Versailles. Robert III spent much of his career in the service of England.

Right: Pole arms became important in the infantry armies of the fourteenth century. This illustration shows a selection of weapons used, all of which had a point for stabbing as well as some sort of axe blade.

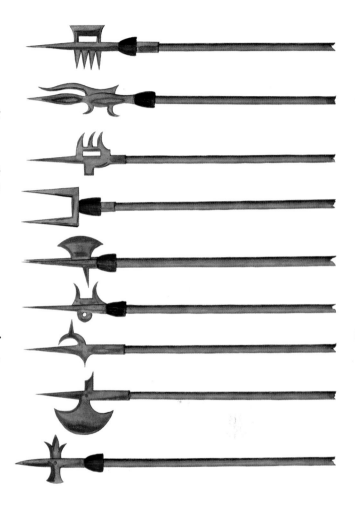

1301–1302

War between German emperor Albrecht I and the Rhineland princes.

1301–1305

Hungarian civil war, caused by a succession dispute.

1302

Peace of Caltabellota ends the War of the Sicilian Vespers. The king of Aragón is confirmed as ruler of Sicily, while the Angevins retain control of southern Italy.

May 'The Matins of Bruges'. Citizens of Bruges massacre French troops stationed in the city, inspiring most of Flanders to revolt.

11 July Battle of Courtrai, Flanders (Battle of the Golden Spurs). Flemish militia annihilate a French army commanded by Robert of Artois.

July Battle of Nicomedia. An Ottoman army led by Osman defeats the Byzantine army of Andronikos II.

Gibelet, the last crusader foothold in Palestine, surrenders to the Mamluks.

his longbowmen at Falkirk only a few years before. Instead, his cavalry trampled their own infantry in their eagerness to reach the despised enemy. The result was disastrous for the French cavalry. They lost speed, thanks to the obstacles that had been placed in their way. Those who did reach the enemy lines were faced by unbroken ranks of tightly formed pikemen, which threw the horses into confusion. Few French men-at-arms would have died in the initial charges – cavalry armour was too good by the fourteenth century, increasingly including even steel breastplates. But once knocked off their steeds, the heavy cavalrymen were vulnerable, and the Flemings were not interested in taking prisoners. King Philip's army was annihilated, with some 700 knights among the total of approximately 20,000 French dead.

The Battle of the Golden Spurs showed that a massed cavalry charge could be halted and defeated by infantry – if the conditions were exactly right. Although many infantrymen had some armour by the fourteenth century, they were far more vulnerable than mounted men-at-arms. To survive, they had to be in a defensible position, to keep from being simply

ridden over. And they needed discipline and an ability to fight as a group; this had been developing for centuries, but it reached a crucial point by the beginning of the century. Also helpful was the fact that the Flemish force at Courtrai significantly outnumbered the enemy.

Such an infantry victory was a desperately risky matter, though, as can be seen by the Battle of Mons-en-Pévèle only two years later. In this engagement, King Philip IV personally commanded a French army against the Flemish rebels led by William of Jülich. The Flemish foot soldiers assumed a position that was *too* defensive, sheltering behind wagons. Not surprisingly, Philip declined to commit his men to a suicidal charge. An impasse followed, ending when the Flemings finally left their secure position to charge the French. They broke into the French camp, nearly killing King Philip in the process. But, away from their defences, the Flemish infantrymen were much

....

This fourteenth-century miniature of Charlemagne and his army on the Spanish March is a good example of cavalry armour of the time.

1303

4 April Battle of Arques. A French army fails to defeat Flemish militia.

1304

First annual Preussenreise ('journey to Prussia'), a crusade to support the Teutonic Knights in their war against Lithuania. Continued until c. 1400.

18 August Battle of Mons-en-Pévèle (modern Belgium). Philip IV of France defeats the Flems under William of Jülich in an inconclusive battle.

Battle of Zierikzee. A major French naval victory over Count Guy of Flanders, enabling the French to raise the siege of Zierikzee.

Siege of Stirling. King Edward I takes Stirling, marking the end of the Scottish 'rebellion' against his overlordship. First known use of gunpowder in the British Isles.

more vulnerable. A French counterattack killed William of Jülich and drove the Flemings from the battlefield, although the engagement was not decisive. At Cassel on 23 August 1328, however, another French king, Philip VI, was able to win a decisive victory over the Flemings – using conventional massed cavalry tactics. Half of the Flemish force died that day. Cassel reinforced the lesson that conditions did indeed have to be perfect – a defensive position, group cohesion and inspired leadership – for infantry to triumph over cavalry.

The Swiss Wars of Independence

Other regions that produced few heavy cavalry also learnt how to win against traditional armies in the course of the fourteenth century. Most surprising was the case of the peasants of Dithmarschen, who won decisive victories over the count of Holstein in both 1319 and 1404, preserving an independent peasant enclave in

William Wallace confronts the nobles of Scotland. He often found himself opposed to the nobles who were willing to make accommodations with Edward I of England.

1305

Peace of Athès-sur-Orge between Flanders and France. Flanders submits to King Philip IV, expiating the 1302 revolt by sending 3000 men on pilgrimage.

July Battle of Apros, Thrace. The Catalan Grand Company, mercenaries who rebelled against their Byzantine paymasters, defeat a much larger Byzantine force under Emperor Michael IX.

23 August Execution of the Scottish resistance leader William Wallace in England.

1306

25 March Robert Bruce has himself crowned king of Scotland, beginning a rebellion against England.

19 June Battle of Methven. An English force under the earl of Pembroke makes a surprise attack on Robert Bruce's camp west of Perth. Bruce is captured, but escapes.

11 August Battle of Dalry. The English defeat Robert Bruce.

Pierre Dubois composes the treatise *On the Recovery of the Holy Land.*

northern Germany for a century. On a larger scale were the wars of the Swiss for freedom from the overlordship of the Habsburg duke of Austria. Three Swiss cantons formed a confederacy in 1291, a pact to resist the Habsburgs. This must have seemed laughable from the Austrian perspective, as with the French at Courtrai, because the Habsburg army included a large contingent of heavy cavalrymen, while the Swiss fought as infantry.

The Battle of Morgarten on 15 November 1315 demonstrated what could be done by well-deployed foot soldiers. They did not fight 'fair' by the chivalric standards of the day, instead waging a battle more reminiscent of guerrilla battles on Europe's frontiers than of a fight in the heartland. Leopold of Austria invaded, only to find the narrow path his army was traversing blocked with a stone wall. As Leopold paused, Swiss fighters closed off the rear, trapping the Austrian troops with a steep slope on one side

The Battle of Morgarten, 15 November 1315, in which Swiss militiamen successfully ambushed a major Habsburg army in a narrow mountain pass.

1307

10 May Battle of Loudon Hill. A Scottish force led by Robert Bruce defeats an English army.

7 July Death of Edward I of England.

13 October The Knights Templars of France are arrested by order of King Philip IV.

1309

The Teutonic Order moves headquarters to Marienburg, Prussia.

Pastoureaux movement ('Shepherds' Crusade') in France. Commoners wanting to crusade massacre Jews and attack the rich. They are dispersed or killed by authorities.

1310

The Knights Hospitallers establish themselves on the island of Rhodes.

The Battle of Laupen, 21 June 1339. Swiss cavalry charge against Habsburg cavalry, against the convention that infantry could stand up to cavalry only if they were in a well-sited and defended position.

and Lake Egeri on the other. They then threw boulders down on their enemies, only a few of whom (including Leopold) escaped by swimming the lake.

Morgarten was the first major Swiss infantry victory over German knights and the least conventional. The Swiss really showed what their infantry could do in 1339, when a Swiss force led by Rudolf van Erbach broke the Burgundian siege of Laupen. At Laupen, Swiss infantry attacked the Burgundian cavalry, a rare and dangerous move that suggests a very highly disciplined force, able to hold together while in motion. But it was the Battle of Sempach in 1386 that established the independence of the Swiss Confederation. In this battle, Duke Leopold III dismounted his cavalry and made them march with their lances against the Swiss. Since men-at-arms were much better armoured than the Swiss foot soldiers, this was a move that might have been effective if the slope had not been so steep. The

men-at-arms, wearing armour that weighed at least 18kg (40lb), tired rapidly, and the Swiss may have been reinforced at the key moment. The result was a heavy defeat for the

....

A Swiss legend tells that the heroic Arnold Winkelried opened the way for a Swiss victory at the Battle of Sempach, 9 July 1386, by throwing himself on the Austrian pikes and opening a path for his fellows.

1311	1312	1313–1314	1314
15 March Battle of Kephissos (near Athens). The Catalan Grand Company defeat the Frankish duke, Walter of Brienne of Athens, and seized his duchy, which they hold until 1388.	Suppression of the Order of Knights Templars by Pope John XXII.	Robert Bruce besieges English-held Stirling Castle.	**18 March** Jacques de Molay, last grandmaster of the Knights Templars, is burned at the stake, along with other high officials of the order.
			23–24 June Battle of Bannockburn. A large English army under King Edward II marches to relieve Stirling, but is heavily defeated by a Scottish army led by King Robert Bruce.

King Robert I Bruce of Scotland (1306–1329), who led Scotland in its fight for independence from England.

Habsburgs, with over 600 men-at-arms, including Leopold, left dead on the field.

Scotland Against England

As we have seen in the last chapter, the Scots also relied heavily on infantry forces that needed careful handling to defeat. Even before the death of Edward I in 1307, there were signs of reviving Scottish resistance to English rule. Most notably, Robert Bruce, one of the claimants for the Scottish crown in 1291, seized the throne in 1306. Although the renewed rebellion was precarious for several years, Robert attracted followers in ever-increasing numbers after the much less talented Edward II had become king of England. Robert proved particularly adept at taking English castles by infiltration, then 'slighting' them – destroying enough of their walls that they could not be used again. King Robert won a first victory over the English at Loudon Hill in 1307, taking advantage of boggy ground and trenches to prevent an effective English cavalry charge. Loudon Hill was a small battle, however. Robert's tactics were only really put to the test in 1314, when Edward II led a massive army north to

suppress the rebellion, hoping to overwhelm King Robert and his followers, just as his father had overwhelmed William Wallace at Falkirk.

Edward's army, including 2500 men-at-arms and about 15,000 infantry, was marching to relieve Stirling Castle when Robert blocked their route only a few miles from Stirling. Robert's force was smaller and consisted mostly of foot soldiers, but he took excellent advantage of the

....

King Edward II of England (1307–1327), whose catastrophically poor military leadership against Scotland helped lead to his deposition and death.

1315–1322

The Great Famine affects most of Europe and kills perhaps 20 per cent of the population.

1315

September Battle of Conor (Ireland). The Scot Edward Bruce and his Irish allies defeat an Anglo-Irish army.

15 November Battle of Morgarten (modern Switzerland). Swiss militiamen ambush a Habsburg army, killing several thousand knights.

narrow, boggy ground. He formed up the bulk of his troops in four closely packed circular formations of pikemen, known as schiltrons, much like the infantry squares that could hold off cavalry attacks as late as the nineteenth century. What followed was a rare medieval battle that lasted for two days.

On the first day, Robert defeated an English champion in single combat, a chivalric throwback rarely seen on battlefields. However, Robert's force was anything but chivalric. The English heavy cavalry tried to outflank the Scots, but could not break through the schiltrons. On the second day, it would be fairer to say that the English lost the battle than that the Scots won it. The weak and unpopular king Edward allowed an argument to develop about which man should command the English vanguard. When the earl of Gloucester won the quarrel, he fought very much as the French commander Robert of Artois had fought at

Robert Bruce's address to his army at Bannockburn, a Victorian sketch by William Bell Scott, which was inspired by Robert Burns' patriotic poem on the subject.

1315–1318

Edward Bruce invades Ireland.

1316

January Battle of Skerries (Ireland). Edward Bruce of Scotland and his Irish allies defeat an Anglo-Irish army.

September Fall of Carrickfergus Castle, Ireland, to Edward Bruce after a year-long siege.

The papal ban on tournaments is revoked, thanks to more careful regulation and the introduction of safety measures.

1318

14 October Battle of Fochart (Faughart), Ireland. An Anglo-Irish force commanded by the lord lieutenant of Ireland defeats and kills Edward Bruce.

Courtrai. Instead of deploying the large number of archers at his command to break the schiltrons (as Edward I had done at Falkirk), he instead ordered frontal cavalry assaults against the still-organized pikemen, over boggy ground that was bad for horses and where the Scots had dug pits beforehand. Even under those conditions, the English men-at-arms might have broken through, but the charge was badly organized and undisciplined. The English archers were eventually brought up, but were scattered by a small Scottish cavalry reserve; after all, unprotected infantry did not really stand a chance against even a small heavy cavalry force. When Edward II fled the field, the English army disintegrated. The next day,

....

King Edward III of England (1327–1377), who came to the throne at age 14 after his father Edward II was deposed.

Stirling Castle surrendered to King Robert. Although a Scottish invasion of Ireland under Robert's brother Edward Bruce from 1315 to 1318 ultimately failed to weaken the English significantly, the unpopular Edward II brought England to a condition of such anarchy that the Scottish strategy was hardly necessary. King Edward's nobles rebelled several times, allowing Robert Bruce to finish his drive to reclaim Scotland. A Scottish force under Sir James Douglas invaded Yorkshire in 1319, inflicting a serious defeat on a northern English army through a daring Scottish advance in schiltron formation. And when Edward II attempted a second invasion of Scotland in 1322, he accomplished nothing and was forced to withdraw because of supply problems. In fairness to Edward, it should be mentioned that this was a time of Europe-wide famine, when logistical support would have been difficult for any army, even one that was much better led.

Edward II was deposed in 1327 by a coalition of nobles that included his own queen. The new rulers (officially the youthful Edward III, but in reality the queen's lover Roger Mortimer) immediately invaded Scotland; the

1319

20 September Battle of Myton. A Scottish army invading Yorkshire under Sir James Douglas defeats an English army raised by Archbishop William Melton of York.

Battle of Dithmarschen. A peasant force defeats the knights of Holstein.

1320

Second 'Crusade' of the Pastoureaux, France. Peasants band together in attacks on the rich and massacres of Jews; suppressed by royal authorities.

Development of sabatons (foot armour) for heavy cavalry.

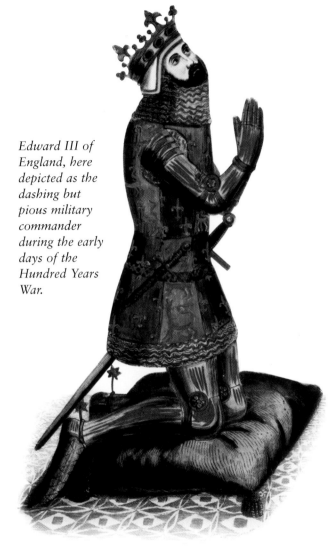

Edward III of England, here depicted as the dashing but pious military commander during the early days of the Hundred Years War.

loss of Scotland was one of the points that had maddened the English into rebellion. But King Robert avoided battle and the English army was literally bogged down by horrible weather and supply problems, eventually withdrawing. In 1328, the English and Scottish governments made what was called in England the 'Cowardice Peace', by which Edward III renounced his claim to overlordship over Scotland and recognized Robert Bruce as the lawful king.

The 1328 treaty did not end contention, however. Robert Bruce died in 1329, leaving the throne to his five-year-old son David. Robert's many rivals, who had spent Robert's reign in English exile, put together a private army and attacked Scotland in 1332 under the leadership of Edward Balliol. Two English victories, at Dupplin Moor (1332) and Halidon Hill (1333), both show that the English could match pikemen with archers, deploying an integrated army in which men-at-arms protected the archers and the archers softened the enemy for a cavalry charge. At Dupplin Moor, Edward Balliol had a force of about 500 men-at-arms and 1000 archers against several thousand

Edward III supports Edward Balliol in his struggle for the Scottish crown against David II (1333).

1321–1328

Byzantine civil war between Emperor Andronicus Palaeologos and his grandson (also Andronicus). The grandson eventually gains the throne.

1322

16 March Battle of Boroughbridge. Sheriff Andrew Harclay of Cumberland defeats rebellious nobles led by Earl Thomas of Lancaster, executing Thomas and other leaders after the battle.

Crusade against the Visconti of Milan.

28 September Battle of Mühldorf. Emperor Ludwig the Bavarian, commanding a largely Bavarian army, defeats his cousin and rival, Frederick I of Austria.

October Battle of Byland. King Robert Bruce defeats Edward II, forcing him to withdraw from Scotland.

Scots. But his army took a strong defensive position, with dismounted men-at-arms protecting the archers, who were positioned well forward on the flanks. The English cavalry charged only after the archers had done their work, which they were able to do because the Scots could not get to them. At Halidon Hill, a victory won by Edward III against a Scottish army led by Archibald Douglas, the English force was similarly disposed. In this case, the Scots dismounted their men-at-arms and sent them against the archers on the wings. But they had to climb a steep, boggy hill and reached the top exhausted and disorganized, easy prey for the English.

The Opening of the Hundred Years War

The English-Scottish war of the 1330s was complicated by French support for the young King David of Scotland. The French provided better armaments for the Scots and did everything in their power to weaken Edward III

Philippa of Hainault, wife of Edward III, musters a northern army to defeat King David II of Scotland at the Battle of Neville's Cross, 1346.

1323–1353	**1324**	**1324–1327**
Aragonese conquest of Sardinia from Genoa and Pisa.	Siege of Metz. First known use of cannon.	War of St Sardos, Gascony. An indeterminate French-English war, sparked by French construction of the fortress of St Sardos on English-held land.

of England. In fact, Philip VI of France seemed determined to bring France's relations with England, which had been strained for centuries, to the breaking point. The long-term point of contention was that, ever since 1066, the king of England had also held land in France as a vassal of the French king – a situation that both rulers resented. Although John had lost the northern part of his family's lands in France (including Normandy) in the early thirteenth century, the duchy of Aquitaine (or Gascony) was still under English rule. Philip VI regarded the weak beginning of the reign of Edward III of England as a good opportunity to impose real French royal control in the province, a process that had failed in the 1290s and 1320s. In April 1337, Philip VI declared the forfeiture of Aquitaine after Edward III sheltered one of his enemies. But when he attempted to confiscate the duchy, he met stiff resistance. Thus began a struggle that lasted, with frequent pauses for fundraising, plague and the insanity of kings, until 1453. Historians know it as the Hundred Years War, a term invented in the 1860s.

By the fourteenth century, the rulers of both France and England had a very sophisticated notion of warfare, based on their advisors' reading of ancient Roman history, the extraordinary endeavours of the European crusaders, and their own sense of what was due to a king. Kings by this period normally paid most of their armies. They equipped navies and bought expensive siege engines, including early cannon. But state bureaucracies did not have the mechanisms for very effective tax collection, and besides the fact that most of Europe had a subsistence-level economy, the early fourteenth century was a time of major Europe-wide famine, as climate patterns began their plunge into the Little Ice Age. As a result,

....

The dramatic death of King John the Blind of Bohemia at the Battle of Crécy, 26 August 1346.

1326

Autumn Queen Isabella invades England, joining with rebels against her husband Edward II.

1327

January Edward II of England is deposed by Queen Isabella and her allies. The 14-year-old Edward III becomes king, and is forced to make a humiliating peace with France.

Edward III invades Scotland. King Robert Bruce avoids battle, and weather and supply problems finally force the English to withdraw.

1328

Treaty of Northampton. The English recognize Robert Bruce as king of an independent kingdom of Scotland with no feudal ties to England.

1 February Death of King Charles IV of France ends the direct line of the Capetian dynasty. Philip VI of Valois, a cousin, becomes king.

23 August Battle of Cassel (modern northern France). A largely cavalry army under King Philip VI defeats the Flemings in support of the refugee count Louis of Flanders.

many kings trying to raise war funds were often frustrated: bankrupt, they nonetheless overspent, planning war on a grand scale and blaming their advisors for the failure to raise war funds that they insisted must be available.

The French opening move of the Hundred Years War was a series of raids on the English coast, using hired Genoese ships. Philip intended a major invasion of England in 1339, but his fleet was dispersed by a storm and his Genoese seamen (two-thirds of the French fleet) – whom the king could not afford to pay – mutinied. For his part, Edward III organized a massive series of alliances against France to support his invasions of France in 1339 and 1340. On 26 January 1340, Edward raised the stakes by proclaiming himself king of France, by right of inheritance through his mother.

Both rulers appear to have desired a decisive battle, but such matters were not always easy to arrange. In 1339, the English 'summoned' the French king to battle by devastating the territory

....

Height was highly desirable on such ships, so castles were built at the stern, bow and atop the mainmast, allowing soldiers to shoot projectiles down at the enemy.

1328–1331

Conquest of Byzantine Nicaea by the Ottoman Turks.

1329

7 **June** Death of King Robert Bruce of Scotland, leaving the throne to his five-year-old son, David.

1330

28 **July 1330** Battle of Kustendil (Velbuzhde). A Serbian army led by Stephen Decanski defeats the Bulgars in a surprise attack while the Bulgars are foraging.

King Alfonso XI of Castile establishes the Order of the Band, an order of chivalry.

Battle of Posada (modern Romania). A Wallachian army ambushes and routs the army of Charles I of Hungary.

1331

27 **September** Battle of Plowce. King Ladislas of Poland heavily defeats a large Teutonic Knight and crusader army.

around Cambrai, burning and destroying an estimated 2118 villages and castles. Philip responded in October with a formal challenge, offering Edward battle on a choice of days, a fight to be held on even ground in a fair appeal to God's judgement in their quarrel. Edward accepted and chose the ground, assuming a strongly defensive position in which he dismounted all his troops and positioned his archers on the flanks. The French troops were naturally unwilling to risk a frontal attack against such a strong position, and fortified their position in turn. After a standoff, the English finally withdrew. Similarly, in the following year the French drew up their battle line at Bouvines, but Philip agreed to a truce because the conditions for battle were unfavourable. And by then both sides had run out of money, with nothing accomplished. By July 1340, Edward III could not even pay his daily household expenses, and three English nobles who had guaranteed some of the king's loans found themselves in a debtors' prison in Flanders.

The Battle of Sluys
Before slinking back to England to raise more money, however, Edward III had won the first great battle of the Anglo-French war, the Battle

This Venetian sketch of the Battle of Zonchio, 1499, gives an excellent impression of the chaos of medieval naval war.

1332

11 August Battle of Dupplin Moor. 'The Disinherited' (Scottish exiles in England led by Edward Balliol) invade Scotland with a private army. The army of King David is defeated, the child-king taken to France for safety, and Edward Balliol claims the throne.

1333

April–20 July Edward III besieges the Scottish town of Berwick, attempting assault by land and sea. Berwick surrenders after the Scots are defeated at Halidon Hill.

19 July Battle of Halidon Hill (near Berwick, Scotland). Edward III defeats Archibald Douglas' Scottish force, which was attempting to raise the siege of Berwick.

1334

First recorded use of mounted archers in western Europe (archers who had horses for mobility but dismounted to fight).

1336

Pope Benedict XII cancels the planned crusade of Philip VI of France.

The French fleet threatens a massive attack on eastern England.

The Battle of Sluys, 1340, from a fifteenth-century illustration. The painting gives a good sense of the crowded chaos of the battle.

....

of Sluys, on 25 June 1340. This sea battle demonstrated clearly the potential of English bowmen. Edward's fleet of about 160 ships sailed for the Zwyn Estuary, planning to invade France from Flanders. But they found a French fleet of 213 ships already in battle array at Sluys, blocking the way upriver with three lines of ships chained together to form a massive sea wall. The French admirals, however, seem to have had no concept of how to wage naval war medieval-style. Medieval fights at sea, especially in the North where most of the ships used were round sailing ships, started as the enemy lines neared. The fighting men of each fleet would then propel as many missiles – stones or bolts from small catapults, crossbow bolts, arrows or even stones thrown down from the fighting tops – as possible to clear the deck of the enemy ship. When two enemy ships came together, one side would try to board the other for bloody hand-to-hand fighting. Since theirs was an

invasion fleet, the English ships had many more soldiers than the French did, including large contingents of longbowmen. The French fleet relied much more heavily on crossbows, which have a longer range but fire more slowly, and for which it is a time-consuming process to replace a bowstring affected by damp. And in

this case, the French had lost most of their hired Italian crossbowmen when they could no longer pay them; they may have had as few as 500 crossbowmen at Sluys, compared to several thousand English longbowmen.

The result was slaughter. The French line was thrown into disarray by the current even before the English fleet engaged, and the English longbowmen devastated the French crews. By the end of the day, the English had taken 190 of the 213 French ships; almost the only French ships to escape were their small number of oared galleys. And, making Sluys the bloodiest European battle of the Middle Ages, between 16,000 and 18,000 Frenchmen died, those who tried to swim to safety from their ships being clubbed by England's Flemish allies as they struggled to the shore.

Since the English Channel lies between England and France, navies remained important for the rest of the war and sometimes met in battle. All of these engagements were fought on the open sea, however, rather than in the all-or-nothing situation to which the French commanders at Sluys had committed themselves. The norm was for battles in which the victor

1337

April Philip VI of France declares the forfeiture of Gascony, officially because Edward III of England had sheltered the refugee count Robert of Artois.

Ottoman Turks capture Byzantine Nicomedia.

Parliament of Westminster forbid all games in England except archery.

1337–1453

Hundred Years War between France and England and their allies.

1337–1338

Earliest reference to gunpowder weapons on a ship, in the refitting records of the English All Hallow's Cog.

King Philip VI seeking refuge after his flight from the battlefield of Crécy, 1346. Philip's poor generalship led to the French defeat.

captured 10 to 20 enemy ships with a comparably small casualty rate, unlike the carnage of Sluys.

Crécy and Poitiers: the Longbow's Triumph

On 12 July 1346, Edward III landed in Flanders with an army of about 15,000 men, intending a frontal attack on France. To pressure King Philip into battle, Edward marched towards Paris, although when Philip offered battle at a fixed place and time, Edward sheered off in another direction. After all, to succeed, the smaller English army had to have the advantage of a good defensive position. Philip's army was about 25,000 strong, with many more men-at-arms than the English could muster.

When the French army was about to catch up, the English chose their ground carefully, near a village called Crécy. Edward's army included fewer than 3000 men-at-arms, whom the king placed dismounted in his centre. At the

---

1338–1339

Edward III of England creates a massive web of alliances against France – an expensive failure.

1338

Spring French ships raid Portsmouth and the Isle of Wight.

5 October French sack of Southampton, England.

1339

Philip VI of France plans a major invasion of England, but his fleet is dispersed by a storm.

21 June Battle of Laupen. The Swiss under Rudolf van Erbach defeat the Habsburgs and their Burgundian allies in a rare battle in which the Swiss infantry charge against knights.

wings, he stationed at least 4000 longbowmen, protected by baggage wagons and shallow pits. Philip VI, no tactician, began to lose the battle. His larger army with its strength of heavy cavalry appears to have made him over-confident, although he may have felt it necessary to commit his troops to battle immediately, before the English were fully in position. Whichever the case, Philip started the battle at about 5 p.m., committing his troops piecemeal as they arrived at the site. His 6000 Genoese mercenary crossbowmen started the attack. It is hard to imagine how Philip thought this could succeed. The crossbow winch had not yet developed, so the crossbows were loaded by placing one or two feet in a stirrup at their head, then pulling back – usually sitting on the ground to do so. At sieges, these vulnerable men were usually protected by shield-bearers carrying huge shields (*pavisses*), but at Crécy the shields were in the baggage train, somewhere miles away from the battle. Not surprisingly, the crossbowmen were repulsed as they tried to advance towards the English longbowmen, who could shoot much faster.

Philip, thinking the Genoese were not trying hard enough to win, ordered his cavalry to ride over them, in an effort to dislodge the English archers. But the cavalry could not penetrate the English 'firestorm' either. The arrows would not have penetrated the French cavalrymen's armour until they were within about 18m (59ft), but faces, limbs and horses all made vulnerable targets. And even if it did not penetrate, the impact of an arrow might topple a man-at-arms or frighten his horse. Charge after charge simply piled up the French dead and injured, who could be finished off by other English infantrymen or be crushed or suffocated by men of their own side. By the end of the day, thousands of Frenchmen lay dead on the field, including nine princes of the blood. King Philip himself was almost killed, and left his royal banner, the *oriflamme*, on the battlefield. One of Philip's first acts after the battle was to order the massacre of the remaining Genoese 'traitors'.

A romanticized view of a British archer in the reign of Edward III. Although infantrymen typically wore some armour by this period, such thorough protection is unlikely.

1340

26 January Edward III of England declares himself lawful king of France at Ghent, a claim upheld by English rulers until 1802 (except 1360–1369 and 1420–1422).

April Pope Benedict XII places Flanders under an interdict for rebellion against the king of France.

English raid on Boulogne. Almost the entire French galley fleet is destroyed.

24 June Battle of Sluys. In a massive naval battle fought in the Zwin Estuary, an English invasion fleet disastrously defeats a French fleet of 213 ships.

30 October Battle of Rio Salado. A Portuguese-Castilian army led by Alfonso XI of Castile wins a major victory over the Muslim Marinid sultan Abu'l-Hasan and Yusuf I of Granada, who are besieging Tarifa. The battle marks the last important North African intervention in Spanish affairs.

1341–1347

Byzantine civil war between Emperor John V and John Cantacuzene, who both claim the throne.

The Battle of Poitiers, fought 10 years later in 1356, was a similar case of the French recklessly attacking an entrenched English position. In the case of Poitiers, Edward III's eldest son, Edward the Black Prince, was conducting a large-scale raid *(chevauchée)* in central France when the French army led by Jean II caught up with them. The Black Prince tried to negotiate a withdrawal, but the French were confident of victory and refused. So, again, the English succeeded in establishing their line in an easily defensible position, this time with woods to the rear and a marsh on the right flank. And again the English archers were well protected. As at Crécy, the French attempted a heavy cavalry charge against that carefully prepared position, only to have their horses fall prey to the English bowmen. A French infantry advance was also thrown back. When King Jean brought up a reserve of dismounted men-at-arms, the Black Prince

King Jean II surrenders to Edward the Black Prince at the end of the Battle of Poitiers, 1356.

1341–1364

Breton War of Succession, after the death of Duke John III. France and England support the two rivals to the duchy, opening a new front of the Hundred Years War.

1342

30 September Battle of Morlaix (Brittany). The earl of Northampton leads an English army to defeat the French in a battle that prefigured the tactics used at Crécy.

1342–26 March 1344 Alfonso XI of Castile with the help of English and French crusaders wins the strategic fortress of Algeciras on the Strait of Gibraltar after a long blockade.

1344

13 May Battle of Pallene. The fleet of the Holy League (the papacy, Cyprus, Venice and the Knights Hospitallers) heavily defeat an Ottoman Turkish flotilla.

28 October A league of the papacy, Venice, Cyprus and the Knights Hospitallers conquer Smyrna from the Turks.

mounted his own men-at-arms and charged them, as well as sending his Gascon fighters to take the French in the rear. The results were even more gratifying (for the English) than Crécy had been: about 3000 Frenchmen were killed at Poitiers, and King Jean himself was taken captive.

An Infantry Revolution?

The English victories at Crécy and Poitiers were impressive triumphs in which infantry played an unusually dominant role. Were they, however, signs of an infantry 'revolution' that made the man-at-arms obsolete? Hardly. Battles like Crécy, Poitiers, Courtrai Bannockburn, and so on showed that a largely infantry army *could* stop a cavalry charge and defeat the cream of western chivalry – *if* the conditions were exactly right. Most vital was that the infantry had to be protected in some way, whether as pikemen in tight, disciplined formation or as archers behind

A tournament, mid-fourteenth century. By this period, protections such as barricades between competitors had made tournaments much safer than in earlier centuries.

1345

26 September Battle of Staveren. Count William IV of Holland invades western Frisia, but the Frisians decisively defeat him, killing William and many of his knights.

21 October An English force commanded by the earl of Darby rout a French force under Louis of Poitiers that was besieging Auberoche, southwest France.

1346

12 July Edward III lands at St-Vaast-La-Hougue with a large English army, intending a frontal attack on Philip VI of France.

18 July The town of Liège rebels against Bishop Engelbert de la Marck, decisively defeating his largely cavalry force in the Liège suburb of Vottem.

August 1346–3 August 1347 Siege of Calais. The English blockade the French city by land and sea until the starving citizens surrender the day after a French force fail to relieve the siege. Most of the citizens are evicted.

26 August Battle of Crécy. King Edward III wins a major victory over Philip VI of France in the first major land battle of the Hundred Years War.

October Battle of Neville's Cross. Queen Philippa raises an army against King David II of Scotland, who was raiding England. David is defeated and captured, and ransomed only in 1357.

1347–1351

First appearance of the Black Death in Europe kills perhaps one-third of the population.

field fortifications that could not be easily penetrated by horses. And, of course, they had to have an enemy commander desperate enough, or foolishly over-confident enough, to charge their carefully prepared positions. The great infantry victories of the fourteenth century, whether in France, Flanders or Scotland, are as notable for the pronounced tactical mistakes of enemy commanders as they are for the skill with which the commander who relied more heavily on infantry used the foot soldiers to his advantage.

Edward III and his successors did not cease to need heavy cavalry. For example, Edward employed 2700–2900 men-at-arms at Crécy, although most of them were dismounted for the battle. Edward himself encouraged knightly skills with at least 55 tournaments between 1327 and 1357 and with the creation of the Order of the Garter, which celebrated knightly exploits in the wake of Crécy. The French soon emulated the practice by creating the Order of the Star, and other states of Europe followed suit. The knights of the Order of the Star vowed never to retreat in battle, which led to 45 of their original 140 members being captured or

killed at the Battle of Mauron in August 1352. Perhaps more practically, the French improved their horse armour after Poitiers, so that at the Battle of Cocherel (1364) and the Battle of Pontvallain (1370) the cavalry stood up better to English arrows. The man-at-arms also proved his continuing worth at the Battle of Roosebeeke, 27 November 1382, when the army of Charles VI of France crushed a Flemish militia force, deploying dismounted men-at-arms in the centre, with mounted cavalry on the wings. Although the battlefield stakes evened after that, the English monarchs continued to rely heavily on both men-at-arms and archers, using them in a variety of tactical options depending on the needs of a given battle. They even mounted archers – for transport on the way to battle, not on the battlefield itself – to give greater speed and flexibility in their efforts to dominate French land. Use of

A Knight of the Garter in ceremonial garb. Ever since the foundation of the Order of the Garter by Edward III, it has been England's highest order of chivalry.

1347	1348	1349	1349–1352
Battle of Waleffe. The bishop of Liège and his ally the count of Looz defeat the citizen militia of Liège.	King Edward III of England establishes the Order of the Garter, an order of chivalry.	Organization of the Great Company (mercenaries) by Werner of Urslingen.	Stefan Dushan of Serbia conquers Bulgaria, Epirus, Thessaly, Albania and Macedonia.
Battle of Imbros. The holy league of the papacy, Cyprus, Venice and the Knights Hospitallers defeat the Turks in a naval battle near Imbros.	Pedro IV of Aragón defeats rebellious nobles at Eppila, ending a civil war.		
	King Louis of Hungary invades the Kingdom of Naples in a failed effort to avenge the supposed murder of his brother Andrew by Queen Joanna of Naples.		

The Victorian imagination at work: nineteenth-century Englishmen gloried in England's victories of the Hundred Years War, even though the details were often wrong.

mounted archers was perhaps the real revolution in fourteenth-century infantry.

A European War

The Hundred Years War was, from its inception, a multi-state war. France and Scotland joined forces against England; England arranged alliances with the countries of the North. Both France and England also took sides in a Breton war of succession. And after a lull in direct hostilities with the Treaty of Brétigny in 1360, the English and French continued to fight by supporting opposite sides in a Castilian civil war. The peace treaty, which had supposedly ended the war, was never even fully confirmed, and war broke out again in 1369. Then, as Edward III was in decline and his son the Black Prince died of a wasting illness, the French constable Bertrand du Guesclin (c. 1320–1380) regained most of the territory taken by the English in the early stages of the war. There was a cessation of the war for some years

– in England, the child Richard II came to the throne, proved deeply unpopular, and was finally deposed and killed; and in France King

The funeral of Richard II of England, 1400. Richard abdicated under pressure from his cousin, but soon died under mysterious circumstances.

c. 1350

Development of breastplates for heavy cavalry.

Battle of Les Espagnoles-sur-Mer (Winchelsea). Edward III of England commands an English fleet to victory against a Castilian fleet of 40 ships sailing for Flanders.

1350–1355 Genoese-Venetian War, beginning with the Genoese seizure of Venetian shipping at Caffa.

1350–1369 War between Pedro the Cruel of Castile and his half-brother Enrique of Trastamara for Castile.

1351

Florentine-Milanese war for control of Tuscany (indecisive).

King Jean II of France establishes the Order of the Star, an order of chivalry.

1352

Giovanna I of Naples establishes the Order of the Knot of Naples, an order of chivalry.

February Battle of the Bosporus (Galata). The Genoese fleet defeat an allied Venetian-Aragonese fleet in a long and bloody battle that continues into the night despite a storm.

14 August Battle of Mauron. The English defeat a French army. Forty-five of the 140 original members of the Order of the Star are captured or killed, since they had vowed never to retreat.

Charles VI went insane in 1389 – but the underlying causes of war continued to smoulder.

The New Arms Race

As France and England (and their allies) struggled for any possible military advantage, princes were eager to embrace any innovation. The most notable of these was gunpowder. A Chinese invention that had reached Europe via the Mongols, gunpowder first appeared in the annals of medieval war in the thirteenth century. Edward I is said to have used igniting pots of gunpowder at the siege of Stirling Castle in 1304, the first appearance of the weapon in the British Isles. And Edward III, doubtless anxious at the numerical superiority of the French, was one of the first European rulers to employ cannon. There appear to have been some English cannon at Crécy (although they seem to have done no good except, perhaps, for frightening

the horses), and certainly 10 cannon took part in the English siege of Calais in 1346–1347.

The first securely dated use of cannon in Western Europe was at the siege of Cividale in 1331, although they may also have been employed at the siege of Metz in 1324. By 1337–1338, we have the earliest reference to gunpowder weapons on a ship, when the English *All Hallow's Cog* was refitted. The earliest guns would have been of limited usefulness. They did not yet use corned gunpowder (a fifteenth-century invention), and so did not get much bang for the buck. They seem to have been impossible to aim and cumbersomely slow to load. Worst of all, they had a tendency to

....

The German alchemist Berthold Schwarz making gunpowder, while an assistant works on a cannon. Both are assisted by demons, suggesting what the artist thought of the new invention.

1353

29 August Battle of Alghero. An allied Venetian-Aragonese fleet of 80 galleys under Nicolo Pisani inflict a crushing defeat on Genoa, capturing 41 of the 60 Genoese galleys engaged.

1353–1363 Papal wars to regain control of the Papal States, led by papal legate Gil Alvarez Carillo Albornoz, archbishop of Toledo.

1354

Ottoman conquest of Gallipoli, their first conquest in Europe.

4 November Battle of Porto Longo (off the island of Sapienza in the Adriatic). Genoese sailors defeat Venice, capturing or destroying almost the entire Venetian fleet.

1355

Conquest of Byzantine-held Adrianople by King Stefan Dushan of Serbia.

explode, killing their crews and other people of their own army – as late as 1460, King James II of Scotland was killed when one of his own cannon exploded. The problem was that bronze cannon were prohibitively expensive. Iron was much cheaper, but Europeans had not yet created blast furnaces that could melt and cast iron. Instead, they crafted cannon as they did barrels, with wrought-iron bars held together by hoops, and a single weak point could be deadly.

As guns became more common, however, they became cheaper and more dependable. The cost of gunpowder fell sharply from the middle of the fourteenth century until about 1500. And by the 1370s gunpowder artillery was equal to the best available stone-throwing artillery, so it came to be used regularly in sieges. By the end of the fourteenth century, cannon were able to breach walls, an achievement first noted at the siege of Odruik in 1377. They had become a standard part of

King James II of Scotland (1430–1460), a warrior king who was fascinated by cannon, one of which exploded and killed him during the siege of Roxburgh Castle.

the medieval siege arsenal. In the second half of the century, Europeans even began to experiment with hand-held firearms.

An early cannon. Weapons similar to those depicted were employed on the battlefield at Crécy, 1346.

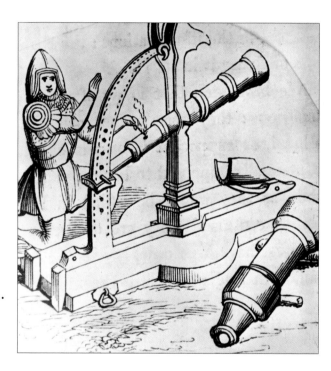

1356	1357-1359	1358	1359
19 September Battle of Poitiers. Edward, the Black Prince, of England is trapped by a large French army during a chevauchée. The English win a crushing victory, capturing French king Jean II and killing about 3000 French fighters.	War between Castile and Aragon.	Peasant revolt in northern France (the Jacquerie).	Pedro the Cruel of Castile attacks Barcelona by land and sea, but is driven off by Pedro IV of Aragón.

The Use and Abuse of Mercenaries

The employment of large bands of mercenaries, who operated under their own commanders, became increasingly common in the fourteenth century. Their military utility was not in question. Mercenary companies provided expert support services, such as the engineers who built and operated siege equipment, or the skilled crossbowmen who entered French service in large numbers. European rulers seemed astonishingly indifferent to expense when planning military endeavours, but nonetheless, mercenaries who had to be paid only during the duration of a campaign must have seemed a bargain compared to a standing army, which would have to be supported year-round. But nobody really came to grips with what to do with discharged mercenaries, men armed and trained to kill but who had no other trade.

The fourteenth century opened with an astonishing mercenary success. The Catalan

The Entrance of Roger de Flor into Constantinople, *an oil painting by José Moreno Carbonero. Roger's Catalan Grand Company rebelled and established an independent state in Greece.*

Grand Company, led by Roger of Flor, consisted of about 6500 infantrymen who had mastered their craft during the Wars of the Sicilian Vespers. The Byzantine emperor Andronicus II hired them in 1302 to help in his wars against the Turks. But the emperor soon became nervous of their ambitious leader, and apparently arranged for his murder. The company was not just a band held together by one man, though. They were highly organized,

---

1360

1360–1389 Ottoman sultan, Murad I, advances into Europe, conquering Thrace, Macedonia and much of southern Serbia.

Conquest of Skåne by King Waldemar IV of Denmark.

15 March Burning of Winchelsea by a French fleet.

8 May Treaty of Brétigny between France and England, for a short time ends the Hundred Years War. King Jean II of France is released on promise of 3 million écus ransom; Edward III renounces his claim to the French throne, but receives much of western France in full sovereignty.

1361

White Company of mercenaries form in Italy under Albert Sterz (later commanded by Sir John Hawkwood).

Waldemar IV of Denmark defeats the Swedes at the Battle of Wisby (Gotland).

The Avignon pope Innocent VI calls for a crusade against pillaging mercenary companies in France.

1361–1365 Crusade of Peter I of Cyprus.

and greatly resented what they saw as Andronicus' betrayal. The Catalans demanded more money, and when they did not receive it they rebelled, invading Thrace. At Apros in July 1305, they defeated a much larger (but less organized) Byzantine army. For several years, the Grand Company looted northern Greece, adding about 3000 independent Turks to their ranks. They then moved on to the independent state of Athens, ruled by the French duke Walter of Brienne. In a major victory of strategically disposed infantry over cavalry, they annihilated the French cavalry that confronted them and killed Walter at the Battle of Kephissos in 1311. They then seized the duchy of Athens, and ruled it as an independent mercenary state until 1388.

Other mercenary companies did not enjoy such staggering success, but they certainly complicated the military situation of Europe with their independence and demands. Most notably, both the French and English kings hired

A Byzantine chrysobull depicting Christ and Emperor Andronicus II (1282–1328). His reign saw the collapse of Byzantium's Asia Minor frontier and the loss of much of Greece.

large numbers of mercenaries to fight in the Hundred Years War, and discharged them on French soil, where they devastated large swathes of territory. The situation got completely out of control after the Battle of Poitiers, when kingless France was in chaos and royal officials lacked the money to hire troops to restore order. These *routiers* are sometimes called 'robber bands', but this was robbery writ large. The Avignon pope, Innocent VI, proclaimed a crusade against them in 1361, but that did not help the situation much. The scope of the problem can be seen in the Battle of Brignais in April 1362, when a large French army (with an estimated 6000 cavalry) was almost completely destroyed by a large army of these *routiers*. Nor was the problem limited to France. For instance, the Battle of Baesweiler in 1371 was fought between Emperor Wenceslas and Duke William of Jülich, after William failed to pay reparations for his rampaging mercenaries, despite the emperor's complaints. Since Wenceslas was defeated and captured, the mercenary misbehaviour continued unchecked.

Mercenaries were most useful in Italy, where the wealthy (and warmongering) mercantile

1362

Pedro the Cruel of Castile wins Catayud from Aragón after a long siege.

A Hanseatic fleet sacks Copenhagen. They go on to besiege Helsingborg Castle, where Danish king Waldemar IV Atterdag captures most of their fleet in a surprise attack.

April Battle of Brignais, on the Rhône. A French army pursuing routiers (discharged mercenaries looting the countryside) suffers a heavy defeat.

1364

16 May Battle of Cocherel. Bertrand du Guesclin of France defeats an English-Navarrese allied army led by the rebellious Charles of Navarre.

28 July Battle of Cascina. Florence defeats Pisa.

First European reference to hand-held firearms.

29 September Battle of Auray. An Anglo-Breton army defeats the French, capturing the French commander Bertrand du Guesclin.

1365

Ottoman conquest of Adrianople.

9 October A crusader army led by Peter I of Cyprus takes Alexandria in a surprise assault, but the soldiers refuse to remain to defend their conquest when a relief fleet arrives.

Pope Innocent VI (1352–1362), who brought about the Treaty of Brétigny between France and England in 1360.

cities had the resources to pay them regularly. Many veterans of the Hundred Years War eventually made their way to the service of one (or more) of the warring Italian states. The most famous band was the White Company, which began operations in Italy in 1361, called there to fight the 'Great Company' (founded in 1349 by Werner of Urslingen). This organization, the union of several independent mercenary companies, brought to Italy fighting techniques that had been perfected at Crécy and Poitiers, and in many raids and sieges. Many of the leaders, such as Sir John Hawkwood and Andrew Belmont, were English. Such leaders showed that mercenaries, when paid regularly, could be loyal and, indeed, invaluable in the wars of Italy.

Since they were full-time professional soldiers, the army with the most and best mercenaries tended to win. For example, Hawkwood's victory over Verona at Castagnaro in 1387 was a model of military professionalism on behalf of his employer, the city of Padua. His largely mercenary army numbered about 7000 men-at-arms, 1000 infantry and 600 mounted English armies. They fought a much larger army of 9000 men-at-arms, 2600 pikemen and crossbowmen, and a large force of untrained militia. Hawkwood fought in the style of the English at Crécy and Poitiers, putting his men

Bertrand du Guesclin (c. 1320–1380), a Breton knight who rose to the position of constable of France, was France's greatest hero of the fourteenth century.

1366

England renounces vassalage to the pope.

Ottoman Turks defeat crusaders led by Amadeus of Savoy and Louis of Hungary at the Battle of Vidin.

1367

3 April Battle of Nájera, Castile. Pedro the Cruel's ally, Edward the Black Prince, defeats Enrique of Trastamara, restoring Pedro to the throne of Castile.

1368

An alliance of the Hanseatic League, Sweden and other regions force Waldemar IV of Denmark into exile, halting Danish expansion.

behind a stream, with archers on the flanks. A Veronese cavalry charge failed against Hawkwood's defences, and the mercenary commander completed his victory with a cavalry charge into his enemy's rear. Hawkwood ended his highly successful career in Florentine service.

Italian Wars

It has been estimated that between 1320 and 1360 there were at least 700 German cavalry commanders active in Italy, commanding a total of at least 10,000 men. Italy was brimming with opportunities for fighting men, both natives and foreigners. During the fourteenth century, a few of the Italian states, most notably Milan and Florence, absorbed a number of their smaller rivals. Other wars were fought for trade advantages, or out of simple rivalry. The biggest player in Italian war, though, was the papacy. The popes, controllers of a significant state of their own, the Papal State, had suffered serious losses during the thirteenth century, culminating

Duke Filippo Maria Visconti of Milan (1412–1447), one of the many small rulers battling for supremacy in fourteenth- and fifteenth-century Italy.

1369

23 March Battle of Montiel. Enrique of Trastamara with a largely French army led by Bertrand du Guesclin defeats the army of Pedro the Cruel and personally kills Pedro to secure the throne of Castile.

Crusaders attempt to capture Alexandria.

Raid on Portsmouth by a French fleet.

Fall of Adrianople to Sultan Murad I.

1369–1374 Charles V of France reopens the Hundred Years War, recovering all of France except Calais and Gascony.

1369–1370 Portuguese blockade of Seville, part of a long struggle for control of the Strait of Gibraltar.

1370

Bertrand du Guesclin named constable of France.

Battle of Pontvallain. Bertrand du Guesclin, constable of France, defeats an Anglo-Breton army, regaining most of Brittany for France.

19 September Sack of Limoges by the Black Prince, an action widely criticized for its brutality.

1371

22 August Battle of Baesweiler. Duke William of Jülich defeats and captures Emperor Wenceslas in a battle over reparations for Duke William's rampaging mercenaries.

26 September Chernomen (Maritza) (modern Bulgaria). In the first Ottoman pitched battle in Europe, Sultan Murad I defeats a larger Serbian army under King Vukashin.

in the decision to move the papal curia itself to the French border town of Avignon in the early fourteenth century. The popes were not, however, willing to give up their territory without a fight, spending at times up to 60 per cent of their annual revenue on war to that end.

As early as 1322 the pope preached a crusade against the Visconti family of Milan. The great drive to regain the Papal State, though, did not begin until 1353. The papal legate, Gil Alvarez Carillo Albornoz, archbishop of Toledo, led the early campaigns. His campaigns highlight the brutality of fourteenth-century war, especially war against perceived rebels and traitors. The papal forces, largely mercenary, combined current fighting and raiding practices with what many regarded to be unfair use of spiritual sanctions. This practice can be seen in the War of the Eight Saints of 1375–78, a rebellion against the papacy engineered by Florence. On the spiritual front, Florence was placed under an

The consecration of Pope Gregory XI at Avignon (1370). This pontiff returned the papacy to Rome in 1378, initiating a new series of Italian wars.

interdict. But on the battlefield, the papal legate in command was more brutal than most European commanders of the day, massacring the citizens of Faenza (1376) and Cesena (1377) after successful sieges. When Pope Gregory XI

returned from Avignon to Rome in 1378, he did so with an army that subdued still more rebels.

At sea, the wars between Italian trade rivals continued with unabated ferocity. Essentially it was a struggle between Genoa and Venice, with each city claiming ports and trade privileges in the eastern Mediterranean. A third Genoese–Venetian war broke out in the 1350s, when the Genoese seized Venetian merchant ships at Caffa. Each city seemed able to draw on an unlimited supply of ships and sailors, which meant that neither side had a clear advantage. Thus in 1352 the Genoese defeated the Venetians in the Bosporus, only to suffer defeat themselves the next year off Sardinia. In 1354, the Genoese captured nearly the entire Venetian fleet at

1372

22 June Battle of La Rochelle. A Castilian fleet under Enrique II defeats an English transport fleet with reinforcements for Gascony through use of fireships.

June The French win La Rochelle from the English through a ruse by the mayor.

1375–1378

War of the Eight Saints. Rebellion against the papacy in the Papal States, organized by Florence.

Florence placed under papal interdict.

1376

Sack of Walsingham, England, by a Castilian fleet.

1376–1389 War of the Swabian City League against Emperor Wenceslas.

A papal army takes Faenza after a short siege and slaughters the citizens.

Sapienza, ending one phase of the hostilities that would last for the rest of the century.

A fourth Genoese-Venetian war broke out in 1372, in a fight over precedence at the coronation of Peter II of Cyprus. The war reached its height after the Venetian fleet was defeated at Pola in May 1379. The Genoese then attacked Venice itself, by both land and sea. The arrival of 18 Venetian ships from the east, however, allowed a counter-blockade of the Genoese fleet to be established. In time, the surviving Genoese surrendered – but the root causes of the long war remained unaddressed.

Ongoing Crusades

The fall of Acre in 1294 largely put an end to Holy Land crusades, although the recovery of Jerusalem remained dear to many Western hearts. In fact, some rulers and nobles, including both Edward I of England and his arch-rival Robert Bruce, symbolized this ongoing

....

Duke Louis II of Bourbon (1337–1410), whose 1390 crusade attempted to suppress Mediterranean piracy by attacking pirate bases in Tunis.

attachment by bequeathing their hearts to the Holy Land. But, although many Westerners in the fourteenth century wrote bold treatises on how to recover the Holy Land, the scope of the problem was simply too large in light of Mamluk military strength and Europe's own internal wars. Crusaders under Peter I of Cyprus sacked Alexandria in 1365 but could not hold it, and Duke Louis II of Bourbon's crusade against Tunis in 1390 was also a failure.

When fourteenth-century nobles decided to prove themselves in war and win a crusading indulgence, they went to the Baltic, where the Teutonic Order gave them carefully organized opportunities to fight pagans while entertaining them in princely fashion. Lithuania – a strong, well organized, and non-Christian state – was a threat to the Order's lands in Prussia, and also a legal opportunity for further conquests (since it was pagan). But the Teutonic Knights did not have sufficient manpower for wars of conquest. And so they engaged in a highly successful propaganda campaign to win crusaders for annual *Preussenreisen*, journeys to Prussia that are first attested in 1304. The Order also hired large numbers of mercenaries – who

1377

February Bloodbath of Cesena. A papal army led by Sir John Hawkwood takes Florentine-held Cesena; papal legate Cardinal Robert of Geneva orders the massacre of the whole population to avenge the murder of some mercenaries.

The French fleet raid English ports from Rye to Portsmouth.

Siege of Odruik. First known case of a cannon breaching walls in Europe.

1378

Florence makes peace with the papacy and pays an indemnity.

1378–1381 Genoese–Venetian War.

30 May Battle of Anzio. A Venetian fleet defeats the Genoese.

1378–1417 Great Papal Schism, with rival popes in Rome and Avignon.

1379

7 May Battle of Pola (Istria). The Genoese fleet win an overwhelming victory over a Venetian force; only six Venetian ships escape.

1379–1380 The Genoese blockade Venice by land and sea, but the Venetian fleet arrive and counter-blockade the Genoese fleet. The surviving Genoese surrender on 24 June 1380.

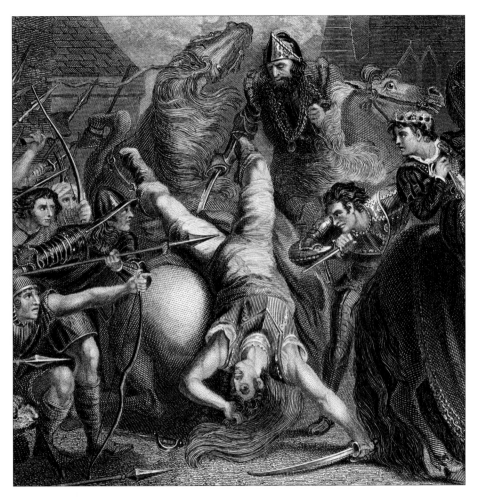

received a crusade indulgence. After the fall of Acre, the master of the Teutonic Order soon transferred his headquarters to Marienburg in Prussia, and all the Order's resources focused on taking and holding territory in the Baltic. It was a long, slow fight. The Order fell into the pattern of two short campaigns each year, in the summer and the winter (when travel was possible). Their objective was usually limited, taking or building a single fortress in enemy territory.

Despite a century of war, the Teutonic Order never succeeded in subduing Lithuania. They were distracted by wars with Poland, whose rulers were understandably alarmed at Teutonic aggression. And the grand dukes of Lithuania fought intelligently and stubbornly for their territory, often allying with other enemies of the Knights. Dashing the Order's hopes, the Lithuanian grand duke Jogaila converted to Latin Christianity in 1386, and married Jadwiga, heiress of Poland. With the Polish–Lithuanian union that followed, the Teutonic Order was forced onto the defensive, and soon lost its supply of low-cost western crusaders.

Crusade also continued in Spain, seen most notably in the Battle of Rio Salado, 30 October 1340, a major Portuguese–Castilian victory over the Muslims. However, this battle marked a turning point in the Spanish reconquista. The Christian force defeated the Marinid sultan Abu'l-Hasan of Morocco, and this proved to be the last time that a North African Muslim state

The English Peasants' Revolt of 1381 began in Brentwood, when peasants protesting the collection of a heavy tax killed a judge sent to punish them.

1380

c. 1380 Invention of the bombard by German friar and alchemist Berthold Schwarz.

8 September Battle of Kulikovo. Prince Dmitri Donskoi of Moscow defeats Khan Mamai of the Golden Horde, the first Russian victory over the Mongols.

French admiral Jean de Vienne burns Gravesend, England.

1381

English Peasants' Revolt.

1382

23 August Khan Toktamish of the Golden Horde captures Moscow, killing much of the population and re-establishing Mongol control.

27 November Battle of Roosebeeke (Westrozebeke). The army of Philip the Bold, who claimed Flanders by marrying the heiress, crushes the army of Ghent and its allies, commanded by Philip van Artevalde.

attempted serious intervention in the affairs of
Spain. In 1344, King Alfonso XI of Castile went
on to take Muslim-controlled Algeciras on the
north shore of the Strait of Gibraltar, leaving
only the emirate of Granada in Muslim hands.
For the rest of the century, Spanish wars were
for the most part a matter of Christian against
Christian, such as the Castilian-Aragonese war
of 1357, or the war for the throne of Castile
between Pedro the Cruel and his brother
Enrique of Trastamara. Castile also fought a
series of naval battles against both Portugal and
the Muslim states of North Africa, for control
of the Strait of Gibraltar.

The Ottoman Turks

Although crusades of conquest appeared to be
faltering in the fourteenth century, defensive
crusades were more necessary than ever, thanks
to the rise of the Ottoman Turkish dynasty in
Asia Minor. The Ottoman sultans proved to be
skilled military strategists, uniting the small

*The Battle of Montiel, at which Pedro the Cruel
of Castile was killed, ending the Castilian civil war,
23 March 1369.*

1383	1384	1385
'Crusade' of Bishop Henry Despenser of Norwich. This was a badly mismanaged English attack on Duke Philip the Bold of Burgundy in the Netherlands, preached as a crusade by the Roman pope.	Castilian naval assault on Lisbon.	Richard II of England leads a campaign against Scotland but accomplishes nothing.
	Battle of Thessalonica. The Ottoman Turks defeat Byzantine emperor Manuel II Palaeologos in the last pitched battle the Byzantines fought with the Turks. Thessalonica surrenders in 1387 after a three-year siege.	**14 August** Battle of Aljubarrota. King João I of Portugal and his English allies defeat an invasion of Portugal by Juan I of Castile (with French allies).

Turkish states of Asia Minor with a combination of force and the appeal of *jihad*, a holy war against the Christian Byzantine Empire. By the 1350s, the Ottomans had won almost all of the Byzantine territory on the Asian side of the Bosporus, and began to turn their attention toward Europe. Sultan Murad I (1360–1389) won an impressive series of victories. He conquered Thrace and established his capital at Adrianople. After that, he went on to annex Macedonia and much of southern Serbia. At Thessalonika in 1384 he defeated the Byzantine emperor Manuel II, in the last pitched battle between the failing Byzantine Empire and the Turks.

As the Turks moved into the Balkans, it is hardly surprising that the Latin Christian states of central Europe should have become concerned. The obvious next Turkish target was Hungary. King Sigismund (1387–1437) responded strongly, co-ordinating Christian resistance in the Balkans. Most notably, he

Ottoman Sultan Murad I is killed by one of his own nobles during the Battle of Kosovo, 15 June 1389.

1386

Union of Poland and Lithuania. Grand Duke Jogaila of Lithuania converts to Christianity and marries the heiress Jadwiga of Poland.

France plans a major invasion of England, but the plan is called off in November, probably because the king of France cannot pay his troops.

9 July Battle of Sempach (modern Switzerland). Swiss infantry militia defeat an Austrian army commanded by the Habsburg duke Leopold III of Austria. Leopold is killed, along with at least 600 Austrian knights.

c. 1386 Earliest known example of a lance rest (*arrêt*) attached to the breastplate, depicted on a tomb.

1387

11 March Battle of Castagnaro, Italy. A Paduan army led by Sir John Hawkwood defeats Verona.

Battle of Radcot Bridge. Rebel nobles led by the Lords Appellant defeat a force of King Richard II's supporters commanded by Robert de Vere, earl of Oxford.

The Merciless Parliament purges Richard II of England's administration.

Publication of Honoré Bouvet's *Arbre des batailles* ('Tree of battles').

Battle of Margate. The English fleet defeats a French–Castilian invasion fleet.

Emperor Manuel II (1391–1425) Palaeologus praying to the archangel Michael.

••••••••••••••••••••••••••••••••••••••

assembled the large western army that took part in the 'Crusade of Nicopolis' of 1396.

The Western army that met Sultan Bayezid at Nicopolis was enormous, estimated to have included as many as 100,000 fighting men. While Hungarians provided more than half the force, there were also French, German, Wallachian, English and other contingents. Bayezid's force was probably about equal in size – but was far more organized in its command structure. The Christian force profoundly lacked unity. The Western crusaders in general defied Sigismund, while many of his Hungarians and Wallachians were disloyal. And at this battle, as in a number of fourteenth-century engagements, the Europeans put too much trust in the power of a cavalry charge, against well-organized foot soldiers who were protected by a forest of planted stakes. The Western men-at-arms were stopped short by the stakes, then shot at by Turkish archers. Dismounted, they broke through and defeated the Turkish infantry. Unknown to them, though, a strong Turkish reserve was lying in wait on the reverse side of the slope. The result was an overwhelming Turkish victory. The battle by no means signalled the end of Western heavy cavalry, but it provided yet another warning that cavalry must be intelligently used, in conjunction with infantry, to win battles.

After Nicopolis, Hungary – and the Byzantine Empire – lay open to the Ottomans. They were saved only by a new invader from central Asia, Timur the Lame, who nearly destroyed the Turkish sultanate at the Battle of Ankara in 1402. The Turkish threat remained, however, and would be a dominant theme of warfare in the fifteenth century.

1388

15 August Battle of Otterburn (Chevy Chase). A Scottish army inflict a serious defeat on a larger English army commanded by Henry Percy of Northumberland ('Hotspur'). Percy is captured.

1389

15 June Battle of Kosovo. A major Turkish victory over an allied Christian force led by Serbian Prince Lazar. Sultan Murad I is assassinated during the battle, which does not affect the outcome.

Queen Margaret, regent of Denmark, decisively defeats her competitor for the throne, Duke Albrekt of Pomerania, and imprisons him.

1390

Sultan Bayezid I 'the Thunderbolt' begins construction of a permanent Ottoman fleet.

A Genoese fleet and crusaders commanded by Duke Louis II of Bourbon fail to take the port of Mahdia (modern Tunisia), a major haven of barbary pirates.

Ottoman sultan Bayezid I takes Widdin as the first step in a planned invasion of Hungary.

1391

Battle of Alessandria. A Milanese army defeats the Florentines, who are commanded by Sir John Hawkwood.

Christian knights, fleeing from the victorious Turks in the aftermath of the Battle of Nicopolis, 28 September 1396.

1392

King Charles VI of France goes insane.

1394

Richard II of England's first Irish campaign.

16 March Death of Sir John Hawkwood, the greatest mercenary captain of the fourteenth century.

1394–1402 Ottoman sultan Bayezid I besieges Constantinople, raising the siege only when threatened by the invading army of Timur the Lame.

1396

March Truce of Leulinghen. France and England agree to a 30-year truce in the Hundred Years War. Princess Isabel of France marries Richard II of England.

25 September Battle of Nicopolis. The Ottoman army inflicts a major defeat on a large crusader force.

Union of Kalmar. Erik of Pomerania becomes king of all Scandinavia.

1399

Summer Timur the Lame inflicts an overwhelming defeat on an alliance of Lithuania, Rus', the Tatars, the Poles and the Teutonic Knights.

Richard II of England's second Irish campaign.

Richard II of England forced to abdicate. Henry of Bolingbroke becomes King Henry IV.

September 1399–1409 Welsh rebellion against English control, led by Owain Glyn Dwr.

The Fifteenth Century: An Age of Change

There was no sudden revolution in European warfare in the fifteenth century. Instead, trends of several centuries' duration continued to develop on the battlefields of Europe. Armies tended to get larger than ever, continuing to strain states' resources to the maximum.

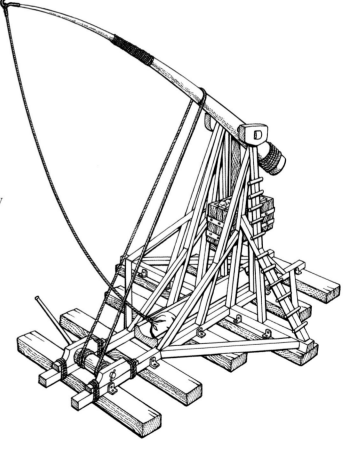

Battles tended to be bloodier than ever, not so much because of improved killing techniques as because both ideological differences and the growing professionalism of armies encouraged soldiers to do the job 'thoroughly'. Arms and armour continued to develop, including a new reliance on the pike by infantry forces. Most importantly, gunpowder technology developed rapidly. By the end of the fifteenth century, warfare in Europe looked – and sounded – very different than it had even a century before.

Left: Henry V protects his fallen brother at the Battle of Agincourt. Henry was in the thick of the fighting. Right: A counterweight trebuchet, still in regular use until the mid-fifteenth century.

The period between 1400 and 1450 saw a considerable improvement in guns and gunnery. For much of the fourteenth century, cannon were more a noisy curiosity than a real aid in battle; in the course of the fifteenth century, they would improve so much that the mere threat of cannon could bring about surrender. The growing effectiveness of gunpowder weapons can be seen in the fact that trebuchets rarely appeared at European sieges after about 1450; although they were still far more accurate than cannon, a cannon (whose very name means 'tube' – something down which to shoot a projectile) could put much greater force behind the missiles that it shot.

Two major inventions helped make guns the dominant force in siege warfare. The first was the invention of the bombard in about 1380, a highly effective form of cannon that directed the force of a gunpowder explosion more directly behind the projectile being shot. By 1420, the largest guns were up to 5.2m (17ft) long, and fired balls of up to 750kg (1650lb). By the 1430s, bombards could reduce most defences. Part of the credit, though, must go to the second invention, that of 'corned' gunpowder, sometime around

the year 1430. This is a process in which gunpowder is dampened with brandy, spirits, vinegar or the 'urine of a wine-drinking man' and then dried to small granules that were perhaps three times as effective as earlier powder. Such a development probably increased the danger to the gunners themselves, as the typical wrought-iron cannon of the

Above: A model of Mons Meg, the great wrought-iron bombard made at Mons in 1449. A gift to the king of Scotland, Mons Meg is now housed at Edinburgh castle.

Left: Berthold Schwarz, a German Franciscan friar and alchemist of the fourteenth century who engaged in early experiments with gunpowder.

1400

30 October Battle of Aleppo. Timur the Lame crushes a Mamluk army, going on to seize Aleppo and Damascus.

1400–1410 A long and confused civil war in Germany ends with the coronation of Sigismund of Hungary as Holy Roman emperor.

1401

Timur the Lame storms Baghdad, massacring the population and largely destroying the city.

fifteenth century had a tendency to burst. However, a shift from stone shot to iron or lead helped to ensure that missiles fit the bore of the cannon better and probably also made dangerous explosions less frequent.

By the middle of the fifteenth century, an attacking force well equipped with artillery could batter down the walls of even the strongest town or castle – as can be seen in the role of great guns in the Turkish conquest of Constantinople, the French conquest of Normandy, and the Spanish conquest of Grenada. At first, defensive builders responded by thickening town walls. The keep of Ham set a record in around 1470 with 11m (36ft) thick walls. By the end of the century, though, engineers were designing squat artillery towers, turning away from the curtain walls that provided such a vulnerable target.

In the fifteenth century, handguns also developed into an effective instrument of war. The first handgun, the *schioppetto*, was introduced perhaps as early as the late thirteenth century. By the second half of the fourteenth century, there is good evidence of handgun use,

Above: A fifteenth-century hand cannon.

Left: Bombards fired balls weighing hundreds of pounds, and were able to break castle and town walls.

1402

20 July Battle of Ankara (Turkey). Timur the Lame (Tamerlaine) destroys the Ottoman army of Bayezid I.

14 September Battle of Homildon Hill. The English under Henry Percy of Northumberland ('Hotspur') defeat a Scottish-French invasion led by Archibald Douglas. Douglas is captured.

1403

21 July Battle of Shrewsbury. King Henry IV defeated rebels led by Henry Percy ('Hotspur'); Percy is killed.

1403–1413 War for control of the Ottoman Empire between the three sons of Sultan Bayazid I; loss of most Ottoman territory in Europe.

1404

27 April Death of Duke Philip the Bold of Flanders.

The peasants of Dithmarschen, Germany, repel an invasion by the Count of Holstein.

almost always in the defence of towns, where it would not be too great a liability that they were heavy, cumbersome and slow (1–1.2m/3–4ft long, and fired with a match). By the 1430s, though, handguns had developed to the point that some field armies included groups of hand gunners. They appear to have been effective – or, at least, very highly resented; by the 1440s, we have accounts that hand gunners captured in battles were summarily executed. By about 1480, the *arquebus*, a more sophisticated gun that was heavier but included a trigger mechanism, had begun to replace the schioppetto. The Milanese army in 1482 included 1250 schioppettos, 352 arquebusses and 233 crossbows, suggesting how the balance of battlefield forces was shifting. It is unlikely that guns were more effective than crossbows, especially with the development of the steel crossbow, wound by a windlass, but smart commanders saw their potential – or enjoyed their imposing racket and air of 'modernity'.

Military Religious Orders

The fifteenth century saw a radical decline and alteration in notions of 'chivalry', even though

some of the most important orders of chivalry were created in this century (most notably the Golden Fleece in Burgundy). Nowhere was the shift in ideals more obvious than in the decline of the military religious orders. The Knights Templars had been dissolved in the early fourteenth century. In Spain, the military orders became largely honorary clubs for the nobility. The Teutonic Knights and the Knights Hospitallers remained, but only in face of extreme difficulty.

By 1400, the Teutonic Knights had constructed more than 260 castles to protect and control their state. They had also made a large number of enemies, though, and the loss of crusader reinforcements after the last of the Baltic peoples converted to Christianity made their position increasingly precarious. Many people must have thought the Order got what was coming to it in 1410, when King Jagiello of Poland/Lithuania put together a large coalition against them. This was truly war on a large

A foot soldier carrying an arquebus, *a firearm developed in the fifteenth century, which gradually replaced the* schioppetto.

1405

A Castilian fleet raids Jersey and sacks Poole.

1405–1406 English conquest of rebel-held Anglesey.

Berwick, Scotland, surrenders to an English attack after a single bombard shot.

1405–1406 Florentine conquest of Pisa.

1407

23 November Duke Louis of Orléans murdered by order of Duke John of Burgundy.

scale: Jagiello's force numbered more than 30,000, while the Teutonic Knights raised about 20,000 (many of them mercenaries) against them.

The Battle of Tannenberg (or Grunwald), 15 July 1410, demonstrates well both the old and the new in battle tactics. The order's grand master, Ulrich von Jungingen, protected his army by digging camouflaged pits. But then he drew back, leaving his carefully created defences for the Poles to occupy. What followed was a largely cavalry battle, as the Knights were charged repeatedly until their formation broke. Tannenberg was a total defeat for the Teutonic Knights, who lost every senior member of the order as well as about 200 knights. The battle marked the first major step of a long decline in both military capability and adherence to the order's moral code. A 13 years' war (1453–1466), in which both rebels and the king of Poland attacked the Order, spelled further

Bran Castle, Romania. First constructed by the Teutonic Knights in 1212, it had become an important defence against the Ottoman Turks by the fifteenth century.

1408

King Sigismund establishes the Order of the Dragon of Hungary, an order of chivalry.

1408–1409 Siege and reconquest of Aberystwyth, Wales, by the English.

1408–1409 Christine de Pisan produces the *Livre des faits des armes et de la chevalerie* ('Book of deeds of arms and chivalry').

1409

Henry IV of England takes Harlech, Wales; Owain Glyn Dwr fled, ends the Welsh revolt.

1410

15 July Battle of Tannenberg (Grunwald). King Jagiello of Poland–Lithuania and his allies crush a major Teutonic Knight army. Most officers of the order and 200 knights are killed.

disaster for the Teutonic Knights, including the loss of Marienburg, their headquarters, in 1457. In 1466, with the Second Peace of Thorn, the order's state was partitioned.

The Knights Hospitallers were more fortunate in preserving a valid goal – the protection of the sea from the advance of Islam. Shortly after the fall of Acre in 1294, the Hospitallers had moved their main theatre of operation to the island of Rhodes, from which they waged naval war first against the Mamluks and then against the Ottoman Turks. They participated in several coalitions against the Turks in the fifteenth century, and retained a good reputation as protectors of Christendom. They also gained the special enmity of the Ottoman sultans. In 1480, the Turks launched a major assault against Rhodes. They breached the walls of the island's main city after two months, but their assault was driven off with

....

The Battle of Tannenberg, *by Wojciech Kossak (1931). The battle, which broke the power of the Teutonic Knights in Prussia, is a strong symbol of Polish nationalism.*

1411

1 February First Peace of Thorn. The Teutonic Order renounces its claim on the province of Samogitia, which becames part of Poland.

Battle of Harlaw. The earl of Mar defeats an invasion of Scotland by Donald, lord of the Isles and northern English nobles.

First mention of the matchlock, a device to light gunpowder in a gun.

1412

Duke Charles of Orléans and his allies make a treaty with Henry V of England against France.

1413–1415

Ottoman sultan Mehmed I regains Ottoman possessions in Europe and conquers Wallachia.

Ulrich von Jungingen, Grand Master of the Teutonic Order, who fell, with most officers of the order, at the Battle of Tannenberg, 1410.

Right: The Knights Hospitallers drive off the Ottoman Turkish assault on Rhodes, 28 July 1480.

....

heavy loss. One military religious order, at least, had survived to fight another day.

The Agincourt Campaign

For the first half of the fifteenth century, Western European warfare was dominated by the renewal of the Hundred Years War between France and England. There had been a long pause in hostilities after the death of Edward III in 1377. His successor, Richard II, had not fought France, at first because of his youth and then because of increasing tensions with his barons, which culminated in his deposition and death in 1399. Henry IV, who stole Richard's throne, had too fragile a hold on power to risk expensive ventures overseas; much of his reign was spent combating major rebellions in both England and Wales. France was not in a position to take advantage of these disorders, because an internal power struggle for control of the mad king Charles VI descended gradually into civil war. By the time Henry V came to the

1414–1418

Council of Constance ends the great papal schism.

1415

6 July Execution of the Bohemian reformer Jan Hus in Constance.

18 August–4 October Successful siege of Harfleur by Henry V of England.

Portuguese conquest of Ceuta on the African side of the Strait of Gibraltar.

September Fifty-eight Bohemian nobles form the Hussite League against Emperor Wenceslas.

25 October Battle of Agincourt. Henry V of England inflicts a severe defeat on the French.

A contemporary portrait of King Henry V of England (1413–1422), the great warrior king whose military leadership and organizational skills had won most of France before his untimely death.

English throne in 1413, however, England was ready to take the offensive again. Henry had already proven his military skill in England's internal wars during his father's reign.

Henry invaded France in 1415 with an army of about 12,000 men, aiming at the conquest of Normandy. His goals appear to have been overly ambitious. The first major step in his strategy was the siege of Harfleur, which took longer than expected, perhaps because Henry had too high expectations of his cannon (which did prove decisive in the end). He lost at least one-third of his army, either dispersed to garrisons or succumbing to sickness (mostly dysentery). So, although the campaigning season had come to an end, Henry took the remainder of his army on an armed tour of Normandy, to advertise his reasonableness as a future lord by ostentatiously keeping his men from looting. But a French army caught up with the English (and their French allies) at Agincourt.

At the Battle of Agincourt, King Henry commanded only about 5000 archers and some 900 men-at-arms against a French force perhaps as much as three times as large. But yet again, the English won a battle against heavy odds through intelligent use of battlefield defences that rendered the French cavalry largely ineffective. Sharpened stakes embedded in a checkerboard before them protected the English archers. The French cavalry were not at great

....

Henry V before the Battle of Agincourt, 25 October 1415. The king was noted for his piety, persecuting Lollard heretics back home in England.

1416

Battle of Gallipoli. A Venetian fleet commanded by Doge Loredano severely defeats the Ottomans.

15 August Battle of Harfleur. An English fleet commanded by the Duke of Bedford wins a major victory over the French and their Genoese allies, securing Harfleur and weakening French naval power.

Battle of San Egideo. The condottiere Braccio da Montone defeats Carlo Malatesta and becomes ruler of Perugia.

1416–1422 King Erik of Scandinavia unsuccessfully tries to seize Schleswig from the count of Holstein.

risk from the English arrows. By the early fifteenth century, men-at-arms wore plate armour, often called 'white armour' because of the way it reflected sunlight. They had abandoned shields, because the armour itself was so strong that even a direct arrow hit would only penetrate at a close range. Horses were also better protected than ever, their 27kg (60lb) or so of armour providing them with much greater safety against archers, too. But if men-at-arms could be stopped and dismounted, they became vulnerable.

What stopped the French cavalry at Agincourt was probably not so much the dense hail of English arrows as the thick mud of the battlefield and the English forest of stakes. It must have been rather like knights attempting to charge a town wall. In repeated charges, the French failed to break through. Men-at-arms fell into the mud, and hundreds suffocated before the English soldiers even touched them. At least

A suit of jousting armour with matching horse armour from the fifteenth century. Jousting armour was heavier than armour used in battle, often weighing as much as 45kg (100lb).

600 French nobles fell at Agincourt, while over a thousand more were captured. In all, probably about 10,000 men perished that day, mostly Frenchmen.

Agincourt did not win Normandy for Henry V, although the loss of French leadership at such a key moment must certainly have helped his cause. The 1415 campaigning season was over, and the English force was riddled with disease. The true gains came only in 1417–19, after the English had prepared the way with major naval victories off Harfleur in 1416 and off the Chef de Caux in 1417. By 1418, Henry had a royal fleet of 39 ships, besides merchant vessels that were pressed into royal service. French disorganization, especially the hatred between the dukes of Orléans and Burgundy and the Burgundian hatred for the Dauphin Charles (heir to the throne), also eased Henry's task.

On 1 August 1417, Henry V invaded Normandy with an army nearly 11,000 strong, and proceeded to take the duchy castle by castle and town by town. He kept his army in the field for two winters, an extraordinary military achievement for the time, made more impressive by the fact that he provisioned it from England

1417

Henry V of England conquers Normandy.

29 June The English defeat a French-Genoese fleet in the Battle of Honfleur.

Henry V of England successfully besieges Caen.

1418

May Fall of Paris to Duke John the Fearless of Burgundy; massacre of 5000 citizens. Dauphin Charles escapes, becoming leader of the anti-Burgundian party.

1418–January 1419 The city of Rouen surrenders to Henry V of England after a lengthy siege.

1419

30 July First defenestration of Prague. Thirteen council members are thrown from the Town Hall window as a declaration of war against Emperor Wenceslas.

30 July Battle of Prague. Hussite victory over the troops of Emperor Wenceslas drives the emperor from Bohemia.

10 September Assassination of Duke John the Fearless of Flanders at the order of Dauphin Charles, leading to a Burgundian alliance with England.

1419–1434 Hussite Wars against German dominance over Bohemia and for the right to follow the religious teachings of Jan Hus.

rather than allowing his men to loot the countryside. Henry proved to be a master at siege warfare, employing the latest techniques, especially in artillery. But we can see in accounts of his sieges, notably of Caen (1417), Rouen (1418–19) and Meaux (1421–22), that siege warfare called for a variety of approaches, as the English army probed for points of weakness. At Caen, the English tried to undermine the wall; the defenders set bowls of water on the walls to detect the vibrations from mining work. The English also tried an escalade at Caen, only to discover that their siege ladders were too short. At Rouen, they relied on starvation to do its work – and were helped by the ruthlessness of the defenders, who expelled their non-combatants from the city. The English refused to let them pass through their siege lines, and they were left to starve where they were.

Even as Henry took Normandy, Duke John the Fearless of Burgundy captured Paris in his

The Battle of Montargis, 5 September 1427, in which a small French force raised the English siege of the town, after breaking dikes to flood the English camp.

1420

First appearance of 'white armour' – plate armour, worn uncovered.

25 March Battle of Sudomer. The Hussites, commanded by Jan Zizka, defeat a royalist Catholic army.

21 May Treaty of Troyes. The representatives of King Charles VI recognize Henry V of England as regent and heir to France, disinheriting Dauphin Charles. Henry marries Princess Catherine of Valois.

Construction of the English ship Gracedieu, an immense 1400-ton vessel, probably three-masted with a bowsprit.

14 July Battle of Vitkov Hill. The Hussites under Jan Zizka defeat a crusading army.

December Fall of Paris to Henry V.

1421

22 March Battle of Baugé. An English force commanded by Henry V's brother Clarence attacks a dauphinist army but is defeated and Clarence is killed.

6 October 1421–10 May 1422 Siege of Meaux. Henry V of England gains this major fortress to secure his hold on Normandy.

21 December Battle of Kutná Hora. Hussites defeat a German/Hungarian royalist army in Bohemia.

private war against the Dauphin, massacring an estimated 5000 citizens. The Dauphin retaliated by arranging Duke John's assassination in 1419, which badly backfired since John's heir responded by making an alliance with England. Burgundian support, added to Henry V's own successes, paved the way for the Treaty of Troyes in 1420. In this agreement, King Charles VI of France agreed to recognize Henry as regent and heir of France; the Dauphin Charles was disinherited and Henry V married Princess Catherine of Valois to seal the agreement. Paris, inclined to support the Dauphin, fell to Henry by the end of 1420.

Although the English suffered a setback at the Battle of Baugé in March 1421, Henry's progress towards the French throne now appeared inexorable. However, before the entire kingdom was in his hands, Henry died, on 31 August 1422, probably of dysentery. He left an eight-month-old son, Henry VI,

Duke John the Fearless of Burgundy (1371–1419). His assassination led his son Philip the Good to support Henry V of England against France.

King Henry V of England and his bride, Catherine of Valois. The marriage sealed the treaty that made Henry regent of France and heir to the French throne.

1422

Turkish siege of Constantinople.

10 January A Hussite force takes and sacks the crusader-held fortress of Nêmecky Brode.

30 June Battle of Arbedo (modern Switzerland). A Milanese force defeats a Swiss invasion of northern Italy.

31 August Death of Henry V of England.

22 April Battle of Hörice. Radical Hussites (Taborites) defeat the more moderate Utraquist faction.

22 October Death of Charles VI of France.

who also became king of France when Charles VI finally died on 22 October in the same year. The infant king's uncle, John, Duke of Bedford (1389–1435), ably maintained Henry VI's claims, defeating armies loyal to the Dauphin in 1423 and 1424. Indeed, by 1428, only one major town, Orléans, still held out for the Dauphin, and it was placed under siege in October 1428.

Joan of Arc

And then came Joan of Arc, one of the greatest imponderables of medieval warfare. She was a peasant girl, a mystic whose 'voices' commanded her to raise the siege of Orléans and see to the Dauphin's coronation as king. She made her way to Charles at Chinon, and convinced him that she did indeed come from God. The prince provided her with arms and a military household and sent her on to Orléans. Joan's military role has been debated ever since. She herself claimed that she never shed blood.

Left: Joan of Arc at the coronation of Charles VII, a painting by the nineteenth-century romantic artist Jean-Auguste-Dominique Ingres.

Joan of Arc's entry into Orléans, 8 May 1429, an event still celebrated in an annual town festival.

She certainly led troops into battle, though, despite the efforts of her co-commanders to limit her position to that of mascot. Her inspirational force cannot, however, be doubted. At Orléans, she convinced the soldiers to make confession, drove out the camp followers, and even led the men in singing hymns. The English

1423

31 July English defeat of the Dauphin's army and their Scots allies.

1423–1430 Ottoman war with Venice.

1424

7 June Battle of Malesov. A Hussite victory over crusaders.

17 August Battle of Verneuil. An English army commanded by the Duke of Bedford and Earl of Salisbury decisively defeats a larger Dauphinist-Scottish army under the Count of Aumâle.

Egyptians devastate Cyprus, reducing it to tributary status.

1424–1426 An attempted Mamluk invasion of Cyprus fails.

thought quite simply that she was a witch, and threatened to burn one of her heralds.

Joan raised the English siege of Orléans on 8 May 1429, an event celebrated in the town for centuries as the 'Mystery of the Siege'. The following month, a French army under Joan and the Duke of Alençon surprised an English army of about 3500 men at Patay, 21km (13 miles) northwest of Orléans. Here we can see the limitations of infantry in battle. The largely infantry English force managed to deploy in a good defensive position, but did not have time to protect themselves with stakes, as they had at Agincourt. A French cavalry charge against the archer vanguard made it through, and an estimated 2000 Englishmen were killed. The Battle of Patay cleared the way to Rheims,

....

Left: The coronation of Charles VII of France (1429). Joan of Arc, the moral if not the military leader of the French army, stands to one side, standard in hand.

Right: The Czech religious reformer Jan Hus (1369–1145), whose execution at Constance in 1415 sparked the Hussite Wars.

where on 17 July 1429 Charles VII was finally crowned king of France. Joan herself, however, was captured by a Burgundian force and sold to the English, who burned her alive on 30 May 1431. By that time, however, England had lost the upper hand in the Hundred Years War.

Religion, Patriotism and the Hussite Wars

Joan of Arc's brief but spectacular career invoked both religious fervour and patriotism to a degree hitherto unknown within the states of Western Europe. Something of the sort had already developed in Bohemia, however. The religious reformer Jan Hus preached a potent blend of evangelical enthusiasm and Czech nationalism against the pervasive influence of Germans. When he was burned as a heretic at the Council of Constance in 1415 – despite a

1426

16 June Battle of Aussig. A large Hussite army that included all factions defeats a major crusader army.

1426–1435 War between the Hanseatic League and Erik VII of Scandinavia over Schleswig, won by the Hanseatic League.

1428

December 1428 Joan of Arc leaves her home for the Dauphin's court.

October 1428–8 May 1429 English siege of Orléans. Successfully raised by a relief force led by Joan of Arc.

1428–1429 Major Hussite raids into Germany, Silesia and Hungary.

1429

12 February Battle of the Herrings (Rouvray). A large Dauphinist army ambushes an English supply train led by Sir John Fastolf. The English rout the French.

18 June Battle of Patay. A French army including Joan of Arc inflicts a severe defeat on the English 21km (13 miles) northwest of Orléans, opening the way for Charles VII's coronation at Rheims.

17 July Coronation of Charles VII as king of France at Rheims.

8 September Failed assault on English-held Paris by Joan of Arc. Joan is wounded.

1430

Philip, the Good, Duke of Burgundy establishes the Order of the Golden Fleece, an order of chivalry.

Shift to use of corned gunpowder, perhaps three times as effective as earlier powder.

1430s–1440s Major wars in Lombardy.

safe-conduct from the emperor – much of the Czech population was outraged. In September 1415, 58 Czech nobles formed a 'Hussite' league against their king, Wenceslas. Matters deteriorated into open warfare by 1419 with the first defenestration of Prague, an incident in which 13 royal counsellors were thrown out of the Town Hall window.

The Hussite Wars, which lasted from 1419 to 1434, display an astonishing amount of military innovation, the work of the Hussite leader Jan Zizka, a professional soldier with wide experience on the battlefields of Europe. He assembled a force of about 25,000 men, which could defeat much larger armies. Perhaps as many as one-third of his men were hand gunners. Their weapons were powerful, able to pierce their enemies' plate armour. But they were very slow to load and fire. Thus, even more than English longbowmen, the Hussite gunners could survive on a battlefield only if they had a strong defensive position.

....

Wenceslas IV of Bohemia and King Charles VI of France at Rheims. Both were weak rulers who failed to deal with rebellious nobles.

Zizka responded to the challenge by developing war wagons – sturdy, fireproofed wagons specially built for warfare. They could be circled and chained together to provide a miniature wooden castle in the middle of the battlefield, which cavalry could not break through. Loopholes allowed a crew of up to 20 men to fire their handguns, and the wagons carried heavier artillery that was dismounted in battle and placed between the wagons. Men wielding heavy war flails (adapted from farm equipment) protected the whole circle. It was not merely gunpowder that won Hussite victories, though. Zizka imposed strict rules for everything from marching to fair distribution of loot, giving his troops a cohesion and discipline that went far beyond the standards of the age.

The Hussites won a series of impressive victories over King Wenceslas and several crusades called into being against them. Unfortunately, these same victories sowed the seeds of their own destruction. The Hussite movement branched off into a radical sect, the Taborites, whose radical apocalypticism repelled the moderates. After the death of Jan Zizka, the military fell into the hands of less scrupulous

leaders, who launched devastating raids into Germany. At the Battle of Lipany in 1434, a league of moderate Hussites was finally able to defeat the Taborites. European armies had by now discovered how to deal with the Hussites' unusual tactics: the Taborites, under their leader Prokop, formed a wagon fort, as was their normal practice. But instead of attempting to charge them, the moderates simply bombarded the wagons. Waiting until the defenders fired their weapons, they then launched a sudden charge before the Taborites were able to reload. This was not, by itself, enough to break through the wagons, but the moderates then feigned a retreat, and this brought the Taborites out into the open in pursuit – where they were massacred.

Italian Wars and Cavalry
The destruction of the Taborites helps to demonstrate that the age of heavy cavalry was by no means over; when conditions were right, the terrifying impact of a mass cavalry charge could still win battles. In most regions, cavalry had to work more closely than ever with infantry for success. However, conditions in

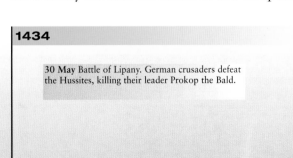

1431

30 May Burning of Joan of Arc in Rouen.

1 June Battle of San Romano. Florentine troops led by the condottiere Niccolo da Tolentino rout the Sienese, who had been besieging the town of Montopoli.

16 December Coronation of the 10-year-old Henry VI as king of France in Paris.

1434

30 May Battle of Lipany. German crusaders defeat the Hussites, killing their leader Prokop the Bald.

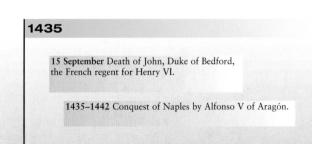

1435

15 September Death of John, Duke of Bedford, the French regent for Henry VI.

1435–1442 Conquest of Naples by Alfonso V of Aragón.

Italy assured that heavy cavalry would continue to predominate there through the fifteenth century. In large part, this was due to the wealth of the cities that competed for pre-eminence: they were wealthy enough to hire mercenary cavalry, preferring smaller numbers of more mobile and elite fighters. There were no large bodies of highly trained infantry to pressure commanders to dismount their men-at-arms.

The fifteenth century in Italy was the great age of the *condotierri*, mercenary captains who signed a contract (*condotta*) to provide troops to their employers. Many condotierri were granted fiefs by the cities that hired them, in an (often vain) attempt to assure their loyalty. In the course of the century, a surprising number of these mercenary leaders became rulers of the cities they protected, whether honestly or dishonestly. They then had to defend their gains against other would-be rulers, and were inclined to try every means to expand their

···

Francesco Sforza, duke of Milan (1401–1466) was an Italian condottiero *who rose to become duke in 1450.*

FRANÇOIS SFORCE.
Duc de Milan.
Mort en 1466.

new territories, in a cycle of violence that involved most of the peninsula. Lombardy in particular saw a number of very large wars in the 1430s and 1440s, with armies that sometimes numbered more than 20,000, as Francesco Sforza worked his way toward control of Milan.

A good example of the quality of mercenary cavalry employed in Italy can be seen in the Battle of Caravaggio, 15 September 1448, at which the Milanese under Francesco Sforza defeated a Venetian force. The Milanese were on the march, and thus vulnerable to the Venetian surprise attack launched against them at Caravaggio. But Sforza not only rallied his forces (who had clearly marched in a state of high alert), but sent some of his men through the woods to attack the rear of the Venetian force. It was an impressive victory, but notable for the discipline of the troops involved rather than for any military novelty. The Italians were responsible for some innovations in fortification building, but otherwise tended to be old-fashioned in military matters, as they realized to their cost when King Charles VIII of France invaded Italy in 1494.

1436

5 July Compact of Basel ends the Hussite Wars. Sigismund is accepted as king of Bohemia, and Hussites are allowed communion with wine as well as bread.

1437

Attempted Portuguese conquest of Tangiers, North Africa.

1438

Battle of Hermannstadt (modern Sibiu). The regent János Hunyadi of Hungary in alliance with the king of Poland and despot of Serbia defeats Ottoman sultan Murad II when he attacks Transylvania.

1438–1442 Siege and conquest of Naples by Alfonso V of Aragón.

The Turkish Challenge

The most innovative armies of fifteenth-century Europe were those of the Ottoman Turkish sultans, since Turkey had established itself as a European power by the end of the fourteenth century. Timur the Lame, who annihilated Sultan Bayezid's army at Ankara in 1402, had brought the Ottoman state to its knees. Bayezid's son Mehmed I (1413–21) restored the state, however, and his successor Murad I (1421–44, 1446–51) returned to the interrupted Ottoman advance into Europe. Murad was backed by the resources of a strong state, innovative both in military training and discipline and in the use of gunpowder technology. He is especially noteworthy for building up an elite infantry corps, the *janissaries*. This force consisted of boys levied as tax from the Christian lands he ruled. The children were taken from their families, converted to Islam, and educated under a system of severe discipline. Technically slaves, the adult

....

Timur the Lame, the last of the great conquerors of the Eurasian steppe. He was preparing to invade China when he died in 1405.

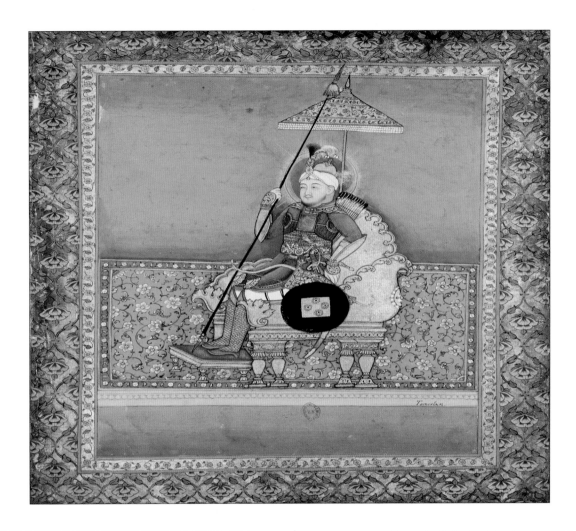

1439

1439–1445 Charles VII reforms the French army, creating Europe's first standing army since Rome.

1440

29 June Battle of Anghiari. A papal/Florentine allied force commanded by Francesco Sforza defeats the Milanese near Arezzo in a mostly mercenary battle.

Margrave Frederick II of Bavaria establishes the Order of the Swan, an order of chivalry.

The Knights Hospitallers repel a Mamluk attack on the island of Rhodes.

1441

The Hungarians under János Hunyadi inflict a major defeat on the Ottoman Turks at Semendria.

janissaries formed a privileged elite that was nonetheless completely dependent on the sultan. They were equipped with the latest military inventions, including grenades and handguns. The corps prided itself on its cohesion as a fighting force, which included matching uniforms and even special marching music. The janissaries formed the first standing army of Europe since ancient Rome.

The Christian crusaders had not lost the Battle of Nicopolis in 1396 because of any basic inadequacy of western fighting equipment or techniques compared to those of the Turks. Turkish armies tended to have the advantage of size, but could be stopped by good leadership. János Hunyadi, *voivode* of Transylvania and regent of Hungary provided such inspired leadership, when Murad II invaded Transylvania in 1438. In alliance with Poland and Serbia, the Hungarian army defeated the Turks at Hermannstadt (modern Sibiu). He inflicted two more crushing defeats on the Muslims in 1441 and 1442. The cause of the West looked promising in 1444, when a major crusade set out, taking advantage of Murad II's abdication and the disorder in the Ottoman sultanate. But

at the Battle of Varna, 10 November 1444, the crusaders lost a closely contested battle, despite the best efforts of János Hunyadi. It is a loss that can be blamed on King Vladislaus III's foolish cavalry charge at a key point in the battle. The crusaders suffered massive losses, but the Turkish force was also shattered, and this dampened their enthusiasm for European conquest.

The Battle of Kosovo

The last significant Ottoman engagement in Eastern Europe for some years was the Battle of Kosovo, 17–19 October 1448. In this encounter, Sultan Murad led an army of about 40,000 men to defeat János Hunyadi's army of 24,000. Hunyadi had decided not to wait for the Albanian Scanderbeg to join him. He might still have won the battle, especially since the German hand gunners who formed the Christian centre fought very well. But when their ammunition ran out, Hunyadi's 10,000 Wallachian allies deserted and most of the remaining Christian force was annihilated.

Janissaries, the elite slave-soldiers of the Ottoman Turkish army, whose headgear designated their rank.

1442

János Hunyadi leads a Hungarian army to victories over the Ottoman Turks in the Second Battle of Hermannstadt (modern Sibiu) and the Iron Gates.

1443

Battle of Snaim (Kustinitza). János Hunyadi defeats the Ottomans.

Sultan Murad II agrees to a 10-year truce that frees Serbia and Wallachia.

1443–1444 Crusade of Varna.

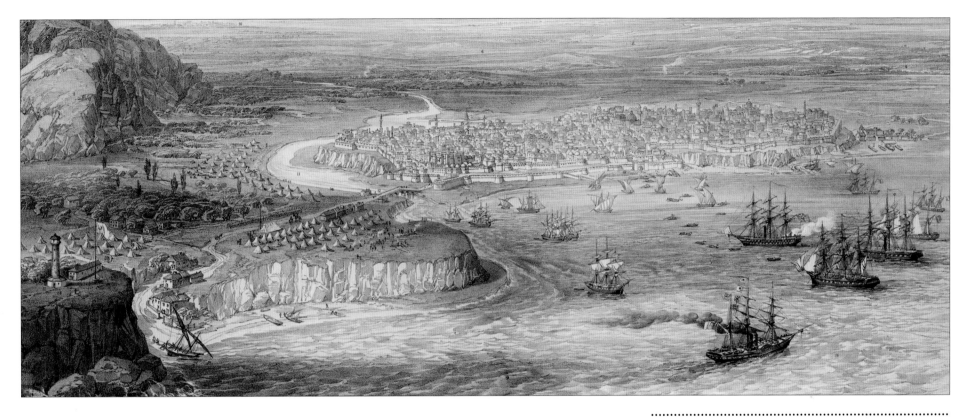

The Fall of Constantinople

When they began their invasion of Europe in the fourteenth century, the Ottomans had bypassed the great city of Constantinople, capital of a rapidly shrinking Byzantine Empire. Constantinople's defences were awesome: surrounded on three sides by the sea, the city was also protected by 16km (10 miles) of sea

Varna, the strategic Black Sea port that was the site of the crusader defeat at the Battle of Varna in 1444.

1444

26 August Battle of St Jakob-en-Birs. A large army of Armagnac mercenaries fighting for France overwhelm a small Swiss force that had attacked them by mistake.

Truce of Tours between France and England. Henry VI of England marries Charles VII's niece Margaret of Anjou.

10 November Battle of Varna. An Ottoman army crushes a mostly Hungarian crusader force in the worst crusade defeat of the fifteenth century.

1448

The French break their truce with England, besieging and capturing Le Mans.

15 September Battle of Caravaggio. The mercenary captain Francesco Sforza (fighting for Milan) defeats a Venetian army that had attempted a surprise attack.

17–19 October Second Battle of Kosovo. Ottoman sultan Murad II defeats Hungarian regent János Hunyadi.

1448–1479 French government attempts to provide a trained military force with a militia system. Louis XI abandons the scheme and employs Swiss mercenaries.

1. Mehmed II establishes his camp in early April 1453, beginning a sustained bombardment of the walls with heavy cannon.

4. On the night of 28/29 May, the Turks penetrate a breach in the wall and open a small postern gate.

5. Constantine XI is killed, ending effective Byzantine resistance.

3. Turkish ships are hauled overland around Pera, and refloated to patrol the Golden Horn, completing the blockade of the city.

2. A small Italian fleet is admitted into the Golden Horn, providing temporary relief for the garrison.

The Siege of Constantinople, 1453.

1449

24 March English capture of Fougères Castle, Brittany, provokes the last phase of the Hundred Years War.

20 May Battle of Alfarrobeira, Portugal. Afonso V defeated and killed his uncle Pedro, duke of Coimbra, ending a power struggle.

May 1449–12 August 1450 The French regain more than 70 English strongholds in Normandy, concluding with the surrender of Cherbourg.

1450

15 April Battle of Formigny. The French crushingly defeat an English army in what was probably the first battle in which field artillery played a significant role.

1453

6 April–29 May Siege and conquest of Constantinople by Sultan Mehmed II 'the Conqueror.' The last emperor, Constantine XI Palaeologos, dies fighting at the breach during the general assault.

17 July Battle of Castillon. An English army commanded by John Talbot, earl of Shrewsbury, is routed, resulting in the loss of Gascony. Talbot is killed.

August 1453 Henry VI of England goes insane.

walls and 6.4km (4 miles) of land walls. The Ottomans made a series of attacks on the city, culminating in the great siege of 1453.

By 1453, the Byzantine Empire was a shadow of its former self – as, indeed, was the city of Constantinople itself. The defenders, led by the Genoese mercenary Giustiniani Longo, could muster a mere 7000 troops and 26 ships. Against them, Mehmed II 'the Conqueror' brought 80,000 soldiers and 120 ships. This time, the Turks were not to be deterred. The siege opened on 6 April, and on 22 April the Turks succeeded in dragging ships overland into the Golden Horn, the great harbour of Constantinople, which had been protected by a great chain. This meant that the sea wall had to be manned, stretching the defenders perilously thin. And the Theodosian Walls, which had stood up to so many enemies for a millennium, could not hold out against Ottoman cannon. Mehmed's artillery train in 1453 included more than 50 cannon that could fire 90.7kg (200lb) shot; 11 that fired 226.8kg (500 lb) balls; and a monstrous cannon, named Urban's Bombard after its Hungarian builder, that could shoot a 362.9 kg (800lb) load. Urban's Bombard was so

large and took so long to cool between shots that it could be fired only six times per day. It was this cannon, however, that succeeded in breaching the city's walls. The inner wall was breached on 28 May, and the final assault began before dawn on the 29th. The last Byzantine emperor, Constantine XI Paleologos, died fighting at the breach. With the fall of Trebizond in 1461, the Byzantine Empire was at an end.

Protecting the West

The plight of Constantinople roused Western Europe to its danger more than ever. While Western authorities talked about strategies to confront the Turks, Sultan Mehmed II moved on to besiege Belgrade in 1456. It seemed that nothing would stop him, but the Franciscan friar John of Capistrano raised thousands of crusaders (mostly Hungarians) and marched

....

Sultan Mehmed II 'the Conqueror' (1444–1446, 1451–1481), who completed the Ottoman conquest of the Byzantine Empire.

1454

Peace of Lodi. Regularized relations between Milan, Florence and Venice.

1455

22 May First Battle of St Albans. In a battle fought in the town, Richard, Duke of York defeats and kills the Duke of Somerset and gains control of King Henry VI.

Turkish shipboard cannon destroys Greek ships that are armed with Greek fire.

1455–1487 Wars of the Roses in England.

19 October The Gascon-English army surrenders unconditionally at Bordeaux, ending the Hundred Years War.

1453–1466 Thirteen Years War: the Teutonic Order versus the Prussian League and the king of Poland, expand to include all Scandinavia, the Hanseatic League and Bohemia. The Teutonic Knights are disastrously defeated.

them to Belgrade to raise the siege. He was assisted by János Hunyadi, whose men, supported by crusaders, broke the Turkish naval blockade on 15 July. Mehmed's last chance, far from his supply lines as he was, was a massive assault on the city walls on 21–22 July, which the crusaders and civilians of Belgrade successfully repelled. Mehmed was forced to withdraw, leaving the Christians to celebrate their victory as the product of divine intervention.

The Turks did not have military affairs all their own way, however, even though the age of great multi-national crusades was over. At the Congress of Mantua in 1459, Pope Pius II won agreement for a massive crusade against the Turks, but national affairs kept the various promises from being kept. Pius finally decided to lead a crusade himself as the best way to gain support for the project, but when he died on 15 August 1464 his crusade died with him. In 1457, however, a papal-Aragonese flotilla won

....

Left: The Ottoman siege of Belgrade, 1456. The people of Belgrade, aided by crusaders, drove the Turks off with heavy losses.

Pope Pius II (1458–1464). Pius' chief concern as pope was the Ottoman threat to Europe. He vowed to lead a crusade himself, but died at Ancona before setting out.

1456

July Sultan Mehmed II unsuccessfully besieges Belgrade, crusaders and civilians of Belgrade fighting off a massive Turkish assault on 21–22 July.

James II of Scotland raids Northumbria.

1457

August Battle of Mytilene. A papal-Aragonese flotilla wins several victories over the Turks, most notably Mytilene.

2 September Battle of Albulena (Ujebardha). Scanderbeg of Albania wins a major victory over the Ottomans, preserving Albanian independence.

Marienburg, Prussian headquarters of the Teutonic Knights, falls to a Polish army.

1459

Pope Pius II calls the Congress of Mantua, a great meeting of Christian powers. The congress agrees to a massive crusade against the Turks, but none of the promises are ever kept.

3 September Battle of Blore Heath. A Yorkish army commanded by the earl of Salisbury defeats the Lancastrians.

several victories over the Turks. Also in 1457, Scanderbeg of Albania triumphed over the Turks at Albulena, preserving Albanian independence. In the Turko-Venetian War of 1463–1479, the Turks did not win a single sea battle, although they took the Venetian land bases in the eastern Mediterranean one by one. Even more terrifying, a Turkish fleet invaded Italy in 1479–1480. The Ottoman Empire would remain the greatest threat to Europe for most of the sixteenth century.

The End of the Hundred Years War

By the end of the fifteenth century, the greatest military power within Christian Europe was once again France, restoring a pre-eminence in war that had been brought into question in some of the battles with the English in the fourteenth century. It is doubtful that anyone would have predicted such success at the beginning of the century. Thanks in large part to the enthusiasm generated by Joan of Arc, the unconquered parts of France had stabilized by the 1430s under the rule of

Charles VII. Nonetheless, half of France was still ruled by a regent acting for the young king Henry VI – who had also been crowned king of France.

England sent troops to protect its holdings in France almost every year from 1415 to 1450. It could rarely afford to send more than 2500 men per year, however. Since the thirteenth century, when the kings of England lost Normandy, England had found it difficult to keep up with France in terms of military preparedness. England was simply a smaller and less wealthy land, despite the overweening ambitions of some of her rulers. Thanks to an advanced system of tax collection, England had achieved considerable success in the first stages of the Hundred Years

....

An overly optimistic 1824 illustration of King Henry VI of England, who suffered from serious mental illness for most of his reign.

1460

10 July Battle of Northampton. Yorkists defeat a Lancastrian force and regain power.

Siege of Roxburgh. King James II of Scotland is killed by an exploding bombard; his army succeeds in taking the town from the English.

Ottoman sultan Mehmed II takes Mistra (Peloponnese).

10 December A Lancastrian army commanded by the Duke of Somerset and Henry Percy of Northumberland defeats and kills Richard, Duke of York at Wakefield.

1461

12 February Second Battle of St Albans. Lancastrians defeat the Yorkist earl of Warwick.

28–29 March Battle of Towton. Edward of York defeats the main Lancastrian army in the bloodiest battle of the Wars of the Roses and soon claims the crown of England.

Ottoman conquest of Trebizond, the last outpost of the Byzantine Empire.

JOHN DUKE OF BEDFORD
REGENT of FRANCE

War, although the English kings had to rely more heavily on infantry than they would probably have liked. Exacerbating the problem was the political confusion and rivalry that marked the long minority of Henry VI, which continued when he came of age and proved himself to be a weak ruler, and easily led. After the Duke of Bedford died in 1435, no strong new leader emerged to protect the young king's claim to the French throne.

Charles VII of France was definitely a late bloomer as military leader. At the time Joan of Arc appeared on the scene, Charles appeared to have given up all hope of ruling France, and may have suffered a mental collapse. After his coronation, however, and especially after Bedford's death, he took a series of methodical steps that made the French re-conquest of their land possible.

In 1439 and then in 1445, Charles instituted army reforms. He established 15 companies, each consisting of 100 six-man 'lances'. A

....

Left: John, Duke of Bedford (1389–1435), commander of the English forces in France after the death of his brother Henry V.

captain appointed by the crown commanded each company. King Charles forbade any other of his subjects to raise troops – and now he had an effective fighting force, the first Christian

....

Free archers, part of the standing army recruited by King Louis XI of France (1461–1483).

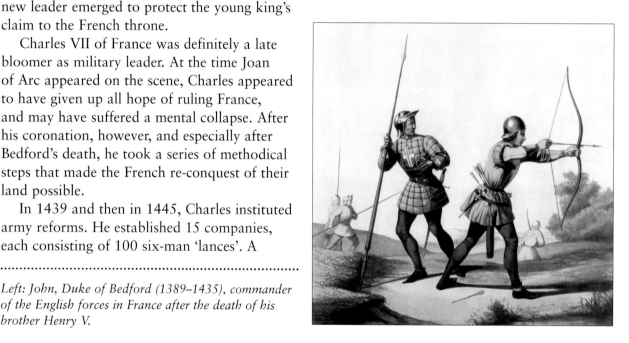

1462

Casimir IV of Poland decisively defeats the Teutonic Knights at Puck.

1462–1479 Turkish-Venetian war. Venice wins all the sea battles, but the Ottomans take Venetian land bases in the eastern Mediterranean one by one.

1463

Ottoman conquest of Bosnia.

1463–1476 Portuguese invasion of Morocco.

1462–1471 Bohemian civil war between Catholics and Hussites.

At the culmination of a long struggle between bishop and townsmen, Archbishop Adolf II conquers Mainz in a 10-hour street fight, during which much of Mainz is burnt.

standing army in Europe, to enforce his edict. In 1448, he went on to call a French militia system into existence. Under this system, each region was required to provide a set number of trained soldiers, proportional to the number of households. These militiamen were supposed to train regularly, using equipment provided by the local community. The system could supply up to 8000 infantrymen, including archers, pikemen, hand gunners, and especially the preferred French crossbowmen. The militia system was an earnest attempt to provide troops who could fight as well as trained mercenaries, but at a fraction of the cost. The fact that Louis XI abolished the system in 1479 in favour of hiring Swiss mercenaries suggests that it was not an unqualified success, as does the fact that Charles VII himself continued to employ large numbers of mercenaries. But that Charles could convince as many militiamen to train and as many communities to buy equipment as he did testifies

....

Queen Margaret of Anjou (1430–1482), wife of Henry VI of England. A major player in the Wars of the Roses, she tried to preserve the throne for her son.

to how well he inspired his countrymen, as does the fact that he raised enough money to pay for mercenaries. Sentiment in France had turned against English rule, which helped the French king to rally support. He even made his peace with the Duke of Burgundy; since Joan of Arc's meteoric career, it had become socially unacceptable to fight on behalf of the English.

All these reforms took time. In 1444, Charles VII agreed to a truce with England, a deal sealed by Henry VI's marriage to Charles' niece Margaret of Anjou. But the French used the period of truce to reorganize, while England sank into ever-deeper political chaos. Then in 1448 the French broke the truce, laying siege to the town of Le Mans. The English in Maine fell back on Normandy. On 24 March 1449, the English capture of the castle of Fougères in Brittany provoked the last phase of the Hundred Years War. The English had been hoping to pressure the Duke of Brittany into supporting them, but instead succeeded in driving him into the French camp.

Between May 1449 and August 1450, the French took more than 70 English strongholds in Normandy. The secret – if secret it was – was

1464

25 April Battle of Hedgeley Moor. A Yorkist army commanded by Lord Montague defeats the Lancastrians.

10 May Lord Montague defeats the Lancastrian Duke of Somerset in a second battle at Hexham. Somerset is captured and executed.

15 August Death of Pope Pius II at Ancona, while preparing to set out with a crusade fleet against the Turks. The crusade dies with him.

1464–1480 Castilian civil war.

1465

13 July An inconclusive battle at Montlhéry between King Louis XI of France and the rebellious noble 'League of the Public Weal'.

The Battle of Formigny, 15 April 1450. A crushing French victory over the English, in which field artillery (not shown) played a decisive role for the first time.

French artillery. Charles VII had assembled an impressive artillery train, including many cannon capable of breaching walls. The vast majority of the English castles and towns in Normandy surrendered without a fight. Not only did their garrisons rightly fear French firepower; they were unpaid and often without provisions, since the English government was in the midst of a financial crisis. The French crushingly defeated an English army at Formigny on 15 April 1450, probably the first battle in which field artillery played a significant role. By the middle of August Cherbourg, the last English centre in Normandy, had surrendered.

The English continued to hold onto Gascony, but not for long. The decisive battle was fought at Castillon on 17 July 1453. The English-Gascon army, commanded by John Talbot, earl of Shrewsbury, neatly reversed the French and English positions at Crécy, Poitiers and Agincourt. This time the French were on the defensive – a fortified artillery park, to be

1466

Second Peace of Thorn. The Teutonic Order cedes Pomerania and the mouth of the Vistula to Poland, also acknowledging Polish overlordship of Prussia.

Battle of Montlhéry. Charles the Bold of Burgundy wins the advantage over Louis XI of France in an indecisive battle.

1467

Death of Duke Philip the Good of Burgundy.

1468

Portuguese destruction of Casablanca, Morocco.

Death of Scanderbeg of Albania; Turkish annexation of Albania.

1468–1474 First 'Cod War'. A series of naval engagements between the English and an alliance of the Danes and the Hanseatic League over fishing rights and trade with Iceland.

The death of John Talbot, earl of Shrewsbury, at the Battle of Castillon, 17 July 1453. This was the last battle of the Hundred Years War.

precise. Talbot launched an attack on their position, probably not realizing how strong it was. His attack was repelled, and the English were overrun. Talbot himself, who had sworn after an earlier capture that he would not again appear before the French in arms, had his head split open by a battleaxe as he fought in doublet and a purple hat. On 19 October 1453, the remaining Gascon and English forces surrendered unconditionally at Bordeaux. The Hundred Years War was over, although no formal treaty ever regularized conditions between the two countries.

The Wars of the Roses

The loss of all of France but a small enclave around Calais was humiliating for the English government. The political situation turned catastrophic, however, when King Henry VI began to suffer bouts of madness in 1453. Long-buried problems came to the surface in the English governing class, most notably the fact that when Henry IV had usurped the throne, in 1399, the lawful heir to the throne (Henry's first cousin) had been in no position to contest the matter at the time. The fact remained: there

were English nobles with a better claim to the throne than the Lancastrian Henrys. Most important of these was Richard, Duke of York.

....

Before his mental illness, Henry VI of England was able to control the rival dukes of York and Somerset, as in this eighteenth-century illustration.

1469

Union of Castile and Aragón with the marriage of Isabella of Castile and Ferdinand II of Aragón.

26 July Battle of Edgecote Moor. The rebellious earl Richard Neville of Warwick and George, duke of Clarence, defeat and capture King Edward IV of England.

1469–1471 Charles the Bold of Burgundy creates the first modern army, a permanent mercenary force that is carefully organized and routinely drilled.

1470

12 July Ottoman conquest of Negroponte, a major Venetian outpost on Euboea.

1471

14 April Battle of Barnet. King Edward IV of England defeats and kills his former ally Richard Neville, earl of Warwick.

4 May Battle of Tewkesbury. Edward IV of England defeats the army of Margaret of Anjou, Henry VI's queen.

10 October Sweden defeats the Danes in the Battle of Brunkeberg, winning Swedish independence.

Battle of Amiens. A French force defeats Charles the Bold of Burgundy, because his Flemish pikemen run away when battle is joined.

Portuguese conquest of Tangiers, Morocco.

1471–1478 War between Casimir IV of Poland and Matthias I Corvinus of Hungary for the crown of Bohemia.

1471–1478 Ivan III of Moscow conquers the principality of Novgorod.

During the years of Henry VI's minority and weak rule, England had no natural centre of gravity. The queen mother, Catherine of Valois, remarried and removed herself from political affairs. And quarrels between leading nobles, unchecked by strong royal power, got completely out of hand. Particularly noteworthy was the animosity between the factions of Richard of York and Edmund Beaufort, Duke of Somerset. Both men were related to the king, and both claimed the right to control the government when the king was incapacitated.

In 1455, war broke out between the rival factions, the first of a series of

Left: According to legend, the Wars of the Roses received their name when the Dukes of Somerset and York quarreled in a garden, York choosing a white rose and Somerset a red one as the emblem of their followers.

Right: King Henry VI, taken prisoner by the Duke of York after the Battle of St. Albans 22 May 1455.

confused engagements that lasted until 1487. The whole has been named the 'Wars of the Roses' because one of the insignia of the dukes of York was a white rose, while one of the Lancastrian badges was a red one. A gentle name for a cruel struggle that was particularly bloody, although armies were only in the field at brief intervals during the whole period. It destroyed many of the noble families of England in a brutal struggle that specialized in deceit and betrayal.

The English had become unused to fighting within England. At the beginning of the fifteenth century, Henry IV had engaged in wars with Welsh rebels, English rebels and the Scots. But by the 1450s, England had lagged behind in gunpowder technology, and what artillery the English did employ had largely been lost to France in the last stage of the Hundred Years War. They soon made up for lost time, however, in a series of bloody engagements that were not particularly innovative militarily but that brought England to anarchy. There were few sieges, since the point of the exercise was not conquest but to claim political leadership. Small armies, at most 5000 per side, were employed.

1472

27 June–2 July Charles the Bold tries and fails to take the French town of Beauvais.

1472–1475 French-Aragonese war for control of the Pyrenees. The conflict ends with Aragonese control of Catalonia and French possession of Roussillon.

1474

July 1474–23 June 1475 Siege of Neuss (near Cologne) by Charles the Bold of Burgundy. Charles' ally Edward IV of England never appears, and Charles is forced to raise the siege when Emperor Frederick III arrives to relieve the city.

1475

Edward IV of England invades France, but is paid to leave without fighting.

The battles were fought on foot, with the men-at-arms dismounted. A great deal of luck was involved in the process – for example, at the Battle of Barnet in 1471, which King Edward IV won because his opponents became so confused in the thick fog that they fought each other. The whole business was very unprofessional, making a strong contrast to the more disciplined forces operating in France by the second half of the fifteenth century.

The First Battle of St Albans, fought on 22 May 1455, is fairly typical. The battle was actually fought within the walls of St Albans, combining elements of street fighting with pitched battle. Richard of York's force won. His men killed the Duke of Somerset – wholesale slaughter of nobles was a hallmark of the war – and Richard gained control of the king. He had lost his position of pre-eminence by 1460, only to regain it in July 1460 with the help of his ally the earl of Warwick. On 30 December 1460,

The death of King Richard III and passing of the crown to Henry Tudor at the Battle of Bosworth, 1485. Richard lost the battle – and his life.

1476

March Battle of Toro. The army of Isabella of Castile and her husband Ferdinand of Aragón secure control of Castile by defeating rival throne claimant Juana and her husband Afonso V of Portugal.

2 March A Swiss army defeats the Burgundians under Charles the Bold at Granson.

22 June Charles the Bold of Burgundy suffers a heavy defeat at Swiss hands in the Battle of Morat (Murten).

A Castilian naval squadron blockading the Strait of Gibraltar defeats a flotilla of Portuguese and Genoese vessels.

however, Richard, who by that time claimed the crown for himself, was defeated and killed at the Battle of Wakefield. In the following year, Richard's heir Edward of York defeated the main Lancastrian army at Towton, after which he was crowned as King Edward IV. King Henry was imprisoned, but when he escaped from the Tower of London the whole round of fighting began again.

The Wars of the Roses finally came to an end only when England ran out of claimants to the throne. After Edward IV's death, his brother Richard III soon seized the throne from his nephew, the young Edward V. The ensuing political unrest provided an opportunity for a new usurper, Henry Tudor, who proclaimed himself Henry VI's lawful heir. Henry Tudor invaded England in August 1485, and Richard III met him in battle at Bosworth on 22 August. Richard's army was much larger. He drew it up in three 'battles' (divisions) across the invaders'

Charles the Bold, duke of Burgundy (1467–1477), whose efforts to become a second Charlemagne led to his ignominious death at the Battle of Nancy.

1477

5 January Charles the Bold of Burgundy is besieging Nancy, France, but a much larger Swiss relieving force attacks the Burgundians under cover of a snowstorm. The Burgundian force is destroyed and Charles is killed.

1478

1478–1489 Russia and Lithuania fight an inconclusive war.

1479

7 August The Habsburg Maximilian secures his claim to the Netherlands by defeating French forces led by Louis XI at the Battle of Guinegate.

1480

Ottoman Turkish invasion of Italy and sack of Otranto on the Adriatic.

Ottoman siege of Rhodes, successfully resisted by Knights Hospitallers.

The more sophisticated arquebus, equipped with a trigger mechanism, begins to replace the schiopetto as the handgun of choice.

line of march. Bosworth should have been an easy victory for Richard. He had military experience, superior numbers and the advantage of the land. But Richard rather brashly charged into the enemy lines when he saw his enemy Henry with only a small guard. One of Richard's nobles, Sir William Stanley, chose that moment to go over to the Tudor side. Richard was cut down and his army soon gave up the fight. The last serious battle of the Wars of the Roses took place at Stoke on 16 June 1487, when Henry Tudor, now ruling as Henry VII, defeated the force of the impostor Lambert Simnel, who claimed to be a son of Edward IV. Henry's army outnumbered the rebels nearly two to one and the result was a massacre, with so many men dying in a ravine that it won the nickname the 'Red Gutter'.

Charles the Bold and the Modern Army

Meanwhile, the Continent saw a series of steps that paved the way for the creation of the first

....

The Swiss led by Hans Waldman utterly rout the Burgundian army of Charles the Bold at the Battle of Morat, 22 June 1476.

essentially professional army. The motive force behind this was the ambition of Charles the Bold, duke of Burgundy (1467–1477). In the fifteenth century, the dukes of Burgundy commanded extraordinary resources. They were wealthy, thanks especially to their control of the wealthy towns of Flanders and the Netherlands. But, as Charles saw the matter, he had a problem: he held two blocks of territory, north and south Burgundy, with the duchy of Lorraine between them. Charles wanted to form a single territorial state, which meant the conquest of Lorraine. Thanks to the complicated politics of that region, Charles' ambition meant that he had to fight the German emperor, a number of local rulers and King Louis XI of France.

Louis XI had further developed the French military in moves that made him more powerful and more unpopular simultaneously. Charles the Bold hoped to take advantage of the hatred caused by the French king's exactions. The Burgundian happily instigated what is known as the War of the Public Weal, a civil war that began as a revolt against Louis, which became in essence the first of several wars between Burgundy and France. Charles tried to convince

Edward IV of England to renew the Hundred Years War against France. He also hired Italian mercenaries and several German princes with their armies. And by 1471, Charles the Bold was well on his way to the creation of a permanent mercenary army.

Charles had a fortune at his disposal, and seemed inclined to spend it all on his dream of conquest. The army he created was a mixed force. According to a detailed record from 1472, the Burgundian army had 15 per cent heavy cavalrymen, who were still essential in pitched battle. But 50 per cent of the force consisted of mounted archers – archers, mostly crossbowmen, who had horses for mobility on the march but who fought on foot – and 10 per cent of foot archers. The 10 per cent of the army that was made up of hand gunners showed the duke's interest in the latest gunpowder weapons. The most innovative part of the force was the 15 per cent of pikemen. These infantrymen, mostly Swiss mercenaries, were known as *landsknechts*. The pike, a spear 4.5–5.5m (15–18ft) long, was just becoming the dominant Swiss weapon in this period. With good unit cohesion, pikemen could wreak

1482

Battle of Loja. A Castilian-Aragonese army is ambushed and defeated by the Muslims of Granada.

1483

Turkish conquest of Herzegovina.

1485

22 August Battle of Bosworth. Henry Tudor defeats and kills Richard III, claiming the crown of England for himself.

enormous havoc among their enemies, such as at St Jakob-en-Birs in 1444, when a much larger force of Armagnac mercenaries trapped 1500 Swiss pikemen. The Swiss were eventually annihilated, but only after inflicting about 4000 Armagnac casualties. Charles the Bold's Ordinance of 1473 introduced the first regular system of training for his troops. He also built up a magnificent artillery train. Charles' army was widely admired for its quality, good equipment, discipline and drill; by 1476, it was considered unbeatable.

The most modern force was only as good as its commander, however. Charles was personally brave and extremely thorough, but he was no Alexander. Despite his deadly earnest, the duke's campaigns have a certain air of dark comedy about them. Thus at Amiens in 1471, when Charles joined battle with a French army, his Flemish pikemen ran away. When he besieged Louis XI's town of Beauvais in 1472, he failed: the siege ladders were too short, and he did not have enough cannon ammunition. And the women of the town in particular put up such a spirited defence that King Louis rewarded them with permanent permission to precede their men

folk in town processions. The Burgundian siege of Neuss, near Cologne, also ended in farce. Charles had paid Edward of England a fortune to bring troops to his aid – but Edward never turned up, and the money was never returned. Emperor Frederick III appeared in May 1475 with a force to break the siege, but when Charles tried to attack the imperial camp he failed to break his way in. The emperor then made peace.

Charles the Bold's army was at the cutting edge of military development, but was only half a step ahead of his leading enemies, King Louis XI of France and the Swiss Confederation (which fought as Lorraine's ally). Swiss pikemen were as tough a foe as anybody in Charles' mercenary army, and enjoyed a greater esprit de corps. One can see this in the two Swiss victories over Charles in 1476, at Grandson and Morat. Charles seems to have trusted too highly to the quality of his army, engaging against the odds (about 15,000 Burgundians versus 25,000 Swiss at Morat). Morat was especially humiliating. Charles was besieging Morat when a large relieving force arrived. There was a two-day standoff when the Swiss arrived. Finally, on

22 June, Charles ordered his troops back into camp, and then the Swiss attacked. Charles fed his troops into the battle piecemeal, where they were heavily defeated. Most of the Burgundian army broke and ran, and German cavalry hunted down the fugitives.

Ideas for the Future

The bold duke of Burgundy's end was as futile as his earlier campaigns had been. He laid siege to the city of Nancy in the winter of 1477, with at most 5000 troops. A relieving Swiss army arrived, outnumbering the Burgundians four to one. Although Charles chose his ground wisely, his small army was enveloped. Charles himself was wounded and killed by looters in the aftermath of the battle. He was a failure in almost everything he undertook, but military leaders in the future applied his ideas with greater success.

....

Jeanne Laisné, nicknamed 'Joan the Hatchet', saved Beauvais when it was besieged by Charles the Bold in 1472. A Burgundian had climbed to the battlement when Jeanne, axe in hand, threw him down, along with the standard he had planted on the wall.

1487

16 **June** Battle of Stoke, Nottinghamshire. In this final battle of the Wars of the Roses, Henry VII annihilates a rebel force supporting the impostor Lambert Simnel.

1492

2 **January** The city of Granada surrenders to Ferdinand and Isabella, marking the end of the Spanish reconquista.

Epilogue: The Limits and Legacy of Medieval Warfare

European armies in the year 1500 were very different from those that took the field at the beginning of the Middle Ages. Cavalry was much more central to the military experience than it had been at the time of Charlemagne, increasing in numbers and importance every century since that time.

Foot soldiers had also changed. Gradually they transformed from disorganized blocks of ill-armed warriors who fought in kindred groups, into units with much better armour that could (usually) be trusted to obey commands, and which fought in groups sorted by their primary weapons. Some even wore uniforms, encouraging a sense of group cohesion. In the year 800, very little of the experience of war included taking or defending fortified places; by 1500, Europe had largely passed through its castle-building stage, and in the game of siege

Left: The death of Charles the Bold at the Battle of Nancy, 5 January 1477.
Right: Niccolò Mauruzi da Tolentino at the Battle of San Romano.

warfare the advantage had passed firmly from the hands of defenders to those of attackers. To a large extent, this development was a result of the introduction of gunpowder weapons to European warfare in the fourteenth and fifteenth centuries.

A Gunpowder Revolution?

Looking back on the phenomenon, it is difficult to understand why the armies of Europe gradually adopted more and more gunpowder technology in the last centuries of the Middle Ages. For most

A scene from The Romance of the Grail, *depicting a battle between several knights in the armour of the later fifteenth century.*

....

firing in every direction but the right one. At the end of our period, cannon remained cumbersome and inaccurate, though able to hurl a missile with greater force than even the most powerful trebuchet. They were of little use on the battlefield, but had proved their abilities when firing from fixed positions. It did not take long to mount small cannon on ships. For example, at the Battle of Gibraltar, fought between small Castilian and Portuguese fleets in 1476, the full-rigged ships employed in the battle boasted wrought-iron cannon, mounted in the waist of the ships. It took until 1513 before shipboard guns succeeded in sinking a ship, however, and such a feat was rare for more than a century.

Harder yet to comprehend is the increasing popularity of handguns. By the time Charles the Bold of Burgundy mustered his armies in the 1460s and 1470s, every 'modern' army also had a considerable corps of hand gunners. It took until the middle of the sixteenth century before

handguns began to decide battles, however, even though it was much quicker and easier to train arquebusiers than archers. In fact, it was only in the nineteenth century that firearms could match the longbow in range, accuracy and speed. The handgun, however, had three points in its favour. First, bowyers and fletchers were skilled craftsmen, who could put out only a limited number of bows and arrows; it was easier to increase production of firearms. Second, many a commander seems to have been attracted by the noise and the smart modernity of firearms, so it was a status symbol to employ them. Third, and doubtless decisively, archers need years of training, while hand gunners can thoroughly master their craft in a few weeks. Thus a bigger army became possible.

The Real Revolution: States Organized for War

The truer revolution in medieval European warfare was not brought about by gunpowder but by the ability of states to organize and channel their resources into war. It took the resources of a state to equip large armies with expensive firearms, as it required the resources of a state to equip infantry with even simple

purposes, guns simply did not pay off until long after the commanders of Europe had adopted their use. The only clear gunpowder successes of the medieval centuries were the great cannon, which could reduce conventional walls of stone by the middle of the fifteenth century. They had, of course, been used with much less success for nearly a century before they reached that point of efficiency, often killing their own crews and

1503

21 April Battle of Cerignola. The Aragonese win a victory over a French force commanded by Louis d'Armagnac, believed to be the first battle in world history to be won by handguns.

1521

8 August Battle of Tenochtitlan. Hernán Cortés, commanding a Spanish and Indian allied army, defeats the Aztecs under Cuauhtémoc, effectively establishing Spanish control of Mexico. The Spanish siege preceding the battle is the last known battlefield use of the counterweight trebuchet.

1526

29 August Battle of Mohács. Ottoman Sultan Suleiman I, the Magnificent, decisively defeats a Hungarian army led by King Louis II, who was killed during the retreat.

arms and armour more generally. Nothing had changed in the average ruler's desire for war, but the financial means to wage it had increased dramatically by the year 1500.

By the end of the Middle Ages, many armies consisted to a large extent of professional soldiers – France had even managed to develop a standing army. These men had to be paid, fed and equipped. Since they had no other profession, they could be trained to a degree unimaginable through most of the period. The medieval knight was a formidable fighter not so much because of his horse but due to his training and discipline; it was the accomplishment of the later Middle Ages to extend that professionalism to the military at large.

Throughout the entire Middle Ages, the natural tendency was for wars to become longer and longer. This development was not caused by any basic rethinking of warfare, but by the gradual development of financial systems able to sustain longer wars, and logistical tools to feed and equip men in the field for long periods. It truly was an extraordinary feat when Henry V of England succeeded in keeping an army in the field for two full years, and it does great credit to his government's organizational skill. By the end of the fifteenth century, winter campaigns were no longer so unusual, as armies' logistical mechanisms developed rapidly. As always, though, commanders' ambitions reached far beyond their administrators' ability to supply. Difficulties feeding and paying troops remained endemic throughout the early modern period.

The Legacy of Medieval War

Warfare in the Middle Ages was the chief catalyst for change, both technological and political. War brought states together, and sometimes ripped them apart. War made and destroyed reputations, determined social organization and created systems of taxation. Medieval warfare also generated a tradition of courtesy to gallant enemies and developed rules of war that have continued to echo to the present day. Medieval Europe was a society geared to war, in which a thousand years of turmoil and confrontation helped give shape to our distinctively Western civilization.

Soldiers with handguns, cannon, and archers operating side by side at the siege of a castle, c. 1468.

1565

18 May–11 September Siege of Malta. A massive Ottoman force unsuccessfully besieges the chief stronghold of the Knights Hospitallers on Malta.

1571

7 October Battle of Lepanto. Spanish, Venetian and papal naval forces under the command of Don Juan of Austria defeat a Turkish fleet commanded by Ali Pasha, in a battle that turns the tide of Turkish domination of the Mediterranean.

1588

August The Spanish Armada. A massive Spanish fleet sent to invade England is defeated in a series of sea battles by the smaller but more manoeuvrable English fleet; most of the armada is destroyed in storms.

Index